The Geographies of
David Foster Wallace's Novels

The Geographies of David Foster Wallace's Novels

Spatial History and Literary Practice

Laurie McRae Andrew

EDINBURGH
University Press

Edinburgh University Press is one of the leading university presses in the UK. We publish academic books and journals in our selected subject areas across the humanities and social sciences, combining cutting-edge scholarship with high editorial and production values to produce academic works of lasting importance. For more information visit our website: edinburghuniversitypress.com

© Laurie McRae Andrew 2023

Edinburgh University Press Ltd
The Tun – Holyrood Road
12(2f) Jackson's Entry
Edinburgh EH8 8PJ

Typeset in 11/13pt Adobe Sabon by
Cheshire Typesetting Ltd, Cuddington, Cheshire, and
printed and bound in Great Britain

A CIP record for this book is available from the British Library

ISBN 978 1 4744 9754 1 (hardback)
ISBN 978 1 4744 9756 5 (webready PDF)
ISBN 978 1 4744 9757 2 (epub)

Contents

Acknowledgements

This book began life as a PhD thesis in the Department of English at Royal Holloway, University of London, and would not have been possible without Royal Holloway's award of a Crossland Scholarship as well as additional funding for research at the Harry Ransom Center, University of Texas at Austin. I owe a debt of gratitude to all those who have read the text and given invaluable advice at different stages of its development, especially Finn Fordham, Adam Kelly and Neal Alexander – although of course any errors and all shortcomings are my own. Thanks to my friends and colleagues at Royal Holloway and beyond for their companionship over the period in which this project has taken shape.

Quotations from materials held in the archive of David Foster Wallace's manuscripts and papers at the Harry Ransom Center are published here by permission of the David Foster Wallace Literary Trust. Thanks to the friendly and welcoming staff at the Harry Ransom Center for their help with this research.

Parts of Chapter 2 are derived from an article published under the title 'Technologically Constituted Spaces: David Foster Wallace, Martin Heidegger, and Technological Nostalgia' in *Critique: Studies in Contemporary Fiction*, 61.5 (2020), copyright Taylor & Francis. Available online: <https://doi.org/10.1080/00111619.2020.1763241>

Special thanks to my family for all their support over the years. This book is for Zoë, whose love and support are its foundation.

Texts and Abbreviations

References to published and collected texts by David Foster Wallace are given parenthetically in the text of this book using the shortened forms shown below. Uncollected texts by Wallace are cited in endnotes.

Broom   *The Broom of the System* (1987). London: Abacus, 2011.

Brief Interviews   *Brief Interviews with Hideous Men* (1999). London: Abacus, 2013.

Consider   *Consider the Lobster and Other Essays* (2005). London: Abacus, 2012.

Jest   *Infinite Jest: A Novel* (1996). London: Abacus, 2016.

Pale King   *The Pale King* (2011). London: Penguin, 2012.

Signifying   *Signifying Rappers*, with Mark Costello (1990). New York: Back Bay Books, 2013.

Supposedly   *A Supposedly Fun Thing I'll Never Do Again: Essays and Arguments* (1997). London: Abacus, 2013.

References to materials held in the archive 'David Foster Wallace Papers, 1971–2008' at the Harry Ransom Center, University of Texas at Austin are given parenthetically in the text using the abbreviation 'HRC' followed by the box number and folder number, separated by a decimal point. For example: 'HRC 38.6' for box number 38, folder number 6.

Introduction

In his 1992 essay on the landscapes of the Midwest, 'Derivative Sport in Tornado Alley', David Foster Wallace wrote: 'the only part of Proust that really moved me in college was the early description of the kid's geometric relation to the distant church spire at Combray' (*Supposedly* p. 11). Space and place, this line suggests, were central to Wallace's literary imagination. But at the same time, the uneasy juxtaposition of geometry and affect, mathematical abstraction and emotional engagement, is an indication that geography, for this writer, was not a simple matter. Interviewing Wallace for a *Rolling Stone* feature (that would never in fact appear in the magazine), David Lipsky recalls being given a tour of Wallace's home: among the assorted furnishings, he notes 'globes from [an] old cartography thing'.[1] This is a tantalising hint at an explicit engagement with practices of geographical representation; no such 'cartography thing' has appeared in print. A clue to its nature, though, might be found in the 'Eschaton' scene in *Infinite Jest*, in which the map of cold war geopolitics and the space of the tennis court are brought into collision, with chaotic results – and to the dismay of the game's overseer Michael Pemulis, who exclaims: '"it's snowing on the goddamn *map*, not the *territory*, you *dick!*"' (*Jest* p. 333). Space and its mediations were not easy to separate in Wallace's imagination, it seems: 'I like to mess with maps a little bit', he admitted in a 1996 interview.[2] He set all three of his novels in recognisable American places – Cleveland, Boston, Peoria – but this geographical familiarity is counterposed with wildly speculative elements. He embellished the landscape of Ohio with an artificial desert of black sand; redrew the diplomatic map of the North American Free Trade Agreement as the 'Organization of North American Nations' and placed a vast ecological disaster zone in the middle for good measure; and populated an ordinary Peoria office building with 'actual, non-hallucinatory' ghosts (*Pale King* p. 317). Wallace's imagination was a deeply spatial one; but one in which space was always a problem, not a solution. This book explores the richly generative problems – aesthetic, social and political – that geography poses in his novels.

David Foster Wallace and the Question of Space

Considering Wallace's proclivity for messing with maps, it is not surprising that the question of space began to assert itself in Wallace criticism from an early stage. In a foundational essay, Paul Quinn highlighted Wallace's 'evocations of, and reflections upon, space, place and region' – unpacking the 'intensely dialectical nature of Wallace's topography' while also insisting on the 'almost tender dimension of his place-writing'.[3] Paul Giles, similarly, insisted upon Wallace as a writer 'morally and philosophically committed . . . to a phenomenology of place'.[4] Lucas Thompson, meanwhile, has drawn attention to the connections with Wallace's literary-historical context that geography can provide: exploring the influence of Cormac McCarthy, Thompson identifies in both writers a shared effort to 'show how landscapes both large and small . . . shape personality and psychology'.[5] And this approach has since been taken up by Jurrit Daalder, who has explored Wallace's connections with the literary tradition of the Midwest in order to place Wallace's work in an imaginative as well as physical Midwestern geography.[6] Space has been on the map of Wallace criticism since its inception.

Probably the most consistently space-focused of Wallace's critics, though, is David Hering. At an early point in the development of Wallace criticism, Hering was already concerned with how Boston geography is shaped in *Infinite Jest*, constructing a 'triangular and circular mapping schema' for the novel.[7] He went on to produce a detailed analysis of the 'toxic postmodern space' of *Jest*'s 'Great Concavity'; and his monograph, *David Foster Wallace: Fiction and Form*, deploys 'spatiality' as one of three central paradigms for reading Wallace's work, focusing especially on a dichotomy of 'regional' and 'institutional' space.[8] Hering's work represents a significant expansion of the developing critical understanding of Wallace as a deeply and fundamentally spatial writer – although his approach also tends to deploy spatial concerns primarily as analogues to other ideas and themes at work in Wallace's writing. His exploration of *Jest*'s Boston is framed by a consideration of how 'geographical shape templates' are 'employed to illustrate and dramatize the themes of choice, absence and addiction'.[9] His reading of the Great Concavity frames this space as one through which 'Wallace articulates and attempts to counter the problems of literary and cultural Postmodernism'.[10] And in his reading in *Fiction and Form*, regional and institutional space are analogues to an underlying (and overarching) conceptual tension 'between monologic and dialogic tendencies'.[11] In these readings, space begins to emerge as a secondary expression of apparently deeper and more primary thematic concerns.

I certainly don't intend to imply that this approach is 'wrong'; Hering's subtle readings have yielded illuminating insights into Wallace's work, helping to elucidate the role of space in the formal and conceptual construction of his writing. As such, these readings establish space as an important focus for the effort, characteristic of the early stages of Wallace criticism, to parse the considerable complexity of Wallace's writing itself – untangling the tightly knotted philosophical and theoretical tangle under the surface of his fiction. My own approach in this book, though, is to put geography in the centre of the frame: to re-read Wallace's novels as responses, first and foremost, to the concrete geographical contexts in which they were composed. This avenue is signposted in Giles's inclusion of Wallace's texts in a 'global remapping of American literature', re-imagining American national territory in the face of globalisation; an attempt to 'describe how globalization works not just as a distant political theory but something that impacts the hearts and minds of the national community'.[12] Quinn, too, made the effort to situate Wallace's place-writing in relation to his historical moment: 'describing late capitalist American space . . . involves rather different challenges than did the eras of colonialism, primitive accumulation, or imperialism. The frontiers are more fluid, internal as well as external'.[13] Heather Houser, meanwhile, has read *Jest*'s narrative geography in line with the novel's ecological as well as social context, pointing out the ways in which 'space has been radically reconfigured under the political scheme that *Infinite Jest* envisions'.[14] These readings point to space as a key vector for the critical effort to contextualise Wallace's work – and such is the project that this book takes up, by developing a fully extended analysis of the interfaces between Wallace's novels and the historical geographies from which they emerged.

As such, this book follows a general trajectory from explication to contextualisation that has increasingly characterised Wallace criticism as the field has grown exponentially over the last ten years. Kiki Benzon, for example, has insisted that 'Wallace's novels . . . provide specific insights into late twentieth and early twenty first century America' – expressing 'the psychological and spiritual effects of a culture governed by neoliberal principles'.[15] Clare Hayes-Brady, similarly, maintains that Wallace's work forms 'a fundamentally political response' to his historical moment that 'became progressively more concerned with the sociopolitical situation of late capitalist America'.[16] Jeffrey Severs has also provided a particularly detailed reading of Wallace's fiction in relation to deep-running concepts of money, work and value in American thinking. Severs moves beyond well-worn Wallacean themes (irony, addiction, media, boredom/attention) in order to reframe Wallace as 'at bottom a rebellious economic thinker' who 'chronicles the long-term infiltration of neoliberal ideology into the American and global scene' and aims to '[resurrect] certain New Deal values in reaction to financial capital's excess in the 1980s and 1990s'.[17] Showing a healthy disregard for Wallace's own insistence that his fiction was not concerned with 'conventionally political or social-action-type situations', these perspectives have helped to root Wallace's texts in their social, economic and political moment.[18] This is the effort that this book extends by reading Wallace's novels through the lens of American geography at the end of the twentieth century.

Having said this, I am not concerned with jettisoning the conclusions of the earlier stages of Wallace criticism. Much of the work of elucidating Wallace's literary mission focused on his own manifesto – the essay 'E Unibus Pluram: Television and U.S. Fiction' – and the interview he gave to Larry McCaffrey, both published in *Review of Contemporary Fiction* in 1993; what Adam Kelly calls the 'essay-interview nexus'.[19] Drawing on Wallace's comments in these texts about a need for 'single-entendre principles' (*Supposedly* p. 81) and a fiction whose 'purpose is to give the reader . . . imaginative access to other selves', in response to a cultural moment in which 'Postmodern irony's become our environment', Wallace readers have promoted his work as a harbinger of a paradigm shift in American literature.[20] As Kelly puts it, critics came to see Wallace's work 'not primarily in terms of aesthetic representation, but of ethical intervention'.[21] For Kelly himself, this translates to a 'New Sincerity'; for Mary K. Holland, it amounts to a 'poststructural realism'; Marshall Boswell prefers a more general 'new literary sensibility'.[22] Whatever the terms, the sense that Wallace's texts were concerned with turning away from postmodernist irony and self-reflexivity and towards a new form of ethical and social engagement has been a guiding theme.

This understanding of Wallace's work has also been extended into the more recent contextualising phase of Wallace criticism. Kelly has gone on to place his notion of the 'New Sincerity' in an 'economic and political landscape ... steeped in Reaganomics' and the 'rise (and rise) of multinational capitalism'.[23] Robert L. McLaughlin also reframes the emphasis on sincerity and directness through a stronger social focus, placing Wallace in a body of writing 'inspired by a desire to reconnect language to the social sphere ... to reenergize literature's social mission'.[24] Similarly, I want to contextualise rather than to abandon the idea, codified in earlier Wallace criticism, that Wallace's work was motivated and structured by a renewed engagement with social forms and relations – even if Wallace himself generally expressed this in terms of relationships on an individual level rather than explicitly political intervention. I take this approach with the important qualifying insistence that the 'disengagement' of postmodernism was a matter of attitude rather than actuality; as Fredric Jameson so comprehensively argued, postmodernism's emphasis on surface and image – its apparent disinterest in its own historicity – is itself best understood as a symptom of a specific historical moment.[25] With this caveat in place, my reading of Wallace's novels will explore how his responses to the geographies of America in the late twentieth century shaped his understanding of the renewed social and ethical purpose of his fiction.

At the same time, the broadly sympathetic accounts of earlier critics have increasingly been joined by dissenting voices, pointing out the places where Wallace's work – as Hayes-Brady puts it – exhibits a 'reluctance or inability to move beyond the borders of his own privilege'.[26] Critics have called into question Wallace's approaches to the question of race in late twentieth-century America.[27] Gender, too, has emerged as a problematic aspect of his work, with Hayes-Brady arguing that 'his writing of both female characters and romantic relationships is patchy at best and enormously problematic at worst'.[28] This critical turn has been cemented in the wake of allegations surrounding Wallace's own relationships with women, prompting Hayes-Brady to reflect on how a 'myth of the male genius' has been mobilised in his reception in ways that are 'enormously troubling'.[29] Indeed, Amy Hungerford has called the edifice of 'Wallace studies' itself into question, outlining her refusal to read Wallace's work on the grounds that 'there was a profound connection between Wallace's treatment of women and his literary project'.[30] A focus on both race and gender has allowed critics to take stock of the problems and limitations as well as the formal and thematic achievements of Wallace's work.

Critics have also used critiques of these aspects of Wallace's writing to reappraise the ideas of 'sincerity' that emerged from earlier criticism, and to push back against the implicit assumption that Wallace's call for direct communication and engagement necessarily represents a politically progressive response to his historical context. Edward Jackson and Joel Nicholson-Roberts have suggested that the 'New Sincerity' as articulated in *Infinite Jest* 'is a reactionary attempt to rehabilitate white masculinity at the direct and violent expense of those outside this category', and Jackson has gone on to argue that Wallace's work is 'indebted to neoliberal logics, which allow [him] to reaffirm masculinity on the basis of its apparently immutable sexual toxicity'.[31] Stephanie Lambert argues both that 'the aesthetic of New Sincerity reproduces the cultural logic of neoliberalism' and that the stories in *Brief Interviews with Hideous Men* (1999) 'repeatedly stage women's violent embodiment as ushering in a visceral, indisputable "real" and urge the reader to find this nourishing and redemptive'.[32] Colson Saylor, meanwhile, has linked the critique of Wallace's approach to race with the question of space, arguing that Wallace's tendency towards a 'conceptualization of space as a universal experience' leads to an effacement of the ways in which 'subjects of color are confined to particular maps and restricted from entering spaces of privilege'.[33] In parts of this book, I also use geography to take forward some of these more troubling questions around Wallace's novels, exploring how space and its representations in *Infinite Jest* and *The Pale King* are bound up with the politics of gender and race in the context of late twentieth-century America. The aim of this critique is not merely to arrive at a decision about Wallace's personal attitudes; rather, identifying the limits to his literary project is also a crucial part of the critical effort to connect this project with its historical context. By approaching Wallace's novels through the particular material configurations of American geography at the end of the twentieth century, this book aims to develop an expanded understanding of the dynamic and sometimes fraught interface between his writing and its historical moment.

Geography in Transition: Space and Capitalism in Late Twentieth-Century America

So: what exactly are these historical-geographical contexts? Wallace critics have drawn on a standard critical vocabulary for the analysis of late twentieth-century America: 'postmodernism', 'late capitalism', and 'neoliberalism' are favoured terms. These terms all refer to a broad understanding of the late twentieth century as a moment of upheaval, a shift towards some new configuration of economic and social structures underlying the literary and wider culture at work at this moment in American history. To develop these historical orientations, I want to give a more specific geographical focus to this sense of a period of major change. I take a starting point from the accounts of Marxist geographers whose work emerged in the 1980s (alongside the beginning of Wallace's own career): the wave of critical spatial analysis heralded by thinkers including Doreen Massey, Dolores Hayden, Edward W. Soja and David Harvey. These geographers contributed to an emerging narrative of a profound shift in the structures of capitalist production and exchange, generally located in the period following the international financial crisis of 1973 – and they insisted that this shift was predicated fundamentally on a change in the geographical arrangements of advanced capitalist economies. A. J. Scott outlined the sense of this change: 'from the perspective of an observer situated in, say, the mid-1950s, the geographical outlines of the world's major capitalist economies must have looked reassuringly stable and predictable' – but by the mid-1980s things were decidedly different.[34] For Scott, the essential change was one of 'regimes of accumulation' (the broad productive and sociopolitical arrangements characterising a specific form of capitalist production): from a 'Fordist' regime characterised by relatively static and rigid spatial arrangements to a 'flexible' one, 'secured by means of socially fragmented but interconnected and organizationally pliable units of economic activity'. As such, American capitalism from the mid-1970s was 'steadily recreated on alternative sociospatial foundations'.[35]

Scott's resultant account of how 'both the social life and the geographic landscape of modern capitalism are being fundamentally transformed'[36] contributed to 'an emerging overall consensus in the social sciences that the period since the mid-1970s represents a transition from one distinct phase of capitalism to a new phase', as Ash Amin put it a few years later – the phase that came to be widely known as 'post-Fordism'.[37] Scott's account works largely on a fairly abstract level, although he does draw attention to the fact that these new geographies of flexible accumulation are also settings for communities, each of which amounts to 'a repository of attitudes, habits, forms of consciousness . . . interpenetrating with local structures of work and life and thickening over time in response to the expansion of collective historical experience'.[38] This is an echo of Hayden's earlier insistence that 'built space provides a concrete, physical statement about how a society organizes itself at the scale of everyday life'; and it is this connection between historic shifts in economic geography and the lived, felt experience of late twentieth-century America that was extended in Harvey's influential 1989 study of the 'origins of cultural change'.[39] Harvey took up the narrative of flexible accumulation, fleshing out its specific ramifications: 'the emergence of entirely new sectors of production, new ways of providing financial services, new markets, and, above all, greatly intensified rates of commercial, technological, and organizational innovation'.[40] But Harvey went further in unpacking the impact of these changes on the experience of everyday life in this period, pointing to a resultant 'space-time compression' in which 'the time horizons of both private and public decision-making have shrunk, while satellite communication and declining transport costs have made it increasingly possible to spread those decisions immediately over an ever wider and variegated space'.[41] Severs has laid some groundwork in connecting Wallace to this context, describing *The Broom of the System* as 'a bracingly Rabelaisian account of a postmodern capitalism that, enduring a crisis of accumulation in the 1970s, sought the flexible modes of a financialized economy that reshaped space and time'.[42]

Harvey's decisive contribution was to link this experience with cultural and aesthetic responses to everyday life: 'the relatively stable aesthetic of Fordist modernism has given way to all the ferment, instability, and fleeting qualities of a postmodernist aesthetic that celebrates difference, ephemerality, spectacle, fashion, and the commodification of cultural forms'.[43] Harvey's link between this historical transition and the culture and aesthetics of postmodernism was reiterated by Jameson, in his famously spatial account of postmodern culture: for him, both culture and economics 'somehow crystallized in the great shock of the crises of 1973 . . . which, now that the dust clouds have rolled away, disclose the existence, already in place, of a strange new landscape'.[44] If this altered landscape of capitalist development partly shaped postmodernism as a cultural phenomenon, then the critical effort to place Wallace's career in the wake of the high postmodernism of the 1970s and 1980s reflects his position at a slight distance from the initial cultural shockwave produced by the mid-1970s crisis: composing his mature fiction from the 1990s, Wallace wrote from a moment in which the origins of transition already belonged to the past. His sketch of Vance Vigorous's 1970s childhood in *Broom* – 'a boy with an intimate but strange relation to the world', who 'through the miracle of television . . . enjoyed a special relationship with Richard Nixon', and whose 'last great historical act came when he was eleven' (*Broom*, pp. 75, 76, 77) – is indicative, perhaps, of a sense of this decade as a foundational but indirectly experienced one; shaping, but coming prior to, the adult Wallace. Wallace's reaction to postmodernist 'detachment' can be placed at the point where the spatial and historical dislocation that began in the 1970s was shifting from novelty to history.

The connection established by Harvey and Jameson between transition in economic geography and change at lived and cultural levels is a foundational assumption of this book; it also helps to link the specific Marxist account of capitalist transition to a much wider sense of the late twentieth century as a period of profound change. American discourse began to register this feeling even before the 1973 crisis: a striking example is Alvin Toffler's 1970 *Future Shock*, in which he argued that 'the roaring current of change . . . [is] so powerful today that it overturns institutions, shifts our values and shrivels our roots'.[45] Historians of this period writing from a range of political perspectives also display agreement on this point. John Ehrman, a broadly conservative-minded historian, points to the 1980s – the foundational decade for Wallace's career – as 'the years when America made the transition from the political and social arrangements built by post-World War II liberalism to the highly competitive, fast-changing, and technology-orientated system we know today'. For Ehrman, 'virtually every area of American life underwent some type of transformation during the Reagan years, and often a drastic one'.[46] One need not read further than the title of Robert M. Collins's *Transforming America: Politics and Culture in the Reagan Years* (2007) to establish his agreement, while William H. Chafe remarks that 'in the period from the early 1960s to the late 1980s, Americans had experienced a wrenching and dislocating series of changes'.[47] Where Marxist accounts tend to pinpoint 1973 as the starting point of the transition, Doug Rossinow argues that 'the recession of 1981–1982 was a watershed in America's social history'.[48] The Marxist narrative of transitional geographies intersects with a broader perception of fundamental upheaval in the social, economic and cultural life of America in the last decades of the century; while my sense of this geographical change is rooted in the Marxist account, it refers also to this much wider perception of an interstitial period in American history.

Severs's work has done much not only to link Wallace's work with 'a moment of great anxiety over transformations in the U.S. economy' (as he says of *Broom* in particular), but also with the concepts and value-systems that make up the 'history of political economy' to which Wallace was (Severs argues) 'more attuned . . . than previous critics have noticed'.[49] This draws attention to Wallace's connection with broader American ideologies; 'ideology' conceived not in the narrow terms of an intentional or even explicitly political programme, but the fuller sense of the system of ideas, beliefs, values and forms of cultural expression that operates in dynamic tandem with the mode of social organisation. The particular link between ideology and novelistic space has been drawn by Lennard J. Davis, whose account of the development of the novel form locates 'the development of novelistic space in a particular set of social and historical processes' and 'a series of more or less hidden, ideological presuppositions'.[50] Eric Bulson similarly insists that 'spatial representations in novels *are* ideological, they are influenced by the culture, history, economy, and politics of a particular time and place, they reflect ways of seeing the world'.[51] And Brian Jarvis has noted a long tendency to 'observe American landscapes through some form of ideological eyeglass', explicating the ideological tendencies that shaped the American geographical imagination in the second half of the twentieth century.[52] To place Wallace's texts in relation to the geographies of economic transition is to see them as mediators of particular sociospatial experiences, and as such they cannot be disconnected from other mediations at work in late twentieth-century America.

Raymond Williams's term 'structures of feeling' is useful here, and I deploy it occasionally in the course of my reading of Wallace. For Williams, 'structure of feeling' refers to the quality of directly lived social experience that is not yet codified into established formations (class relations or social institutions, for example). Neither, though, can it be reduced to 'subjective' or 'individual' experience and thus divorced from the realm of the social. As Williams puts it, 'we are concerned with meanings and values as they are actively lived and felt . . . defining a social experience which is still *in process*'.[53] Since it refers to experience that is not immediately reducible to established forms of social organisation or modes of thinking, the term is particularly useful for periods of historic transition, during which those established forms and modes come under particular strain. For Williams, this is primarily 'the rise of a class' or 'contradiction, fracture, or mutation within a class'.[54] We might also wonder, though, whether the uprooting of the geographies of Fordist production and the formation of Scott's 'alternative sociospatial foundations' might produce specific structures of spatial feeling, representing breaks in established ideologies of space and challenges to America's settled geographical imagination. And for Williams, structures of feeling are inscribed not only in the content but also in the form of literary texts: 'this is a way of defining forms and conventions in art and literature as inalienable elements of a social material process . . . as the articulation . . . of structures of feeling'.[55] My proposition, developed across the course of this book, is that Wallace's attempts to envision and enact a new form of fictional engagement beyond postmodernism, and his writing of geographies and narrative spaces across his novels, can both be seen as linked expressions of an emergent structure of spatial feeling associated with the transitional geographies of late twentieth-century America.

Literary Geographies and 'Geocriticism'

To connect Wallace's texts with this historical-geographical context is also to draw his work into a second sphere of literary scholarship: the increasingly interdisciplinary work being done on the intersections between literary texts and practices on the one hand, and geographical spaces and processes on the other. It is to take up what geographer Adam David Morton calls a 'spatial history perspective' on literature – to ask (as Morton does of Cormac McCarthy's novels): 'in what ways can the historical frontiers of geography be traced through literature and the novel form, linking to the endeavour of literary geographies?'[56] The link is to 'literary geographies', a field that has (like Wallace criticism) grown considerably over the past decade. But it might also be to the second and broadly contemporaneous grouping of 'geocriticism', an umbrella that covers Bertrand Westphal's 'geocentric' form of *géocritique* – in which analysis proceeds from a particular location and aims to encompass all textual representations of that location – and Robert T. Tally Jr.'s more general literary 'cartographics': 'a set of critical practices that seek to engage with the issues of spatial relations in connection with cultural and social theory'.[57] Literary geography and geocriticism form a rich critical and conceptual soil in which this book is grounded.

These strands of spatial literary thinking can be traced back to a common theoretical touchstone: Henri Lefebvre. Lefebvre's vastly influential *The Production of Space* (1974, English translation 1991) provides a deep and wide-ranging analysis of the state of French urban space in the postwar period, but probably more influential than these specific arguments is the larger underlying project of the book. Marxist geographers who encountered the text in French certainly found a starting point in Lefebvre's insistence that 'every mode of production with its subvariants ... produces a space, its own space'; Hayden was quoting Lefebvre's book as early as 1983, nearly a decade before its appearance in English.[58] But Lefebvre was also an important influence on the cultural turn exemplified by Harvey's work. Indeed, Lefebvre's core project was to break down what he saw as an artificial division of space into separate physical, conceptual, and imaginative dimensions: a division he saw as 'exemplify[ing] a very strong – perhaps even the dominant – tendency within present-day society and its mode of production'.[59] His alternative is a conception of space formed from three distinguishable but dialectically interconnected parts: firstly, 'spatial practice', which corresponds to concrete material processes in space and 'embraces production and reproduction, and the particular locations and spatial sets characteristic of each formation'. Secondly, 'representations of space' form 'conceptualized space, the space of scientists, planners, urbanists'. Lastly, 'representational spaces' are 'linked to the clandestine or underground side of social life'; this is 'space as directly *lived* through its associated images and symbols ... space which the imagination seeks to change and appropriate'.[60] But these are not separate containers into which particular practices and concepts can be separated: literature and culture in particular cross between categories, so that 'a certain type of artist with a scientific bent' is placed under 'representations of space', while 'some artists and perhaps ... a few writers' belong to 'representational spaces'.[61]

The point of Lefebvre's model is to erase the supposed ontological boundary between 'actual' space and the spatial representations found in literary texts and other cultural forms; to insist that practices of planning, building, representing and imagining are equally 'real' aspects of the production of space. This insistence is parsed by Edward W. Soja through the term 'Thirdspace': the 'real-and-imagined' geographies formed through the intersection of physical ('first') and imaginative ('second') spaces.[62] This project has made Lefebvre particularly influential in subsequent approaches to culture and space; the accounts of Harvey and Jameson are explicitly indebted to it.[63] But it also appears prominently in accounts seeking to lay out the methodological groundwork for spatial approaches to literary texts in particular;[64] and, as literary geographer Sheila Hones points out, the basic approach – codified through Soja's version – has become a 'relatively conventional one' that is 'commonly understood by literary geographers'.[65] The project of breaking down the boundaries between real and imagined geographies is now a bedrock upon which literary geography stands.

The conceptual intervention of Lefebvre and Soja also intersects with a history of disciplinary convergence between literary and geographical scholarship – a history set out by the geographer Marc Brosseau in an important 1994 article (on which I draw in the following account).[66] Human geographers, especially those with an interest in regional geography, began to take a systematic interest in literary texts from the mid-twentieth century; but this interest was largely illustrative, taking literature as a secondary record of the geography 'out there' in the world. This attitude was echoed in literary criticism; by Ricardo Gullon, for example, who insisted on maintaining a distinction between 'literary and territorial (geographic) space'.[67] This sense of literary scholars and geographers viewing one another across a conceptual chasm persisted, despite William E. Mallory and Paul Simpson-Housley's effort to stage a 'meeting of the disciplines' in 1987.[68]

In the 1980s, however, a new movement of humanist geography emerged in the Anglo-American academy; and these geographers began to see literature not just as a secondary record but also as a producer of place. Organised around the affective and perceptual category of the 'sense of place', humanist geographers saw places as 'centers of felt value' (as Yi-Fu Tuan put it).[69] And, since 'felt value' is a property of perception and behaviour as much as physical space itself, the distinction between geography and its imaginative representation was softened. A window opened onto the idea of literature as a productive practice of place; thus Douglas Porteous argued that there was 'no necessity for a sharp divide in approach between geographers and literary critics in the common task of furthering our understanding of human experience and landscape'.[70] For Douglas C. D. Pocock, meanwhile, 'setting achieves existential significance in literature and life through events or experiences . . . it is the latter which converts setting into place, thereby linking environment and person'; the forging of existential ties with place is not just reflected but effected in literary texts.[71] As Neal Alexander has put it more recently: 'literature draws extensively upon . . . geographical perceptions and, by augmenting or transforming them imaginatively, plays an important role in creating senses of place'.[72] In this sense, the humanist geographers carried out a project not wholly dissimilar to Lefebvre's; though concentrated on geographies of affect rather than political economy, these geographers also began to see the composition of literary texts as an active component of the production of space. Certainly, humanism formed an important strand of American thinking about geography and literature in the late twentieth century, and in Chapter 4 I return to humanist geography's understanding of literary practice in relation to Wallace's writing of place in *Pale King*.

Brosseau's 1994 article, though, was also an intervention. Brosseau's charge against geographers – including both Marxists and humanists – was that their approaches had been predicated on 'a generally unexamined mimetic conception of literature' characterised by a 'near total absence of theoretical or aesthetical considerations on the literary text, how it functions, and produces or subverts meaning'. For Brosseau, 'geographers have not been looking for what might be disruptive, subversive, or a source of new questions in the novel but mostly what can be reassuring, what can approve or provide answers for their quest' – 'the text offers no resistance'. Brosseau's solution was for geographers to 'spend more time on the text itself'; to examine 'the specificity of its form' and its 'singular use of language', and elucidate 'the particular way it generates another type of geography ... the particular way it writes people, society and space'.[73] Brosseau's call amounted to a merging of disciplines at a methodological as well as thematic level – while at the same time, his attention to the production of geographies through literary form recalls Williams's argument that the forms and conventions of literature give shape to structures of feeling. And Brosseau's call was echoed later from within literary scholarship by Andrew Thacker, who argued for a 'critical literary geography' that would move beyond 'effortless mapping of represented landscapes in literary texts' and ask 'how social spaces diachronically help fashion the literary *forms* of texts'.[74] Taken together, Brosseau and Thacker lay out the double movement now at the centre of literary geography: social space produces literary form, and literary form produces social space.

Both the intensifying convergence of literary and geographical scholarship and the conceptual foundations of Lefebvre and Soja have paved the way for an increasingly developed understanding of literature as a fundamentally geographical practice, inextricable from other forms of spatial practice at work in a larger social whole. This understanding is expressed in Nedra Reynolds's suggestion that we 'see writing as a set of spatial practices informed by everyday negotiations of space'.[75] It also underpins Hones's conception of literary texts as 'spatial events', their meanings emerging from practices of composition, dissemination and reception as they happen in space: 'the text . . . comes into being in the interaction of differently contextualized processes, and these processes are each in themselves generated in the context of countless interactions across space and time'.[76] Hones focuses on the promotion and reception of texts, but Angharad Saunders has also turned attention to practices of writing: 'understanding composition as a spatial practice'.[77] For Saunders, this spatialisation of literary practice revolves around the idea of the 'scene' of writing: the relational geography of social interactions and relationships in and through which texts are composed. The scene of writing, as Saunders puts it, is built around the 'tangle of life lines – of people, places and things' that works through the text's composition, and that suggests a view of the text as 'an assemblage of movements, relationships and practices', revealing 'the social and spatial nature of a novel's making'.[78] If there is a distinction to be made between 'geocriticism' and 'literary geography', it is the attention that the latter pays to the geographical practices that make texts as well as the represented spaces contained within them: as Saunders puts it, the 'move beyond the geography in the text to . . . the geography of the text'.[79]

Insofar as this spatial understanding of literary composition connects the making of the text with the social situation that frames it, it provides a means of linking Wallace's practice, and its aim of producing a renewed interface with the world (elaborately articulated in his essays and interviews), with the profound changes that characterised the transition to a post-Fordist economic geography. In order to construct this link, I draw in this book on the extensive archive of Wallace's manuscripts and papers held at the Harry Ransom Center, University of Texas at Austin, the availability of which has led Hering to identify an 'archival turn' in Wallace criticism.[80] In Chapter 1, I follow Hones's attention to the promotion of texts by considering publicity material related to *Broom*, exploring how this material places the text in relation to conceptions of regional geography. In Chapters 2 and 3, I turn to the process of writing itself: I begin to deploy a 'genetic' element, tracing the composition of represented spaces between draft and published versions of *Jest*. This approach becomes more prominent in Chapters 4 and 5, as I turn to the unfinished *Pale King*; here, I use drafts, notebooks and marginal annotations, in tandem with the published text, to develop an understanding of Wallace's concerns about his own fictional practice and its relation to place in late twentieth-century America.

It is primarily in relation to Wallace's unfinished last novel that his critics have begun to develop the idea of a genetic approach to his work; indeed, some attention to the novel's composition is prompted, if not necessitated, by the radically unfinished state in which we receive it.[81] As Tim Groenland points out, drawing on the terminology of genetic criticism, 'the work as Wallace left it could be considered . . . as consisting entirely of *avant-texte*, or as a "genetic dossier" for an unrealized work'.[82] The published text of the unfinished novel, assembled by his editor Michael Pietsch, organises this material into an object of study, but it represents one of many possible approaches to the collection of unfinished work that constitutes the novel. But I see the lack of a finished version of *Pale King* as an opportunity as well as a loss. Indeed, textual criticism tells us that, as Sally Bushell puts it, 'the concept of a single, stable state [of any text] is in part an illusion', meaning that we ought to 'understand the nature of the text as process' rather than a single, finished object. The lack of a 'final' text of *Pale King* brings this process more fully into view, and Hering has assimilated Bushell's approach to argue for a reading of *Pale King* in 'processural' terms, using extensive archival research to develop a full picture of the novel's development.[83] In parts of this book, I adopt this approach to both *Infinite Jest* and *Pale King*, using comparisons across draft and published versions of the texts to explore the literary production of space in process – a method that allows me to adopt and develop literary geography's focus on literature as a spatial practice, involving various forms of negotiation with the geographies in which it takes place.

I have attempted to place this book on the continuum between analysis of geography within Wallace's novels and the geography of them. This enables me to dovetail literary geography's attention to writing as a spatial practice with Williams's insistence on literary texts as the practical expression of structures of feeling, and connect this in turn to Wallace critics' identification of his writing as an ethical and social intervention as well as a set of aesthetic forms and principles. Throughout this book, my aim is to combine close attention to the forms of Wallace's novels – their specific arrangements of language – with an awareness of the geographical practice that produced them. Deploying this approach allows for a productive approach to the question, posed by David James, of 'how we might at once attend to the specificity of narrative form while evaluating the responsiveness of new writing to empirical conditions and transformations in the built environment' – and a response to his call for a combination of 'culturally oriented thinking about the politics of place . . . with a more attentive concern with the local details of language and style', forming a 'dual focus that seems crucial for reading the aesthetics of spatial representation in historically responsible ways'.[84] This literary-geographical endeavour provides a way of thinking about Wallace's novels that fully connects their aesthetic form, and their intent to engage with the world, to the spatial structures of feeling that surrounded the geographies of late twentieth-century capitalist transition.

Overview of Chapters

To draw these critical, historical and genetic components together, I organise my readings of the novels through three keywords, one for each text: 'regional' geography in *Broom*; 'metropolitan' geography in *Jest*; and 'postindustrial' geography in *Pale King*. I use these keywords in the spirit of Raymond Williams: not as simple descriptors of content but as conduits for 'a history and complexity of meanings'. They are not merely labels to pin upon the texts, but terms that pose 'active problems of meaning [that] are always primarily embedded in actual relationships' – relationships understood in turn as 'diverse and variable, within the structures of particular social orders and the processes of social and historical change'.[85] These keywords link Wallace's novels both to established traditions of American geographical thinking, and to the challenges posed to these traditions by historical change. They are the hinges around which I articulate Wallace's novels with the geographies of economic change and the ideologies of American space.

Chapter 1 considers the relationship between *Broom* and the changing landscape of American 'regional' geography in the 1980s. It extends an existing debate around the depth of Wallace's 'regionalism' by examining the connection between the material history of regional development in this transitional period and the conception of 'region' as a literary category. Understanding literary representation as part of a wider process of regionalisation, it reads the space of the 'Great Ohio Desert' as a reflection on the production of regional images in and through networks of capitalist production and exchange. It goes on to read the architectural forms that comprise the novel's portrait of Cleveland in their historical contexts, seeing architecture as a point of contact (and conflict) between local identity on the one hand, and cosmopolitan and international culture and aesthetics on the other. I then turn to Wallace's dramatised placement of literary and textual production within these ambivalent architectural settings, and discuss how this placement is connected with Wallace's early exploration of literary practice as a negotiation between the scales and locations whose reconfigured arrangement had brought notions of regional identity under strain in the late twentieth century. I close with a reading of the poster produced by Penguin to promote the series within which the novel appeared, exploring how this other side of literary practice is also embedded in the ambiguities of American regional geography in this period.

Chapter 2 follows Wallace's move to 'metropolitan' Boston in 1989. Beginning from the critical idea of the 'city novel', I consider *Jest* in relation to Boston's social and topographical history in the late twentieth century, connecting this with broader challenges to ideas of metropolitan space and life – and with Edward W. Soja's category of the 'postmetropolis'. I develop this connection through a reading of the eclectic postmodern architecture Wallace invented for his re-imagined Boston. Then, I turn to the tentative excursions into the city's public spaces that appear in the first half of the novel via Joelle van Dyne and Don Gately, and explore how Wallace drew on traditionally gendered assumptions about urban space and geographical knowledge in order to give formal expression to the problem of representing the late twentieth-century city as a coherent social space. I show how a sense of social dissolution and loss associated with Joelle's walk is countered by a nostalgia for the sociospatial form of the old industrial city in Gately's drive, both expressive of a wider structure of feeling emerging in response to the conditions of post-Fordist urban space.

Chapter 3 takes up this thread, staying with *Jest* to consider how a perception of lost community informs Wallace's sense of a need for a new form of fictional engagement; and how the metropolis itself provides the conceptual and formal material for this new form. I use biographical and textual sources to root Wallace's resumed composition of the novel in Boston's recovery networks. Then, I read *Jest*'s engagement with a perceived urban social alterity alongside William T. Vollmann's *The Rainbow Stories* (1989), exploring how urban encounters with social difference lie at the root of the novel's concern with empathy and the possibility of fiction as an ethical intervention. I go on to examine the formal and narrative significance of urban walking in Wallace's effort to build these concerns into the larger formal development of his text, reading the practice of walking as an analogue for the connective formal procedures that *Jest* engenders, and an act central to the prospect of a renewed metropolitan community. I trace this process into the novel's penultimate chapter, using draft materials to indicate the organising role of the city's geography; drawing on the work of urbanist Kevin Lynch, I posit urban walking as the key process in a reader-centric and open-ended process of constructing an 'image of the city'. I see this process as fundamentally entwined with the novel's effort to produce an active and ongoing sense of possible community; but I also explore how this project encounters tensions and limits around questions of both race and gender, showing how gendered and racialised experiences appear to exceed the strategies Wallace was developing to connect his practice to the social conditions of the late twentieth century.

Chapter 4 turns to Wallace's unfinished last project, *Pale King*, approaching the novel through the connected discourses of 'postindustrial' society and of 'place' and its supposed decline in post-Fordist America. Drawing more heavily on archival material, I read connections between work and space as a major theme in the novel's early period of composition. I explore the development of Toni Ware's story, showing how Wallace both develops and disrupts relationships between characters and place in a way that is closely connected to changing structures and geographies of postindustrial labour. I then follow the composition of the text's opening scene, tracing the careful balancing of pastoral and postindustrial registers in this section. Finally, in the construction of the story of Claude Sylvanshine, I find Wallace's initial interest in the possibilities of place-writing developing into a profound concern over the nature and efficacy of literary practice in the context of economic and geographical transition.

In Chapter 5, I follow this thread into Wallace's last work on *Pale King* after 2005, which became increasingly centred on Peoria and its 'Regional Examination Centre' – a narrative geography that I connect with broader responses to the quintessentially postindustrial form of the 'Edge City'. Via the introduction of the 'David Wallace' character, I read this space as one resistant to incorporation into historical and personal narratives, before exploring how Wallace responded by configuring this postindustrial space as one (literally) haunted by an industrial past; a literary intervention that aims to reconnect place with history, forming the basis of a possible rehumanisation of American geography effected within postindustrial workspace itself. Again, though, I explore how this strategy finds limits as questions of gender and race run through the text, placing strains on the rehumanising strategy that Wallace situates in the spaces of postindustrial life.

In selecting these keywords for my reading, I do not intend to present them as exhaustive; as a matter of economy of focus, they necessarily limit my approach to the exclusion of other prominent aspects of Wallace's textual geographies. If Giles's attention to the poetics of globalisation and Houser's concern with the spaces produced by ecological degradation appear only marginally, for example, this is not intended as a negation of their importance. It should also be noted that my focus on the novels excludes some of Wallace's explicitly geographical short fiction, such as the early story 'Here and There' and the later piece 'The Suffering Channel'. To keen Wallace readers, these omissions might seem glaring; I hope that the depth of attention I am able to bring to the novels themselves is adequate compensation. Reading Wallace's novels through the lens of historical geography, I aim to bring into view the full significance of his spatial imagination. Approached through my three keywords, he emerges as a profoundly complex – if sometimes problematic – geographical thinker for whom negotiating the challenging geographies of historical transition was an inescapable part of both the social life and the literary practice of late twentieth-century America.

Notes

1. David Lipsky, *Although of Course You End Up Becoming Yourself: A Road Trip with David Foster Wallace* (New York: Broadway Books, 2010), p. 301.
2. Kunal Jasty, 'A Lost 1996 Interview with David Foster Wallace' (21 December 2014), <https://medium.com/@kunaljasty/a-lost-1996-inter view-with-david-foster-wallace-63987d93c2c> [retrieved 28 February 2022].
3. Paul Quinn, '"Location's Location": Placing David Foster Wallace', in Marshall Boswell and Stephen J. Burn (eds.), *A Companion to David Foster Wallace Studies* (New York: Palgrave MacMillan, 2013), pp. 87–106 (p. 87, 94).
4. Paul Giles, 'All Swallowed Up: David Foster Wallace and American Literature', in Samuel Cohen and Lee Konstantinou (eds.), *The Legacy of David Foster Wallace* (Iowa City: University of Iowa Press, 2012), pp. 3–22 (p. 10).
5. Lucas Thompson, '"Books Are Made out of Books": David Foster

Wallace and Cormac McCarthy', *The Cormac McCarthy Journal*, 13.1 (2015), 3–26 (p. 12).

6. Jurrit Daalder, 'Wallace's Geographic Metafiction', in Ralph Clare (ed.), *The Cambridge Companion to David Foster Wallace* (Cambridge: Cambridge University Press, 2018), pp. 220–34.

7. David Hering, 'Infinite Jest: Triangles, Cycles, Choices & Chases', in Hering (ed.), *Consider David Foster Wallace* (Los Angeles: Sideshow Media Group, 2010), pp. 89–100 (p. 100).

8. David Hering, 'Theorising David Foster Wallace's Toxic Postmodern Spaces', *US Studies Online* 18 (Spring 2011), <http://www.baas.ac.uk /issue-18-spring-2011-article-2/> [retrieved 28 February 2022]; *David Foster Wallace: Fiction and Form* (New York: Bloomsbury, 2016), especially pp. 41 ff.

9. Hering, 'Triangles', p. 89.

10. Hering, 'Toxic Postmodern Spaces'.

11. Hering, *Fiction and Form*, p. 8.

12. Paul Giles, *The Global Remapping of American Literature* (Princeton: Princeton University Press, 2011), p. 174.

13. Quinn, '"Location's Location"', pp. 87, 90.

14. Heather Houser, '*Infinite Jest*'s Environmental Case for Disgust', in Cohen and Konstantinou (eds.), *Legacy*, p. 118.

15. Kiki Benzon, 'David Foster Wallace and Millennial America', in Philip Coleman (ed.), *David Foster Wallace: Critical Insights* (Ipswich, Massachusetts: Salem Press, 2015), pp. 29–45 (pp. 29, 32).

16. Clare Hayes-Brady, *The Unspeakable Failures of David Foster Wallace* (New York: Bloomsbury, 2016), p. 197.

17. Jeffrey Severs, *David Foster Wallace's Balancing Books: Fictions of Value* (New York: Columbia University Press, 2017), pp. 2, 23, 24.

18. Larry McCaffrey, 'An Expanded Interview with David Foster Wallace', in Stephen J. Burn (ed.), *Conversations with David Foster Wallace* (Jackson: University of Mississippi Press, 2012), pp. 21–52 (p. 26).

19. Adam Kelly, 'David Foster Wallace: The Critical Reception', in Coleman (ed.), *Critical Insights*, p. 48.

20. McCaffrey, 'Expanded Interview', pp. 22, 49.

21. Kelly, 'Critical Reception', p. 49.

22. Adam Kelly, 'David Foster Wallace and the New Sincerity in American Fiction', in Hering (ed.), *Consider*, pp. 131–46; Mary K. Holland, *Succeeding Postmodernism: Language and Humanism in Contemporary American Literature* (New York: Bloomsbury, 2013), pp. 165 ff; Marshall Boswell, *The Wallace Effect: David Foster Wallace and the Contemporary Literary Imagination* (New York: Bloomsbury, 2019), p. 6.

23. Adam Kelly, 'The New Sincerity', in Jason Gladstone, Andrew Hoberek and Daniel Worden (eds), *Postmodern/Postwar – And After* (Iowa City: University of Iowa Press, 2016), pp. 197–208 (p. 195).

24. Robert L. McLaughlin, 'Post-Postmodern Discontent: Contemporary Fiction and the Social World', *Symploke*, 12.1–2 (2004), 53–68 (p. 55).
25. Fredric Jameson, *Postmodernism: Or, The Cultural Logic of Late Capitalism* (London: Verso, 1991), especially pp. 16–31, 364–76.
26. Hayes-Brady, *Unspeakable Failures*, 193.
27. See Samuel Cohen, 'The Whiteness of David Foster Wallace', in Len Platt and Sara Upstone (eds), *Postmodern Literature and Race* (Cambridge: Cambridge University Press, 2015), pp. 228–44; Tara Morrissey and Lucas Thompson, '"The Rare White at the Window": A Reappraisal of Mark Costello and David Foster Wallace's *Signifying Rappers*', *Journal of American Studies*, 49.1 (2015), 77–97; Jorge Araya, 'Why the Whiteness? Race in *The Pale King*', in Coleman (ed.), *Critical Insights*, pp. 238–51; Hayes-Brady, *Unspeakable Failures*, pp. 167 ff; Lucas Thompson, 'Wallace and Race', in Clare (ed.), *Cambridge Companion*, pp. 204–19.
28. Hayes-Brady, *Unspeakable Failures*, p. 167.
29. Steve Paulson, 'David Foster Wallace in the #MeToo Era: A Conversation with Clare Hayes-Brady', *Los Angeles Review of Books* (10 September 2018), <https://www.lareviewofbooks.org/article/david-foster-wallace-in-the-metoo-era-a-conversation-with-clare-hayes-brady> [retrieved 28 February 2022].
30. Amy Hungerford, *Making Literature Now* (Stanford: Stanford University Press, 2016), p. 147.
31. Edward Jackson and Joel Nicholson-Roberts, 'White Guys: Questioning *Infinite Jest*'s New Sincerity', *Orbit: A Journal of American Literature*, 5.1 (2017), 1–28 (p. 23), <https://doi.org/10.16995/orbit.182> [retrieved 28 February 2022]; Edward Jackson, *David Foster Wallace's Toxic Sexuality: Hideousness, Neoliberalism, Spermatics* (New York: Bloomsbury, 2020), EPUB edition accessed via British Library electronic legal deposit, paragraph 8.46.
32. Stephanie Lambert, '"The Real Dark Side, Baby": New Sincerity and Neoliberal Aesthetics in David Foster Wallace and Jennifer Egan', *Critique: Studies in Contemporary Fiction*, 61.4 (2020), 394–411 (395, 401).
33. Colson Saylor, 'Loosening the Jar: Contemplating Race in David Foster Wallace's Short Fiction', in *The Journal of David Foster Wallace Studies*, 1.1 (2018), 119–49 (p. 129, 132).
34. A. J. Scott, *New Industrial Spaces: Flexible Production Organization and Regional Development in North America and Western Europe* (London: Pion, 1988), p. 1.
35. Ibid. pp. 10, 14.
36. Ibid. p. 108.
37. Ash Amin, 'Post-Fordism: Models, Fantasies and Phantoms of Transition', in Amin (ed.), *Post-Fordism: A Reader* (Oxford: Blackwell, 1994), pp. 1–40 (p. 1).

38. Scott, *New Industrial Spaces*, p. 39.
39. Dolores Hayden, 'Capitalism, Socialism, and the Built Environment', in Stephen Rosskamm Shalom (ed.), *Socialist Visions* (Boston: South End Press, 1983), pp. 59–81 (p. 69).
40. David Harvey, *The Condition of Postmodernity: An Enquiry into the Origins of Cultural Change* (Oxford: Basil Blackwell, 1989), p. 156.
41. Ibid. p. 147.
42. Severs, *Balancing Books*, p. 37.
43. Harvey, *Condition*, p. 156.
44. Jameson, *Postmodernism*, pp. xx–xxi.
45. Alvin Toffler, *Future Shock* (London: Bodley Head, 1970), p. 3.
46. John Ehrman, *The Eighties: America in the Age of Reagan* (New Haven: Yale University Press, 2005), p. 2.
47. William H. Chafe, *The Unfinished Journey: America since World War II*, seventh edition (Oxford: Oxford University Press, 2011), p. 474
48. Doug Rossinow, *The Reagan Era: A History of the 1980s* (New York: Columbia University Press, 2015), p. 84.
49. Severs, *Balancing Books*, pp. 36, 5.
50. Lennard J. Davis, *Resisting Novels: Ideology and Fiction* (New York: Methuen, 1987), pp. 53–4.
51. Eric Bulson, *Novels, Maps, Modernity: The Spatial Imagination, 1850–2000* (New York: Routledge, 2006), p. 11, original emphasis.
52. Brian Jarvis, *Postmodern Cartographies: The Geographical Imagination in Contemporary American Culture* (London: Pluto, 1998), p. 2.
53. Raymond Williams, *Marxism and Literature* (Oxford: Oxford University Press, 1977), p. 132, original emphasis.
54. Ibid. p. 134.
55. Ibid. p. 133.
56. Adam David Morton, 'The Frontiers of Cormac McCarthy', *Progress in Political Economy* (15 December 2015), <http://ppesydney.net/the-frontiers-of-cormac-mccarthy/> [retrieved 28 February 2022].
57. Bertrand Westphal, *Geocriticism: Real and Fictional Spaces*, trans. Robert T. Tally Jr. (New York: Palgrave MacMillan, 2011), pp. 112 ff; Robert T. Tally Jr., *Spatiality* (London: Routledge, 2013), p. 113.
58. Henri Lefebvre, *The Production of Space* (1974), trans. Donald Nicholson-Smith (Oxford: Blackwell, 1991), p. 31; Hayden, 'Capitalism', p. 63.
59. Lefebvre, *Production of Space*, p. 8.
60. Ibid. p. 33, 38–9, original emphasis.
61. Ibid. p. 38–9.
62. Edward W. Soja, *Thirdspace: Journeys to Los Angeles and Other Real-and-Imagined Places* (Malden, Massachusetts: Blackwell, 1998), pp. 11 ff.
63. Harvey, *Condition*, p. 226; Jameson, *Postmodernism*, pp. 364 ff.
64. For example: Andrew Thacker, *Moving Through Modernity:*

Geographies of Modernism (2003) (Manchester: Manchester University Press, 2009), pp. 16–22; Eric Prieto, *Literature, Geography and the Postmodern Poetics of Space* (New York: Palgrave MacMillan, 2013), pp. 89 ff; Tally, *Spatiality* pp. 116–19; Phillip E. Wegner, 'Spatial Criticism', in Julian Wolfreys (ed.), *Introducing Criticism in the 21st Century* (Edinburgh: Edinburgh University Press, 2015), pp. 233–58.

65. Sheila Hones, *Literary Geographies: Narrative Space in* Let the Great World Spin (New York: Palgrave MacMillan, 2014), p. 67.

66. Marc Brosseau, 'Geography's Literature', *Progress in Human Geography*, 18.3 (1994), 333–353.

67. Ricardo Gullon, 'On Space in the Novel', *Critical Inquiry*, 2.1 (Autumn 1975), 11–28 (p. 18).

68. William E. Mallory and Paul Simpson-Housley (eds.), *Geography and Literature: A Meeting of the Disciplines* (Syracuse, New York: Syracuse University Press, 1987).

69. Yi-Fu Tuan, *Space and Place: The Perspective of Experience* (1977) (London: Edward Arnold, 1979), p. 4.

70. Douglas Porteous, 'Literature and Humanist Geography', *Area*, 17.2 (June 1985), 117–22 (p. 120).

71. Douglas C. D. Pocock, 'Geography and Literature', *Progress in Human Geography*, 12.1 (1988), 87–102 (p. 90).

72. Neal Alexander, 'Senses of Place', in Robert T. Tally Jr. (ed.), *The Routledge Handbook of Space and Literature* (London: Routledge, 2017), EPUB edition accessed via British Library electronic legal deposit, paragraph 13.3.

73. Brosseau, 'Geography's Literature', pp. 338–9, 347, 345, 348.

74. Andrew Thacker, 'The Idea of a Critical Literary Geography', *New Formations*, 57 (Winter 2005–2006), 56–73 (p. 60, 63), original emphasis.

75. Nedra Reynolds, *Geographies of Writing: Inhabiting Places and Encountering Difference* (Carbondale: Southern Illinois University Press, 2004), p. 6.

76. Hones, *Literary Geographies*, p. 6.

77. Angharad Saunders, *Place and the Scene of Literary Practice* (London: Routledge, 2018), p. xxii.

78. Ibid. pp. xxviii, xxvi, xii.

79. Angharad Saunders, 'The Spatial Event of Writing: John Galsworthy and the Creation of *Fraternity*', *Cultural Geographies*, 20.3 (July 2013), 285–8 (p. 285).

80. Hering, *Fiction and Form*, p. 9

81. See Toon Staes, 'Work in Progress: A Genesis for *The Pale King*', *English Studies*, 95.1 (2014), 70–84; Jeffrey R. De Lio, 'Sovereignty of the Dead: Authors, Editors, and the Aesthetic Text', *The Comparatist*, 36 (May 2012), 123–36; Tim Groenland, *The Art of Editing: Raymond Carver and David Foster Wallace* (New York: Bloomsbury, 2019).

82. Tim Groenland, 'Recipe for a Brick: *The Pale King* in Progress', *Critique: Studies in Contemporary Fiction*, 58.1 (2017), 365–7 (p. 366).
83. Sally Bushell, *Text as Process: Creative Composition in Wordsworth, Tennyson, and Dickenson* (Charlottesville: University of Virginia Press, 2009), p. 1; Hering, *Fiction and Form*, p. 125.
84. David James, *Contemporary British Fiction and the Artistry of Space: Style, Landscape, Perception* (London: Continuum, 2008), pp. 3, 16.
85. Raymond Williams, *Keywords: A Vocabulary of Culture and Society* (1976) (London: Fontana, 1983), pp. 17, 21–2.

Chapter 1

'This strange, occluded place': Regional Geography, the Midwest and *The Broom of the System*

Introduction: Region, Regionalism, Regionalisation

'They are also Midwesterners', Mr. Bloemker notes of the residents at his nursing home in *The Broom of the System*. To Bloemker, this Midwestern-ness is troubled and ambiguous: 'this area of the country, what are we to say of this area of the country, Ms. Beadsman?' (*Broom* p. 142). The issue is geographical, economic and cultural – the experience of a people who stand in an ambiguous productive relationship with the rest of the nation: 'we feed and stoke and supply a nation much of which doesn't know we exist. A nation we tend to be decades behind, culturally and intellectually' (p. 142). And this geographical experience has a psychological dimension; the locational and existential unease of life in an area of America 'both in the middle and on the fringe', both 'the physical heart and the cultural extremity' (p. 142). Bloemker's residents, in his diagnosis, are troubled by a need to 'come to terms with and recognize the implications of their consciousness of themselves as part of this strange, occluded place' (p. 142). But there is also an ambivalence in the novel about how seriously we are to take Mr Bloemker's interpretations: he rehashes the theme in very similar terms later in the novel (p. 369), so that by the time we hear of him 'acting as if he were whispering to someone under his arm when there was clearly no-one there, and asking Judith and Candy how they perceived their own sense of the history of the Midwest', we come to recognise a less-than-healthy obsession (p. 446). Midwestern-ness is doubly pathologised here: both the psychology associated with this geographical identity itself, and the interpretation and expression of that psychology, are problematic. In this ambiguous fashion, Bloemker's orations signpost a dimension of *Broom* – with its primary setting in and around the Midwestern city of Cleveland, Ohio – that is concerned with the distinctive late twentieth-century experience of the Midwest as a particular American region, and with the ways in which this region can be spoken about.

The notion of the 'regional', and of the Midwestern-ness of Wallace's writing, is the geographical category that has been most extensively brought to bear on Wallace's work by his critics – though this has led to some disagreement. 'Regionalism' emerged in Paul Giles's treatment of Wallace and globalisation: for him, Wallace's work both shows 'affiliations to a tradition of Midwestern realism' and 'speaks to a new kind of American regionalism'.[1] Giles finds an echo in Paul Quinn, who suggests that 'it seems counterintuitive to read David Foster Wallace as . . . a regional writer', since 'it is hard to imagine . . . some future tour of the Midwest rebranded, along the lines of Hardy's Wessex, as Wallace Country' – but nevertheless finds it 'surprisingly instructive, if provocative, to examine [Wallace's] evocations of, and reflections upon, space, place and region', concluding that Wallace presents us with a form of 'radically revised regional writing'.[2] Josh Roiland is less equivocal: for him, Wallace 'was nothing if not spiritually Midwestern', an identity 'closely tied to the subtleties of its land, to the extremes of its weather, and to the expansiveness of its people'.[3] Jurrit Daalder, too, writes that 'for David Foster Wallace . . . the heartland is where home is', substantiating his observation that *Broom* 'offers a series of critical reflections on the Midwest' by elucidating links between Wallace's writing and a tradition of Midwestern fiction, looking back to Sherwood Anderson's *Winesburg, Ohio* (1919) (an annotated copy of which is among Wallace's books held at the Harry Ransom Center) and Sinclair Lewis's *Main Street* (1920).[4] Similarly, Andrew Hoberek suggests that 'it is . . . largely accurate to see Wallace as . . . a Midwestern regionalist, and this in turn points to an even deeper lineage for his concerns and strategies'.[5]

Other critics, though, have expressed scepticism about Wallace's 'regional' status. Samuel Cohen sees the Midwest as a 'home to which [Wallace] was in some ways always alien', arguing that, in truth, 'Wallace was not of Illinois'.[6] Clare Hayes-Brady sees 'the geographic disruption of Ohio, defamiliarizing the familiar landscape' as a strategy for 'disorienting the subject'.[7] Mark McGurl's reading of *Pale King* turns away from 'midwestern regionalism, a form . . . arguably relevant to this writer', and instead emphasises Wallace's interest in 'institutional' spaces: 'his relation to institutions is what makes Wallace, in literary historical terms, most interesting'.[8] David Hering echoes this dichotomy, using an expansive reading of the 'relationship between the idea of the region and institutional . . . space' to suggest 'a deep ambivalence over [Wallace's] own sense of regional identity'. Hering argues that 'to locate Wallace specifically as a Midwestern author is to commit something of a category mistake'; instead, he sees Wallace as a 'performative Midwesterner' who is able to 'stage, where expedient, a Midwestern persona'.[9] Still, these perspectives – divergent as they are – establish the question of Wallace's relationship both to a broad tradition of 'regional' American writing, and to a specific lineage of Midwestern literature and culture. These critics have begun to orientate Wallace's early writing in relation to discourses of regionalism and regional identity, particularly as they were configured in the latter decades of the twentieth century.

What is missing in these critical accounts, though, is a precise sense of what 'region' and 'regional literature' mean – and what a reading of Wallace through these categories might tell us about *Broom*'s relation to the changing geographical contexts of the 1980s. To a degree, these terms are common currency in American literary culture, but some more attention to what they say about the relationships between America's material geography and its culture is necessary for a more firmly historicised understanding of Wallace's geographical engagements in *Broom*. Ann Markusen provides a concrete starting point: 'a region is a historically evolved, contiguous territorial society that possesses a physical environment, a socioeconomic, political, and cultural milieu, and a spatial structure distinct from other regions and from the other territorial units, city and nation'.[10] Accordingly, literary 'regionalism' is writing that is set in such a distinct territory, and takes this distinctiveness as part of its subject: as Karl Beckson and Arthur Granz put it, regional literature is that in which 'a particular locale . . . is conceived of as a subject of interest in itself'.[11] An eloquent expression of American regionalism in an earlier context is Mary Austin's 1932 essay 'Regionalism in American Literature', which proceeds from the insistence that 'there is no sort of experience that works so constantly and subtly upon man as his regional environment'. This environment 'arranges by its progression of seed times and harvest, its rain and wind and burning suns, the rhythms of his work and amusements', and thereby 'forces upon him behaviour patterns such as earliest become the habit of his blood, the unconscious factor in all his mechanisms'. This is why, for Austin, literary regionalism answers to a project of writing 'life as it is lived there, as it unmistakably couldn't be lived anywhere else', and hence of 'completely knowing, not one vast, pale figure of America, but several Americas, in many subtle and significant characterizations'.[12] Regionalism, in this traditional formulation, is the transposition of the economic stratification and specialisation of American geography into the stuff of literary expression.

Wallace came close to this regionalist sentiment in a review of Michael Martone's collection of Midwestern stories *Fort Wayne Is Seventh on Hitler's List* (1990). Wallace praises Martone for invoking 'an Indiana limned in marvellously offhand detail as environment and not setting: wind and soybeans, flat black land, ... tornadoes as religion, basketball as mantra, diners and single-car crashes and endless road construction and agribusiness and cake factories'. He owns that he, 'the reviewer, who's from rural Illinois, might be prejudiced by sentiment', and in a passage that mixes criticism with regional identification, admits that:

> if, for example, you don't know that Eckrich is a conglomerate of evil-smelling meat plants, or that Speech Team is to the Midwest's nerds what computer science is to Cambridge's, that elevators are for grain and not for people, or that the Maumee River has catfish to die for and flows into Fort Wayne and the St Joseph's and St Mary's from Defiance, Ohio ... some of Martone's impeccable detailing might be just data to you.[13]

Here, regional identity is more than a matter of geographical familiarity; it is a texture of habit and instinctive response, rooted in long experience of geographically specific social life. The review is equivocal in its valorisation of Martone's regionalism: ultimately, Wallace recommends the book to a non-Midwestern readership on the basis that it provides 'less ... the emotional cartography of a region than ... the timeless theme of people in circumstances'.[14] But this piece does illustrate Wallace's attention to the distinctive fabric of life and experience in a particular region; and in doing so, it also links back to what we know about Wallace's literary juvenilia: according to D. T. Max, his early attempts at writing included a prose poem about the cornfields of rural Illinois.[15] Regionalism was a familiar geographical sentiment to Wallace; Bloemker's obsession with Midwestern identity may not be portrayed with full sympathy, but there seems to be something of Wallace in it.

How does this attention to regional identity connect Wallace with the geographies of economic transition that form his historical and spatial context? Regionalism is a long-running mode of geographical imagination in American culture; partly owing, as Sergio Perosa has pointed out, to 'the enormous expanse of its geography and its deep regional differences'.[16] And even if regionalism – as Roberto M. Dianotto charges – carries associations of provincial conservatism, discursively fencing off particular locations from the historical change imaginatively located at national level and/or in the metropolitan centres,[17] we should keep sight of the fact that regions are always (as Markusen insists) 'products of material forces in history'.[18] Modes of regional differentiation change along with the material structure of sociospatial relations in which they are formed; and with this, the structures of feeling attached to regions shift, too. Edward L. Ayers and Peter S. Onuf insist on an understanding of regions not as 'areas filled with a certain kind of cultural ether, but rather as places where discrete, though related, structures intersect and interact in particular patterns'.[19] To read through the lens of 'region' is therefore to connect texts with the material geographies that underlie regional differentiation.

In its literary and cultural dimensions, Raymond Williams points to this use of the term, including it among his cultural 'keywords': for him, the historical development of the regional idea 'depends ... on the term of relation' – that is, the particular material relationship between the region and the larger national and international structures of which it is understood to form a part.[20] It is the imaginative elaboration of this term of relation that links 'regional' literature with a larger set of historically contingent sociospatial relationships. The basis of regionalism does not lie in the depiction of static and given regions (even if some regionalists might present it as such), but in the way in which literary representation combines with social, economic and political processes to produce geographical differentiation at connecting material and imaginative levels. If, as Gordon MacLeod and Martin Jones put it, 'regions are historically constructed, culturally contested, and politically charged rather than existentially given and neutral', literature plays an active and shaping role in this process.[21] This historical approach to region as process rather than locale has increasingly informed literary-critical accounts of American regionalism: 'viewing region and regionalism as constructs rather than as natural formations and recognizing the processes of negotiation, contestation and conflict in forming their definition', as the editors of one volume put it.[22] Judith Fetterley and Marjorie Pryse declare that they are 'not trying to establish regionalism as a fixed literary category, but rather to understand it as the site of a dialogical critical conversation' – arguing that 'as both a literary and a political discourse, regionalism . . . also becomes the site of contestation over the meaning of region, one that reveals the ideological underpinnings of regionalization'.[23] Meanwhile, Tom Lutz argues that 'a central issue has been the relation of different groups to ongoing technological, economic, and social change, or, in other words, the relation of the region to the rest of the social world'.[24] This relational and contingent understanding of 'regional' literature and culture has become increasingly commonplace in critical accounts.

Critical notions of regionalism have moved away, then, from what Williams called the 'fly-in-amber quality' more traditionally attributed to the 'regional novel', and towards a historicising use of the term.[25] It may be true, as Hering charges, that Bloemker's speeches in *Broom* are 'flatly undramatized',[26] and this may be in part a function of Wallace's immature style – but allowing his spiel to stand conspicuously as a discourse, working in slightly awkward relation to the language of the novel, also reminds us that (as Fetterley and Pryse suggest) 'region' might best be seen as 'a discourse . . . rather than a place'.[27] Important work in this direction has been done by Hsuan L. Hsu, who trains his focus on how 'attending to the literary dynamics of regional production helps us understand how texts mediate the complex and multidirectional influences among regions, cities, the nation, and the world'.[28] By resisting 'the common perception of regions as privileged sites of spatial identification steeped in nostalgic feelings about rootedness and community', Hsu brings into view 'the ideological work that regionalist literature performs by producing affectively charged localities, as well as the large-scale economic pressures that are provisionally resolved by regional identifications'.[29] Hayes-Brady has noted the importance of a 'renegotiation with . . . geography' to the 'reappropriative experimentation that animated [Wallace's] work'; by taking up a historical approach to literature's regionalising role, I want to train a stronger focus on how Wallace's renegotiations connect with wider re-imaginings of regional geography and identity.[30] In reading *Broom* through the 'regional' keyword, I am less interested than previous Wallace critics in testing the sincerity and authenticity of his regional affiliation to the Midwest. Instead, I want to shift attention towards what the category allows us to see of the novel's intersections with material and imaginative processes of regionalisation; a process taking place against the backdrop of the economic and spatial transitions of the 1970s and 1980s. Regionalisation plays a prominent role in the formation of America's image of its own territorial mosaic; the debate about Wallace's regional 'identity' therefore speaks to the broader question of how his writing situated itself in relation to a traditional American mode of spatial imagination, at a time when the nation's material geography was undergoing fundamental shifts.

The 1980s, the 'new American regionalism' and the 'Great Ohio Desert'

If David Harvey sees 'space-time compression' as a major effect of the transition from Fordist to flexible regimes of accumulation (see Introduction), he also emphasises that this dissolution of geographical differentiations is far from a simple, one-directional process. At the same time, in fact, 'heightened competition under conditions of crisis has coerced capitalists into paying much closer attention to relative locational advantages, precisely because diminishing spatial barriers give capitalists the power to exploit minute spatial differentiations to good effect'. The result is what Harvey calls the 'central paradox' of post-Fordist geography: 'the less important the spatial barriers, the greater the sensitivity of capital to the variations of place . . . and the greater the incentive for places to be differentiated in ways attractive to capital'. On the other hand, for individuals and communities caught up in the maelstrom of transition, 'the fashioning of some localized aesthetic [image] allows the construction of some limited and limiting sense of identity in the midst of a collage of imploding spatialities'.[31] Even as geographical differentiations seem to be effaced by the increasing spatiotemporal flexibility of capitalist production, the process of forming such differentiations – from above and below – is surprisingly intensified.

To recall Williams's phrase, the upheavals of the last decades of the twentieth century entailed paradoxical changes in the regional 'term of relation'; changes taking place precisely as Wallace turned to the task of writing the Midwest in *Broom*. And Harvey's broad argument provides a bridge to more focused accounts of regionalisation in the late twentieth century, and the 1980s in particular: a decade that saw the fruition of the postwar 'metamorphosis in the regional distribution of population, jobs and income' identified by William Issell.[32] This regional metamorphosis is a focus for Edward W. Soja, who commented in 1989 on the 'changing configuration and political meaning of the nested hierarchy of regionalized and nodal locales . . . currently in the midst of a dramatic reformation . . . filled with new contradictions and possibilities that challenge established modes of understanding' – or, as he more pithily puts it, 'the patterned mosaic of subnational regional differentiation [has] become more kaleido scopic, loosened from its former rigidities'.[33] The regional fluidity of capital was also matched by a rapid increase in the mobility of people – producing a 'remarkable interregional migration', according to Ann Markusen and Virginia Carlson.[34] At the same time, confirming Harvey's paradox, American historians have noted an intensification of regional feeling in this period: James T. Patterson remarks that 'passionate regional loyalties, which had been expected to decline as TV and other mass communications tied the nation more closely together, more than held their own as the years passed', while Robert M. Collins finds that 'a resurgence in regionalism pitted the Sunbelt South and Southwest against the Frostbelt states of the industrial Northeast and Midwest'.[35] Regionalisation intensified as American geography became increasingly unfixed.

It is unsurprising, therefore, that critics have identified the 1980s with the 'revitalised interest in American literary regionalism' identified by Michael Kowalewski, countering the dismissal of regional writing as 'merely a historical trend' and emphasising 'the urgency of its present manifestations': a 'new American regionalism'.[36] As Lutz has it, this was a decade in which 'regionalist literature was once again recognised for its literary value and once again became an important focus of critical work'.[37] Herb Wylie and colleagues link this new regionalism with the historical and cultural contexts of postmodernism, and echo Harvey in noting that centralising and globalising tendencies 'have also created a certain cultural and political dislocation and anxiety, which have thrown attention back on local cultures . . . attention that may prove beneficial to a focus on regionalism'.[38] Indeed, this trend was expressed by Wallace's contemporary and correspondent Jonathan Franzen in 1996, when he lamented 'a world in which the rich lateral dramas of local manners have been replaced by a single vertical drama, the drama of regional specificity succumbing to a commercial generality'.[39] But this return to the 'drama of regional specificity' did not necessarily entail a counterfactual return to bounded localities and stable geographical relationships. Instead, practitioners of this 'new regionalism' in the 1980s emphasised the intense inter-regional connectivity that defined new forms of regionalisation and regional identity in this period. Wendell Berry suggested that Mark Twain 'taught American writers to be writers by teaching them to be regional writers' – but anxiously separated this regionality from 'provincialism', the 'conscious sentimentalization of or condescension to or apology for a province'.[40]

This effort to distinguish regionality from provinciality is echoed more strongly in Jim Wayne Miller's 1987 call for a 'cosmopolitan regionalism', building on the unexpected fact that 'improved means of transportation and communication . . . abet the combination of global and regional perspectives' in order to present 'a regional perspective which . . . is appreciative of . . . the ways in which small and great traditions are connected'.[41]

The intensified and paradoxical regionalisation of the 1980s was giving rise to a form of regional writing that rejected a focus on bounded locales in order to probe the relationships between regional and larger scales, and aimed to build new regional aesthetics out of shifting material geographies. These new regionalisms form a context through which to approach the suggestion of a new or revised regionalism in Wallace's writing, raised by both Giles and Quinn. Indeed, Giles's sense of the 'new kind of American regionalism' expressed in Wallace's fictions is 'one reliant less upon the distinct properties immanent within any given place than upon the cartographies relating "here" and "there" to all-encompassing global networks' – a sense that chimes with the cosmopolitan tendencies highlighted by other practitioners and critics of the new regionalism.[42] While there is no evidence that Wallace engaged directly with this new regionalist trend beyond Martone's writing, these accounts provide an important comparative touchstone and contextual starting point for my reading of *Broom*'s regional portrait of the Midwest.

The 'new regionalism's' concern with how regional identities intersect with larger economic, social and cultural structures finds its most obvious echo in *Broom* in the form of the comic portrait of the 'Great Ohio Desert'. The most audaciously imaginary of the novel's narrative spaces, the 'G.O.D.' first appears in a descriptive passage that lays out the landmarks of the novel's version of Ohio: 'with its miles of fine ash-black sand, and cacti and scorpions, and crowds of fishermen, and concession stands at the rim' (*Broom* p. 46). The latter feature introduces the (slightly heavy-handed) running joke that this space provides – its reduction of landscape to a commercialised and artificial operation: 'you can just buy a wander pass at any gate. They're only about five dollars. The really desolate areas can get pretty crowded, of course' (p. 143). As Graham Foster puts it, this is the notion of a distinctive local topography reconfigured as 'a theme park, a constructed fake'– and indeed, we hear that the desert's construction has resulted in the destruction of real-world locations: the community of Caldwell and the Wayne National Forest (*Broom* p. 54).[43] This, as Aisling O'Gara points out, is an evident satire on 'the ability of capitalistic enterprise to shape the landscape'; the reality of the Midwest as a distinctive physical and social geography has been displaced, it would seem, by an artificial and commodified image.[44]

At the same time, though, the joke also encompasses less obvious reflections on both the nature of regionalisation in the 1980s, and the specific image of the Midwest in this period. Tied up with the changing economics of inter-regional relationships were concurrent political and ideological shifts in the administration of regional geography. William Alonso contrasted the prevailing approach to regional policy in the United States during the 1980s to that of the middle of the century: 'an ideological sea change has taken place in the United States . . . away from planning and state intervention and toward a much greater emphasis on market processes', a change which 'clearly means that the style of regional planning which flourished in the 1950s through the 1970s will not be seen again for a long time, if ever'.[45] Instead, as Robert Goodman explored in 1979, centralised government planning was replaced by intensified economic competition between regions left to fight for capital investment in what Goodman terms 'regional wars for jobs and dollars', as business moved 'freely between areas of maximum opportunity, taking advantage of the regional competition it fosters as its migration wreaks havoc with local economic conditions'.[46] The response was for state governments to present the distinctive features of their social and topographical landscapes as incentives for investment. Traditional ideas of regional distinctiveness were recruited into the advertisement of geographical differences as opportunities for development and exploitation, recalling Harvey's account of capital's manipulation of local difference in this period; as Michael French explains, 'the enthusiasm and effectiveness of local boosters affected the timing and character of regional development'.[47] At the same time, regional images increasingly became harnessed to the branding and marketing processes of consumer capitalism – as Midwest historians Andrew R. L. Clayton and Susan E. Gray have noted, 'especially after World War II, the most ubiquitous appearance of the word "Midwest" was in the service of advertising and marketing'.[48] The G.O.D.'s replacement of regional landscape with a commodified image also reflects this transmutation of regional distinctiveness into an asset to be exploited in the new inter-regional competition, as regionalisation turned from a process overseen by federal government to one driven by the scramble for private investment. If Andrew Lang complains that 'this whole thing's just gettin' too goddamn commercialized' (*Broom* p. 421), his judgement also speaks to the way regionalisation increasingly operates within flexible and decentred structures of capitalist competition.

If the relative stability provided by centralised planning had provided the framework for a conception of regionality as the 'commonplace of what has never been debased by industry [and] capital', as Dianotto puts it, *Broom* is instead attentive to the inseparability of regional images and contemporary capitalist structures of production and exchange.[49] In fact, the G.O.D. represents a spatial product geared precisely to the unease that surplus production provokes: it is because 'industrial investment and development in the state are at an all-time high' that the Governor suspects that 'things are just too good . . . the state is getting soft . . . It's getting to be one big suburb and industrial park and mall. Too much development' (*Broom* p. 53). There are specific Midwestern resonances at work here: James R. Shortridge identifies 'a close and continuing association between Middle-western identity and the concept of pastoralism', with this association forming 'the unwavering fact of Middle-western experience – a root identity equivalent to New England's puritanism'.[50] This pastoralism is linked with a traditional mode of imagining the Midwest in relation to the western frontier of the territorial United States: where the frontier represented 'near wilderness, sparsely occupied by a somewhat unstable society', the Midwest has been identified with the establishment of settled society in its wake, a regional mythology incorporating the imagined process of 'civilising' the American 'wilderness'.[51] This image filters through the nostalgia that colours the G.O.D.'s inception: Ohio's Governor lamenting its people's 'forgetting the way the state was historically hewn out of the wilderness' (p. 53).

The Governor's retrospective pastoralism is a reflection of the nostalgia that 'has become a more pervasive aspect of Middle-western identity since 1960' and that 'intensified during the late 1960s and the 1970s', according to Shortridge; a nostalgia that hinged on the image of the region as a link to a past unadulterated by intensified global capitalism.[52] But Wallace does not allow us to lose sight of how the G.O.D.'s commodified version of this image is also physically produced by a globalised system of capitalist production, figured by 'Industrial Desert Design' – who also 'did Kuwait' as well as 'this really kick-ass desert project on the west side of Kerkira, Italy' (*Broom* pp. 54, 234). And these elements are pointedly placed in 1972 (p. 53): on the eve of the global economic crisis that played a key role in prompting the transition towards flexible accumulation, as well as in the year of a domestic energy crisis provoked by the international action of the Organization of Petroleum Exporting Countries (OPEC); this latter context is signposted by the connection between the G.O.D. and Kuwait, and would surely have been unmissable from the perspective of the mid-1980s.[53] Severs notes that, published in 1987, *Broom* 'arrived at a moment of great anxiety over transformations in the U.S. economy'; the G.O.D. uses the lens of Midwestern regional identity to project this anxiety back to its origins in the previous decade, and begins to uncover its connection with the process of regionalisation in the wake of these upheavals.[54] Drawing on popular conceptions of the region, the space of the G.O.D. is configured as an image of a pastoral Midwest protected from the transition to an increasingly global post-Fordist capitalism – but simultaneously revealed as an image that is produced in and through that economic structure itself, and recycled as a commodity.

The G.O.D., then, is a satire on 'the gleeful incorporation of capital into culture' (as Hayes-Brady puts it), and a reflection of the shifting terms of relation that connect regional geographies with global networks of capital – but at the same time, it also functions as a critique of a nostalgic regionalism built on an image of the Midwest as a symbol for the 'authentic' values of America, mobilised in reaction to the flexible and decentred capitalism of the late twentieth century.[55] Indeed, this form of Midwestern nostalgia became a still more prominent aspect of the American geographical imagination as the sociospatial consequences of economic change became increasingly manifest: Shortridge noted in 1989 that 'the image of the Middle West has risen again in the public mind', providing a soothing 'emblem of old securities such as family, community, and sense of place'. But, as Shortridge also points out, these images of stability and certainty map problematically onto a region whose social and economic realities were increasingly complicated by processes of deindustrialisation and shifting regionalisation: 'the image of cowboys and yeoman farmers is flattering in some ways but is hard to reconcile with the largely urban and commercial present realities of the region'.[56] This was a period in which the decline of manufacturing industry had a profound impact on the physical and social geography of the region: as John C. Teaford's account illustrates, 'the late 1970s and early 1980s were the most dismal years of the post-World War II era. Plant closings accelerated, municipal governments teetered on the brink of bankruptcy, and the Midwest led the nation in unemployment'.[57] These events themselves remain something of a lacuna in *Broom*; Hering is right to note that an

understanding of 'the region's topography as economically configured' would not clarify in Wallace's writing until later in his career,
and Chapters 4 and 5 of this book will explore how 'postindustrial'
geography would shape *The Pale King*.[58] But in the G.O.D. we can
already see how the Midwest provided a geographical focus for
Wallace's interrogation of the 'nostalgia mode' that Fredric Jameson
identified in postmodernist culture: a mode Jameson saw as 'an
elaborate symptom of the waning of our own historicity, of our lived
possibility of experiencing history in some active way'.[59] Rather than
allowing for a concrete historical consciousness, this form of regionalism subsumes the material geography of the Midwest into a nostalgia industry; a commodified regional mythology offered as a hollow
alternative to the challenges of late twentieth-century transition.

Through the G.O.D., regional geography and its representations
cohere as an important point of connection between Wallace's first
novel and the spatial reconfigurations of American capitalism in the
1970s and 1980s. Although the concrete social conditions of the
Midwest, as its economic terms of relation with national and global
economic structures was reconfigured in these decades, remain
largely absent from the novel, this initial satire suggests that geography was already shaping a developing concern with how literary
traditions like regionalism could relate to the challenging sociospatial context of the late twentieth century. And indeed, there is a clear
trajectory from the 'G.O.D.' into Wallace's more mature writing in
the form of one of his major journalistic essays of the 1990s: first
published in *Harper's*, 'Getting Away From Already Being Pretty
Much Away From It All' (originally titled 'Ticket to the Fair') returns
to the construction of a theme-park-style space in the Midwestern
landscape, albeit in the much more down-to-earth context of the
1993 Illinois State Fair. And, like the G.O.D., this fair is depicted
as a festival of capital and consumption, a fact most evident in the
extended description of the 'Expo Building', in which 'Every interior
inch . . . is given over to adversion [*sic*] and commerce of a very
lurid sort' – 'a Xanadu of chintzola' (*Supposedly* pp. 118, 120). For
Quinn, Wallace establishes this spectacle of consumer capitalism
in order to push back: in particular, Quinn highlights the moment
at which Wallace reports the discovery of real grass underneath an
imposed surface of artificial turf (*Supposedly* p. 89), a moment that
points Quinn towards the way in which, across Wallace's writing,
'the seemingly flat surfaces of commodified or synthetic spaces . . .
are sifted for traces of the real'.[60] There is a line of continuity from
the apprentice satire of the G.O.D. into Wallace's more developed

exploration of the relationship between his writing and the social contexts it attempts to address.

Certainly, there is a concern for 'the real' and its relationship to the spectacle of capital at work in this essay – but this is a category that remains difficult to pin down. Wallace frames the Fair's 'garish and in all ways exceptional Spectacle' as the apotheosis of a childish solipsism, sustaining the child's view of the world as 'For-Him alone, unique at its absolute center' (*Supposedly* p. 90); its appeal lying in a retreat from the real and relational world. But at the same time, it is through the framework of this spectacle that 'the sheer *fact* of the land is to be celebrated' (p. 91, original emphasis). Indeed, the 'fact of the land' beyond the Fair's festival of consumption is far from a straightforward presence: an early and poetic paragraph that places the fair in the landscape of the Midwest and its geological origins – 'These gentle rises and then dips down to rivers are glacial moraines, edges of the old ice that shaved the Midwest level' – ends with a reflection that 'by the time I left for college the area no longer seemed dull so much as empty, lonely . . . You can go weeks without seeing a neighbor. It gets to you' (p. 84). If the fair's spectacle is associated with a kind of solipsism bound up in the consumer capitalism of the late twentieth century, the real landscapes of the region itself are connected with an alienation that is unpacked more fully later, when Wallace associates this experience with the configuration of the landscape around large-scale capitalist agriculture: 'You're alienated from the very space around you . . . because out here the land's less an environment than a commodity' – and 'It's probably hard to feel any sort of Romantic spiritual connection to nature when you have to make your living from it' (p. 92). Expanding on the satire of the G.O.D., the essay works both to establish a portrait of the fair as an embodiment of rampant consumerism and to close off the possibility of a nostalgic retreat into an 'authentic' regional space beyond this spectacle.

How, then, can writing speak to the reality of the late twentieth-century Midwest as a spatial and social environment? This question is figured subtly in the essay through a series of references to the hugely destructive 'Great Flood' that took place in the Midwest over the summer of 1993: local journalists are found 'talking about the apocalyptic floods to the immediate west, which floods are ongoing'; we hear that 'The serious flooding's well to the west of Springfield', and later that 'the East St. Louis levee's given way; National Guardsmen have been mobilized' (*Supposedly* pp. 85, 88, 113). These moments amount to an insistent but never fully developed acknowledgement of very real regional events with major social consequences, a shadow side to the artificial spectacle of the fair – but their isolation and lack of elaboration produce a sense of a text in which this reality struggles to gain a foothold between a spectacle of consumption and an alienating economic landscape. In fact, it is only when one reference is embedded within Wallace's account of the opening of the fair itself that a sense of the significance of these references is allowed to unfold, as the state Governor speaks 'plainly and sanely and I think well – of both the terrible pain of the '93 flood and . . . of the special importance of this year's State Fair as a conscious affirmation of real community' (pp. 90–1).

Only through the spectacle of the fair, in other words – as compromised as this spectacle might be – can the social significance of this important material context begin to be articulated. Elsewhere, in a similar vein, Wallace catches a brief glimpse of the construction of the fair's physical architecture, as 'Workmen crawl over structural frames. We wave at them; they wave back' (*Supposedly* p. 86) – momentarily, the artificial space of the fair discloses both its material 'structural frames' and the real labour that has produced them. And later, we hear that 'The first sign of the Help Me Grow area is the nauseous bright red of Ronald McDonald's hair' – but this ubiquitous signifier of international consumer capitalism also points towards a regional social programme, albeit one rather condescendingly described as 'a statewide crisis line for over-the-edge parents to call and get talked out of beating up their kids' (p. 88). It is these details that serve to substantiate the essay's otherwise dubious suggestion that this festival of capital is in fact what satisfies an 'urge physically to commune, melt, become part of a crowd' – and the claim that 'The real Spectacle that draws us here is Us' (pp. 108, 109), an authentic sense of communality that counters the commodified nostalgic images of the region satirised in the G.O.D. Having turned a satirical lens on this pastoral image of the Midwest in *Broom*, in 'Getting Away' Wallace worked towards a complementary point that signals the connections between his work, the 'new American regionalism' of the 1980s, and the altered regional mosaic of the United States in these decades: that the sociospatial reality of the Midwest can be authentically known and expressed only in and through its imbrication within the overarching structures of late twentieth-century capitalism.

Writing the 'heartland city': Architectural Form in *Broom*'s Cleveland

I want to bear in mind this sense of a need to write the Midwest by way of its unstable terms of relation with the shifting geographical structures of the American and global economies as I return to *Broom*, and its construction of a Midwestern geography whose correspondence to the immediate reality of the 1980s is closer – but not necessarily simpler – than that of the G.O.D.'s satirical space. While the G.O.D. is an ostentatiously invented zone that allows for play with regional images and their construction within the larger structures of capitalism, *Broom*'s primary narrative focus falls on a more grounded locale: the city and suburbs of Cleveland, Ohio. But if this setting anchors the text in a real Midwestern geography, it does not do so straightforwardly. Rather, the fluid mobility of people and capital that had restructured the regional terms of relation in post-Fordist America is built into the early arrangement of the narrative itself, which opens not in Cleveland but Mount Holyoke College in Massachusetts (near Amherst, where Wallace first wrote the novel). Having begun with this regional displacement, the novel's mode shifts repeatedly between the implied authority of extradiegetic narration (*Broom* pp. 28–31, 32–44), non-contextualised dialogue that leaves the reader with no direct sense of spatial context at all (pp. 22–7), text-within-text in the form of Rick Vigorous's journal (pp. 32, 44), and a nested narrative involving a protagonist who 'has to fly all the way to Switzerland', suddenly invoking a global scale (p. 24). But at the same time, against these spatiotemporal and narrative jumps we encounter anxious flurries of redundant and excessive geographical information – 'the Shaker Heights Nursing Home, in Shaker Heights, right near Cleveland, Ohio, which was where Lenore lived, in East Corinth' (p. 31) – invoking an anxiety of regional orientation that reflects Bloemker's focus on the psychological hazards of Midwestern geography. The early part of the novel, then, is structured by both a fluid geographical mobility and an alternate performance and withholding of Midwestern narrative cartography; a formal expression of the paradoxical return to local and regional specificity within the transition to a flexible and decentred economy, and an echo of the new combinations of locality and cosmopolitanism that the 'new regionalism' was exploring in the 1980s.

Eventually, after forty-four pages, *Broom* settles into a descriptive section that places the novel firmly in its primary frame: 'in that part of downtown Cleveland called Erieview Plaza, right near Lake Erie', and in 'the city of East Corinth, Ohio, which was where [Lenore] had her apartment' (*Broom* pp. 44–5). Alongside its evident enthusiasm for geographical specification, the narrative voice in this belated placing sequence implies a local familiarity ('that part of downtown Cleveland called . . .') in contrast to the disorienting jumps that characterise the narrative to this point. And indeed, this section is key to establishing the novel's image of Cleveland, introducing both the real spaces (Erieview Plaza) and imagined landscapes (East Corinth) that Wallace blends to form his portrait of the city. And yet it is unsurprising, given the role of inter-regional mobility in the mode of regionalisation taking place in the 1980s, that this narrative centre is initially framed through an approach by road: Lenore 'going seriously fast . . . preparatory to being flung by I-271 northward into the city itself . . . with her car tracing the outline of the city of East Corinth, Ohio' (pp. 44–5). This is a Midwestern locale whose cartography is traced in motion along the national lines of connection formed by Interstate highways. Cleveland may provide a geographical centre for *Broom*, but it is one that also reflects the shifting structures of regionalisation in the American economy of the 1980s.

In fact, in a 1987 interview Wallace apparently insisted that he had never actually been to Cleveland: 'a middle-westerner . . . he wanted a heartland city that he could imagine instead of describe'.[61] This preference for 'imagining' over 'describing' might seem to imply a diminishing of the importance of the material, historical city to his writing of 'heartland' geography – and Mary Shapiro has argued as much, suggesting that this was a city Wallace 'might as well have picked out of a hat to represent the Midwest'.[62] A closer look at the architecture and topographical arrangement of his version of Cleveland, though, suggests that subtler interplays between real and imagined versions of the regional city are at work. This interplay is particularly evident in Wallace's approach to one of the novel's recurring spatial nodes: the Bombardini Building, where Lenore and Rick work. There are, we hear, 'two reliable ways to identify the Bombardini Building' (*Broom* p. 45). Pointedly, neither relies on the building itself, the form of which is only briefly described in the course of the novel; instead, building on the mobile epistemology that structures the opening sections, we approach this space indirectly. The first means of identification involves 'a look from the Erieview tower, high and rectangular not far from the Terminal section of Cleveland's downtown', and the 'huge dark shadow' this tower casts over the surrounding space of the city (p. 46). This, too, is pointed, although some investigation into the history of Cleveland is required to see it as such. The (real-world) Erieview Tower does indeed form a centrepiece for the 'part of downtown Cleveland called Erieview Plaza' (p. 44) – a section of the city that was extensively redeveloped in the early 1960s, with the Tower itself completed in 1964. Wallace's mention of the tower's 'high and rectangular' appearance is an oblique nod to the 'International Style' modernist aesthetic that characterises the Tower and the Plaza development as a whole; a project overseen by the New York-based architect I. M. Pei (whose architectural legacy will reappear in *Jest*, and in Chapter 2 of this book).

For Pei, the project was 'bold, aesthetic and realistic'– but his judgement was not universally accepted by the city's inhabitants.[63] As Teaford relates, Midwestern developments like Erievew Plaza 'in the fashionable "International Style" of modern architecture . . . had little interest in regional or local diversity'; a sentiment echoed in the judgement of the Cleveland Fine Arts Advisory Committee, one of whose members argued (according to Teaford) that 'New York-designed Erieview Plaza . . . reflected the condescending, parochial outlook of New Yorkers toward Cleveland'.[64] It was an architectural development, in other words, that embodied tensions between Midwestern regional identity and the aesthetic dominance of the East Coast. And these aesthetic misgivings were joined by social tensions, according to Thomas F. Campbell, as Cleveland residents judged that 'too many of the city's resources and too much administrative attention were being concentrated on this downtown project to the neglect of the neighbourhoods'[65] – creating a cosmopolitan downtown in a global style that provided little felt connection with the social reality of the city. Wallace's re-imagining of the heartland city stands literally in the problematic shadow of reconstruction imposed from above and without. Using the shadow of the Erieview Tower to find their way to Wallace's own invented building, the novel's reader seems to pre-empt Bloemker's worries about the cultural politics of Midwestern orientation.

This context lies below the surface of the text, but it bears some significance for Wallace's writing of his own Bombardini Building. The mention of the shadow is followed by an extensive elaboration:

> the sun, always at either a right or a left tangent to the placement of the Tower, casts a huge, dark shadow of the Building over the surrounding area – a deep, severely angled shadow that joins the bottom of the Tower in black union but then bends precipitously off to the side . . . (*Broom* p. 46)

This part of the description scans simply enough, but a second glance reveals that there is an odd confusion of (Erieview) Tower and (Bombardini) Building at play: the shadow ought to belong not to the Building but to the Tower. Confusions are at work between real and fictional buildings; between the historical legacy of architectural development and Wallace's own fictional practice of re-imagining the city. The conflation echoes the ambivalence over the cultural politics of reconfiguring and re-imagining space that surrounds the Erieview development and its legacy, blurring the distinctions between this material reconfiguration and Wallace's fictional one. These confusions are embodied in the form of the remainder of the description:

> In the morning, when the shadow casts from east to west, the Bombardini Building stands sliced by light, white and black, on the Tower's northern side. As the day swells and the shadow compacts and moves ponderously in and east, and as the clouds begin to complicate the shapes of darknesses, the Bombardini Building is slowly eaten by black, the steady suck of the dark broken only by epileptic flashes of light caused by clouds with pollutant bases bending rays of sun as the Bombardini Building flirts ever more seriously with the border of the shadow. (p. 46)

As though dramatising an attempt to compensate for the earlier Tower/Building conflation, the passage repeatedly (and redundantly) names 'the Bombardini Building' in full. But confusions continue to arise: 'the shadow casts' feels odd – usually shadows *are* cast, they do not themselves cast. This is followed by a disarming conjunction of the incompatible directional signals 'in and east', together with an unexpected double-pluralisation of 'shapes of darknesses' – a phrase that gestures towards the visualisation of 'shapes' while in fact withholding the empirical information the reader requires to perform such a visualisation.

Eventually, the passage moves away from this slipperiness and towards an emphatic attempt at placing the building: 'the Bombardini Building, then, is easy to find, occurring nowhere other than on the perimeter of the sweeping scythe of the Midwest's very most spectacular shadow' (*Broom* p. 46). The phrase 'nowhere other than' together with the repetition of the specifying 'of the' suggests another anxiously dramatised gesture of orientation, similar to the others scattered across the novel's opening sections; an orientation now placed explicitly within the named regional frame of the Midwest. Balancing these attempts at regional placing against the disruptions of the Tower's shadow, Wallace embeds the connection between his regional re-imagining and the conflicted material legacy of regional development into his descriptive mode. And despite the firm placement that ends this description, the disorienting effect of the shadow is later reprised as the perspective is reversed, and Rick describes the view from within the building: 'It is a windy day. Clouds scud. The wind whips at Lake Erie, the shaggy lake. My office window is sliced neatly in black. Half. In the lit half, the wind makes Lake Erie shaggy' (*Broom* p. 300). Even as the Erieview development delivers on the promise of its name, connecting narrative space with regional landscape, the Tower's shadow splinters the view of one of Cleveland's most distinctive natural features, and this fracturing is echoed in the collapse of Rick's usual verbosity into monosyllabic stuttering and repetition; the regional vista and the language of spatial description itself are simultaneously in the process of breaking up.

The ambiguity of the architectural history embodied by the Tower and its shadow is reflected again in the second means of identifying the Bombardini Building: 'the white skeleton of General Moses Cleaveland, which found itself in shallow repose in the cement of the sidewalk in front of the Bombardini Building, its outline clearly visible' (*Broom* pp. 46–7). This joke is more obvious: the city's historical founder recurring as a sign and orienting marker for its re-imagined contemporary architecture. But there is also a subtler gesture at orientation in process – 'found itself' – which forms another echo of Bloemker's discourse on the troubled process of regional self-awareness. And this is set against the second part of the joke: 'the General's rest . . . largely untroubled save by the pole of a sign which jutted disrespectfully out of Cleaveland's left eye socket . . . reading: "THIS SPACE RESERVED FOR NORMAN BOMBARDINI, WITH WHOM YOU DO NOT WANT TO MESS"' (p. 47). Bombardini, the businessman and landlord whose mission is to 'grow to infinite size' and thus leave no 'room for anyone else in the universe at all' (pp. 91–2) – an obvious figure for the spatially omnivorous force of capital – has literally staked his claim to this historical marker of regional identity.

Through the problematised placing of the Bombardini Building, Wallace overlays his own practice of imagining this heartland city with the historical reconfiguration of Midwestern space, which is in turn inextricably caught up in the shifting geo-cultural politics of inter-regional relationships. This is an example of the 'systematic use of architecture' Hering has identified in Wallace's work; here, Wallace's text makes contact with particular historical forms and practices of architecture that are tied up with the complexities of

Midwestern identity in the late twentieth century.[66] This is architecture not just as a thematic correlative, but as a point of connection with material and cultural practices of regionalisation; conflicting historical and contemporary claims are made tangible through both the physical construction and the literary representation of built space. Wallace's novel, then, provides one of the instances identified by David Anton Spurr, in which 'architecture and modern literature come together in ways that appear to break down the barriers between the two art forms, or at least to construct bridges between them'.[67] Indeed, Wallace's own construction of his fictional building coincided with a wave of construction of office space that, as Teaford notes, took place in Cleveland in the first half of the 1980s.[68] And as Clayton and Gray establish, the practice of architecture (like that of literature) has a longer, prominent historical role in the social identity of the Midwest: 'the architectural creativity of the turn of the twentieth century that produced . . . a peculiarly Midwestern urban landscape . . . helped mould an enlarged conception of the Midwest as a commonwealth'.[69] With this legacy of local architectural innovation in mind, it is easy to see how the design and imposition of Erieview Plaza from New York represented a particular bugbear for Midwesterners. Architecture forms a contested practice in which larger shifts in the terms of relation between region, nation and globe are mirrored, and Wallace's own production of narrative space was deliberately embroiled in this contestation.

Wallace also appears to nod towards this older tradition of twentieth-century Midwestern architecture in the space of the Shaker Heights Nursing Home, a prominent setting in the opening part of the novel. A number of key architectural features that Wallace attributes to this building are worth noting. It has 'just one story' (*Broom* pp. 29), and is distinctly geometric in form, a decidedly modernistic feature that filters into the descriptive phrasing of the passage that describes in detail: 'pentagonal' shapes, 'concentric circles', 'interior planes' (pp. 37–8). At the same time, this form also involves a permeation between the interior and exterior portions, with 'ten areas arranged in a circle' and linked by 'a courtyard filled with chalky white gravel and heavy dark plants . . . the interior planes of each section walled in glass and accessing into the courtyard' (p. 38); a merging of interior and exterior architectural space suggestive of an architectural form that exists in close relation to the landscape around it.

In these features, the building recalls aspects of the 'Prairie School' of architecture led by Midwesterner Frank Lloyd Wright in

the early twentieth century: a movement that produced buildings
whose strongly modernist features, though linked with the innova-
tions of the International Style (Lloyd Wright himself had a prominent place in a defining exhibition of International Style architecture
at the Museum of Modern Art in New York in 1932), were at the
same time intended to complement the landscapes specific to the
Midwest. The Prairie School architects, Teaford suggests, 'not only
shared Midwestern roots but also found a common inspiration in the
heartland landscape. They appreciated the beauty of the Midwestern
prairie, and their architecture was intended to complement the
region's flat expanses'.[70] Lloyd Wright himself wrote: 'We of the
Middle West are living on the prairie. The prairie has a beauty of its
own and we should recognize and accentuate this natural beauty, its
quiet level.'[71] As H. Allen Brooks outlines, the resultant architecture
– as 'a regional manifestation of the international revolt and reform
then occurring in the visual arts' – was based on a 'clear, precise,
and angular' approach.[72] Teaford links this aesthetic directly to the
Midwestern landscape, noting that Prairie School buildings 'were
stark, clean, and ground-hugging like the broad, uncluttered prai-
ries of Illinois'.[73] Architectural modernism, in this regional context,
involved an aesthetic negotiation between internationalism and the
particularities of local landscape.

There is a degree of conjecture involved in linking Wallace's
nursing home to this architectural lineage; and it is true that the
circular arrangement of Wallace's building is a divergence from the
angular approach more typical of the Prairie School. But the Prairie
School provides an intriguing complement to Wallace's architectural invention, not least since the aesthetic tensions embodied in
the combination of local landscape and cosmopolitan form were
also reflected in Lloyd Wright's effort to speak simultaneously to
a more abstract nationalism: 'the hope that one day America may
live her own life in her own buildings', tied up with an appeal to the
'ideal' of 'Democracy'.[74] In both aesthetic and ideological terms, the
Prairie School was constructed around an attempt to reconcile plu-
ralising localism with a singular national identity – directions that
seemed inherently opposed in Austin's contemporaneous literary
regionalism. This architecture embodies the ambiguous and unstable
terms of relation that structure regional identity: ambiguities and
instabilities that were exaggerated in the transitions of the 1980s,
when Wallace revisited Midwestern architectural form through his
imagined Nursing Home. Indeed, the interconnection of different
scales embodied in the architecture of the Prairie School recurs in

the argument made by architect Kenneth Frampton, around the time of *Broom*'s composition, for a 'critical regionalism' in architecture. Such a regionalism would present 'a manifest critique of universal civilization' (the homogenising effect of late twentieth-century capitalism). But it would do so without relying 'simply . . . on the autochthonous forms of a specific region alone', avoiding 'simple-minded attempts to revive the hypothetical forms of a lost vernacular'.[75] Reflecting the anti-provincialism of the literary 'new regionalism', Frampton's argument indicates that a notion of architecture as the site of contestation between national, international and regional claims was of renewed relevance against the backdrop of the 1980s.

With this in mind, it is worth paying attention to the manner of Wallace's description of the Nursing Home, which begins from a detached and top-down perspective reminiscent of an architect's blueprint: 'The Home was broken into ten sections, areas they were called, each roughly pentagonal in shape . . .' (*Broom* p. 38). Along with the geometric terms of the building's description, this initial viewpoint is suggestive of the controlled, rationalised space associated with International Style modernism – the conceptual framework of this architecture's universalising aesthetic. But this detached description of the building is followed in the next paragraph by an abrupt shift to a different point of view:

> Down a corridor, through a door, around the perimeter of one area, past a gauntlet of reaching wheelchaired figures, out a glass panel, through the steamy crunch of courtyard gravel, through another panel, and halfway around the perimeter of area F, Mr. Bloemker led Lenore to her great grandmother's room . . . (p. 38)

Static and detached description is supplanted by a mobile, ground-level perspective, as a rapid sequence of short clauses, linked by a disorienting series of directional markers, produces a sense of being led abruptly and blindly through the space. This shift in perspective reflects a disjuncture between the top-down point of view of the International Style and the grounded, immediate experience of the space, inscribing this gap into the text's descriptive form – and producing the sense Hering describes of a space that is 'almost as hard for the reader to picture as it is for the inhabitants and visitors to negotiate'.[76] This is an architectural – and a fictional – form conditioned by a slippage between cosmopolitan and local perspectives, and the dislocation that this slippage produces. While Lloyd Wright sought a synthesis of the regional and the international in the forms of his architecture, Wallace's descriptive opacity reflects the confusions

engendered by a built form caught up in the increasingly paradoxical relationships between regional identity, national ideology and
internationalist aesthetics that emerged from the transitions of late
twentieth-century capitalism; it is not coincidental that in an office
at the heart of this labyrinthine space sits the 'disoriented' Bloemker,
orator of problematic Midwestern identities (*Broom* p. 34).

The Bombardini Building and the Shaker Heights Nursing Home
are built forms that incorporate both the architectural history of the
Midwest and the tensions inherent in regional identity – tensions
present in the longer history of Midwestern development, but
brought to the surface by the transitional forms of regionalisation
taking place in the 1980s. In both cases, Wallace draws out aspects
of architectural form and history and turns them into features of his
own descriptive and narrative style, entwining these architectures
with his fictional practice. Alongside these architectures, two more
narrative spaces also draw specific attention to a 1980s proliferation
of broadcast media and its attendant geography of cultural production: the fictional outlying town of East Corinth, which 'lay in the
shape of a profile of Jayne Mansfield' (*Broom* p. 45), and the interior
space of the 'Gilligan's Isle' bar, themed around the television sitcom
Gilligan's Island. These spaces represent a geography literally shaped
by the cultural products of cinema and television, cultural forms
associated with Coastal centres of production – Hollywood and New
York.

This overlaying of Coastal cultures onto Midwestern spaces is
suggestive of the general 'image of the Midwest as a cultural colony'
identified by Teaford as a factor in the reformation of Midwestern
regional identity, and the perception of Midwestern cities especially,
in the late twentieth century – as 'New York City and Los Angeles
were to dominate television broadcasting, and producers and execu-
tives on the East and West Coasts would determine what millions
of heartlanders would watch every evening'.[77] If the shadow of
the Erieview Tower frames the Bombardini Building, the primary
workplace of *Broom*'s Midwesterners, the cultural projections of
Hollywood and New York onto East Corinth and Gilligan's Isle literally shape their domestic and leisure environments. In these narrative spaces, Wallace's use of architectural and urban form extends to
a figure for the tensions between Midwestern spaces and cosmopolitan culture, and an inscription of the sense that – as Olivia Banner
observes of the later story 'The Suffering Channel' – the 'Midwest,
consumes . . . cosmopolitan New York, produces'.[78] These are architectures which answer to Raymond Williams's understanding of the

'regional' category as 'a function of cultural centralization' – 'an expression of centralized cultural dominance'.[79] It is worth noting, though, that Wallace selects images that belong not to the explosion of broadcast media in the 1980s but to an earlier moment: both Jayne Mansfield and *Gilligan's Island* were mid-century phenomena (the latter televised between 1963 and 1967, notably contemporaneous with the construction of Erieview Plaza). Again, Wallace's image of the Midwest responds both to intensifying regional insecurities of the 1980s and to longer lineages of twentieth-century culture.

But should we read these spaces as simply reflective of the subsumption of Midwestern regional identity by a dominant Coastal and cosmopolitan culture? It is worth looking closely at the mode in which these spaces are described in *Broom*. East Corinth in particular seems an obvious joke:

> leading down from Shaker Heights in a nimbus of winding road-networks, through delicate features of homes and small businesses, a button nose of a park and a full half-smiling section of rotary, through a sinuous swan-like curve of a highway extension and tract housing, before jutting precipitously westward in a huge, swollen development of factories and industrial parks, mammoth and bustling, the Belt curving no less immoderately a couple miles south into a trim lower border of homes and stores and apartment buildings and some boarding houses ... (*Broom* p. 45)

Hayes-Brady sees this as 'the neoliberal city made literal'; Severs reads it as a debased form of town planning that has 'made a mockery of the social body of the community'.[80] But a closer inspection of the passage reveals that it is animated by a jostling between the superimposed Hollywood image and the insistent materiality of a typical Midwestern suburb. 'Button nose of a park' clearly renders the Mansfield image dominant, reducing the park itself to a function of this image. But as the passage progresses, the dominance of the image softens: 'huge, swollen development of factories and industrial parks' could stand without the Mansfield image to frame it. By the end of the passage, the 'trim lower border' – still a feature of Mansfield's profile, but less obviously so, with 'border' more associated with geographical space than the human figure – is overwhelmed by the piled-up list of geographical features ('homes and stores and apartment buildings and some boarding houses'). East Corinth is not, as O'Gara argues, 'entirely artificial': the passage shows us the stubborn insistence of regional space itself, even as it is inscribed with the images of a dominant Coastal culture.[81] As the passage progresses, the overlaying of a Hollywood image onto the physical and social space of the Midwest becomes more like a double exposure, with the cosmopolitan cultural reference and the regional landscape simultaneously visible. East Corinth forms a point of contestation between the local scale of a Midwestern town and the overarching scale of a homogenising culture: an example of how literary narrative can express 'anxieties, contradictions, and possibilities situated at the boundaries between different scales', as Hsu puts it.[82]

This is a process also reflected in the description of 'Gilligan's Isle'. This space is important to the unfolding of the novel's plot, providing a meeting point for different characters in two separate scenes (*Broom* pp. 138–45, 301–5). A setting for substantial dialogues, it is marked as a prominent social space in the novel's narrative geography. But like East Corinth, this social frame at first appears pointedly artificial – conditioned by 'decades of pop mythology attached to television', as Matthew Luter puts it:[83]

> The inside of the place was round, the walls painted to look like the filmy blue horizon of the ocean, and the floors were painted and textured to resemble a beach. There were palm trees all over, fronds hanging down ticklishly over the patrons. Sprouting from the floor were huge statued likenesses of the whole cast . . . The bar itself was made of that vaguely straw-like material that the huts on the show were made of. (p. 139)

The terms of the description seem to emphasise the artificiality of the space – 'to look like', 'to resemble' – while the 'filmy' appearance of the walls underscores the association with recorded and broadcast culture. This, perhaps, is one place through which Wallace 'imagines American geographic space as a level playing field where the mass media operate in all zones simultaneously', as Giles puts it.[84] But at the same time, the passage insistently reminds us of the physical architecture behind this artificiality: for all the overlaying of television's images, this is a 'painted and textured' space, one composed of 'material'. This insistence on materiality is redoubled in the sensual aspect of the 'ticklish' fronds, which counters the general emphasis on visual effect, while the strangely organic 'sprouting' statues offset the insistent artificiality. The suggestion of a generic global frame in the desert island theme, filtered through a national, Coastal-dominated system of cultural production, is contested by an insistent materiality; the bar becomes a space in which the sense of the Midwest as cultural colony is both registered and countered. Flannery O'Connor – an earlier regionalist whom Wallace counted among the writers who 'really rung [his] cherries'[85] – complained of stories that 'might have originated in some synthetic place that could have been anywhere or nowhere . . . [that] hadn't been influenced by the outside world at all, only by the television'. O'Connor argued for a strong emphasis on regional identification in response (since 'the best American fiction has always been regional').[86] Gilligan's Isle, though, reflects the extent to which late twentieth-century places are often both synthetic and localised, mediated and material; dualities within which regional identities must be rethought and recast. It is appropriate that, while Shaker Heights forms his workplace, Gilligan's Isle is the backdrop for Bloemker's anxious Midwestern spiel (*Broom* p. 142).

In constructing his imagined version of this heartland city, Wallace entwined architectural and cultural legacies in order to make visible the practices of producing regional space – both material and cultural, economic and imaginative – whose histories spanned the twentieth century but that were increasingly conflicted in the transition that followed the 1970s. *Broom* deploys real and invented architectural references to engage with a culturally contested process of regionalisation, characterised by the tensions between international and cosmopolitan aesthetics on the one hand, and local social and physical geographies on the other. These features of the novel indicate an interest in architectural form and history that would continue to frame Wallace's approach to writing geographies in his subsequent novels; the remaining chapters of this book will continue to explore how built spaces and topographies inform the construction of metropolitan and postindustrial spaces in *Jest* and *Pale King*. Already, though, the overlapping of Wallace's own process of imagining the heartland city with historical processes of reconstructing the Midwest suggests a conscious connection between his own literary practice and the wider forces at play in the production of regional space.

Regional Geography, Literary Practice and Textual Production

From the regional satire of the G.O.D. to the re-imagining of Cleveland's topography, *Broom* was self-consciously concerned with its own placement in a geography of literary practice and production that, bound up with the shifting relationships between regions and scales produced by the transition to a flexible post-Fordist capital-

ism, was implicated in a reconfigured process of cultural regionalisation. And if Bloemker's regionalist discourse is pointedly situated
within built spaces that embody the negotiations between locations
and scales that produced regional space in the late twentieth century,
then it is also notable that Wallace's invented Bombardini Building
– in its ambivalent relation to the Coastal monolith of the Erieview
Tower – plays host to the transplanted 'Frequent and Vigorous
Publishing', a firm exiled to the Midwest from New York (*Broom*
p. 65). Rick's publishing house is caught between issuing '*The
Frequent Review*' – 'a literary thing' that occasions the nested stories
that appear throughout *Broom* – and 'publishing monosyllabic prop-
aganda praising . . . a clearly ineffective and carcinogenic pesticide
to be disseminated among . . . Third World countries' (p. 65). This
ambiguous architectural space is also a site for literary and textual
production poised between the heartland city, an East Coast literary
culture, and the global structures of transnational capital.

It is unsurprising, then, that textuality has an ambiguous status
in *Broom*. This is evident in the first appearance of Rick's journal, a
text-within-the-text that serves to incorporate a dramatised practice
of written expression into the novel's narrative construction, and
which opens with a return address:

> *Richard Vigorous*
> *62 Bombardini Building*
> *Erieview Plaza*
> *Cleveland, Ohio*
> ***Reasonable reward for proper and discreet return.***
> (*Broom* p. 32, original italics and boldface)

The appearance of the address both signals the introduction of the
journal and plays a role in establishing the regional setting in this
early part of the novel: textuality and regionalisation are overlaid
here. But its inclusion, as the boldface mention of a reward for
return emphasises, is also motivated by an anxiety about the possibility of the physical loss of the textual object; placement and
the prospect of misplacement are both in play. This is appropriate, since it is also Rick who recounts the submissions to *The
Frequent Review*: nested pseudo-literary narratives that introduce
secondary diegetic levels, shifting away from the novel's primary
Midwestern frame and towards other scales and places. Thus we
hear, as I have already noted, of the skin-disease-sufferer who flies
'all the way to Switzerland' (p. 24), but also of the character who
'wanders the streets of New York City' (p. 181) – the cosmopolitan

publishing centre from which 'Frequent and Vigorous' itself has been transplanted – and the vague 'isolated cabins deep in the woods of whatever state the story [of the crying child] takes place in' (p. 105). The novel's regional setting is punctured and unsettled by these interruptions from a larger network of literary composition, publishing and exchange.

The narrative complications produced by the nested stories are further compounded by the introduction of an unexpected echo across narrative levels: in the cabin story, the crying child is given peas 'which the woman had been too sleepy and gorged even to unfreeze and cook' (*Broom* p. 109), while in the primary Cleveland frame, Lenore eats 'frozen peas' in the Spaniard house (p. 161). The migration of incidental detail across narrative levels gives a hint of metalepsis: what Gérard Genette calls (in intriguingly spatial terms) the 'deliberate transgression of the threshold of embedding', a disorienting conflation of previously separate diegetic spaces.[87] If the economic and political upheavals in America's regional geography were uprooting regions like the Midwest from their established system of relationships, the play with diegetic levels in Wallace's novel – much like the mobility built into its narrative construction – gives formal expression to this process. Text and narrative are thus mechanisms for an ontological decentring of novelistic space that is distinctly at odds with traditional literary regionalism; the act of narration itself is what fractures Austin's sense of 'life as it is lived there'.[88] For Wylie and colleagues, the new regional literature of the 1980s is not associated with a conservative recuperation of 'local colour' aesthetics. Instead, this new regionalism deploys more experimental approaches, 'to see what shape it may take within the centralizing and homogenizing pressures of global consumer culture and to see whether it can break out of its traditional stereotype as an aesthetically conservative form'.[89] In the narrative play at work in *Broom*, we can see something of this re-examination of the formal possibilities of regional identification. Complementing the deployment of architectures as sites for the interplay of regional identity and cosmopolitan culture, publishing and textual practice operate as problematised processes of regionalisation, and literary production itself becomes associated with the disorientation that Bloemker attributes to 1980s Midwestern identity.

It is also significant that these stories – appearing within the text of *Broom* itself via Rick's oral retellings to Lenore – undergo shifts between textual and spoken modes of storytelling. As such, they are complexly located and relocated between a cosmopolitan

network of textual production and the localised frame of oral narration. Storytelling itself is an act that, in this late twentieth-century
moment, is poised between practices occurring at differentiated but
overlapping geographical scales – a fact that also helps explain the
spatially and narratively disruptive role attributed to these nested
stories in the novel. And much as the G.O.D. was later reprised and
reconfigured in Wallace's State Fair essay, this play with the differently scaled frames of storytelling – and their relationship to the
construction of the Midwest – reappears in another of Wallace's
1990s essays: 'Derivative Sport in Tornado Alley', a piece whose
publishing history itself reflects some of the questions that had
emerged in *Broom*. The piece was first published in the quintessentially cosmopolitan, New York-based *Harper's* in 1992, a context
that foregrounds the same question of the framing of the Midwest
from outside which *Broom* had filtered through architecture and
topography – and draws inevitable attention to the question of the
mediation of regional space and identity, a recurrent concern for
Wallace critics. In his reading of the essay, Quinn suggests that it
'brings home . . . Wallace's habitual *mediation* of his home region',
noting that 'he is always aware of contexts of publication and
reception, sometimes exhilaratingly, sometimes excruciatingly so'.[90]
Hering agrees, pointing out that in Wallace's writing 'the Midwest
is rarely, if ever, afforded the chance to exist as an unmediated
environment'.[91] Certainly, as Wallace's stature grew, so did his self-
conscious awareness of his own position within the Coastal literary
industry whose presence in *Broom*'s Bombardini Building plays such
a destabilising role.

But the publication of 'Derivative Sport' in *Harper's* was also
paralleled in the same year by a second appearance: this time in a collection of essays on the Midwest titled *Townships*, edited by Michael
Martone – whose Midwestern stories Wallace had reviewed with
such enthusiasm – and published in Iowa City by Iowa University
Press. The text itself, then, was doubly positioned: both stationed
outside the Midwest and looking back in, and at the same time
situated within a regional publishing context as part of a collection of Midwestern voices. In this sense, it echoes the shuttling of
Broom's nested stories between national literary networks and localised frames of narration. Accordingly, the positioning of the essay
between the Midwest and the Coast is signalled as a framing concern
in its opening line: 'I left my boxed township of Illinois farmland to
attend my dad's alma mater in the lurid jutting Berkshires of western
Massachusetts' (*Supposedly* p. 3). Within this frame, the essay turns

on the recounting of a distinctly spurious tale about a tennis game interrupted by a tornado – a climactic story prefaced as Wallace, 'strangely eager to speak of weather', identifies 'my township' as 'a proud part of what meteorologists call Tornado Alley' (p. 15). It is notable that Wallace's eagerness is to speak, not to write, of weather; this text, whose narrative, composition and publication were all self-consciously divided between local and national scales of literary production, also begins to signal the interplay of textual and spoken narratives that had appeared in *Broom*.

Regional folklorist Larry Danielson has explored the role of oral tornado narratives – like the one Wallace foregrounds in this essay – in the regional identity of the Midwest, suggesting that these stories form a 'commonplace in the contemporary oral tradition of the central United States', linked to a longer history in which they have proved 'compelling to the regional imagination' of the Midwest.[92] The importance of this oral tradition in the construction of Midwestern regional identity explains the significance of Wallace's eagerness to 'speak' of weather; and the turn towards this spoken form is reflected in the climax to the tale, narrated in terms that mark it as an imitation of oral storytelling:

> I seem to remember whacking a ball out of my hand at Antitoi to watch its radical west-east curve, and for some reason trying to run after this ball I'd just hit, but I remember the heavy gentle lift at my thighs and the ball curving back closer and my passing the ball and beating the ball in flight over the horizontal net, my feet not once touching the ground over fifty-odd feet, a cartoon, and then there was chaff and crud in the air all over and both Antitoi and I either flew or were blown pinwheeling for I swear it must have been fifty feet to the fence the one court over, the easternmost fence, we hit the fence so hard we knocked it halfway down, and it stuck at 45° . . . (*Supposedly* 19)

Here Wallace deploys a loose syntactic structure to imitate the patterns of spoken narration, with the increasing informality of the diction in the latter clauses ('chaff and crud in the air all over', 'I swear it must have been') a further signal in this direction. The increasingly tenuous scenario, and the blasé terms in which it is related, also link the tale to the tradition of the tornado story as described by Danielson: 'the account that describes the bizarre consequences of the storm, uncolored by melodrama and tragedy', typically related in a tone that is 'largely unemotional, dramatic or incredible though the information may be'.[93] This textual performance of spoken storytelling amounts to a claim to regional belonging by way of a deeply rooted oral tradition. But at the same time, the appearance of the textual marker ''' towards the end of the passage undercuts this subtly, drawing attention back to the textuality of the piece – and hence the doubled geographical context of its publication. The tension between spoken and textual forms, and their complex relationship to the wider processes of regionalisation taking place in the wake of the transition to a new flexible form of capitalism, evidently continued to preoccupy Wallace several years after *Broom*'s initial composition.

Considering this reflexive aspect of Wallace's engagement with the literary production of regional geographies, it is intriguing to follow these concerns out of the content of Wallace's texts and into the publication and promotion of *Broom* itself – material practices belonging to the Coastal, cosmopolitan system of literary production whose relationship to regional space and identity is explored in both *Broom* and 'Derivative Sport'. Sheila Hones has established the role that promotion plays in the 'spatial event' of the literary text, pointing out that paying attention to how the promotion of texts is framed by material and imagined geographies can play an important role in fully illuminating the geography of the text itself.[94] The promotional material produced by Penguin for the release of *Broom* in 1987 included a large wall poster for the 'Contemporary American Fiction' range in which the novel is included (a copy of which is held in the Harry Ransom Center's Wallace archive [HRC 4.4]). The front side of the Penguin poster clearly signals a geographical aspect to the promotion of these texts: it is taken up mostly with a reproduction of a painting from Jasper Johns's 'Maps' series (from 1963), underneath which is emblazoned the tagline 'celebrates the wealth of a nation'. The choice of Johns's painting itself is an illuminating one: a representation of American territory in an abstract expressionist style strongly associated both with New York and with an international cosmopolitanism, incorporating European influences. The poster appeals to the literary 'wealth of the nation' from a decidedly Coastal perspective.

The composition of the Johns painting itself is arranged according to a familiar cartographic view of the continental territory of the United States; individual states' names (or their abbreviations) are shown in stencilled font, with boundaries clearly visible in the centre of the composition (where the Midwestern and Northern states are shown), and different colours used to differentiate the states. Across the painting, though – and particularly towards the edges of the national territory – these boundaries are obscured or effaced entirely, with the edges of the composition squeezed by the encroachment of strong, seemingly random brushstrokes. On the eastern side of the map in particular – where the Midwest borders the Northeastern Coastal states – the geography seems to blur and blend; though not to become entirely undifferentiated, as strong blues and yellows contrast with greys and deep reds. Regional boundaries are both suggested and deformed; the painting neatly reflects Soja's account of how, through the late twentieth century, 'relatively stable mosaics of uneven regional development have suddenly become almost kaleidoscopic'.[95] Selecting this image to promote the series, Penguin seem to indicate that theirs is a series deeply connected with contemporary American geography – but a geography whose regional composition has become newly unstable and unfixed.

The reverse side of the poster provides a more prosaic but no less revealing picture of how geography and regionality functioned in Penguin's promotion of the novel and the series. The texts included in the range are shown in a list organised by region, each illustrated with a neat cartographic outline, as if to offset the territorial confusion introduced by the Johns painting on the other side. Six regions are represented: Pacific Coast, Mountain States, Midwest, Southwest, South, and Northeast (with a separate section for writers 'living abroad') – it is notable that a considerable majority of titles belong to the Northeast region (a list that is placed adjacent to Penguin's own New York address). Also notable is that, despite Wallace's Midwestern origins and for all the overt concerns with the images and topographies of the Midwest that I've explored in this chapter, *Broom* itself is not placed among the Midwest's offering, but instead listed under the Southwest (Wallace being based in Tucson at the time of the poster's production, presumably). This placement of Wallace's text is a clear indication that it is the location of literary production, not the content of the novel itself, that is privileged here – and of just how mobile the association between region and text had become in the 1980s. The poster shows that regional identity was still deployed as a key aspect of literary production and promotion, possessing (as the 'new regionalism' recognised) a continued literary-cultural weight; but, in this 1980s context, regionality is conceived not as a set of distinctive areas from whose specificities works themselves emerge, but as a network of literary production organised by and around the metropolitan publishing centre of New York. Reflecting the play with publishing and narrative production within the text itself, the poster shows us how the promotion of *Broom* involved a deliberate insertion into a pre-existing cultural geography – but also how publishing works as a practice that itself actively reconfigures this geography

Conclusion

Reading Wallace's first novel through the 'regional' keyword brings into view how, from this early stage, his texts interacted closely with the shifts and developments in the American geographical imagination during the transitional period in which he wrote. The satire of the G.O.D., together with the mobility that is embedded in the novel's formal approach to narrative space, reflects the forms of intensified regionalisation that connected the Midwest with the fluid and flexible structures of the new post-Fordist configuration of American capitalism, while also articulating a critique of nostalgic regionalism as a mode of response to this context. Instead of this nostalgia, Wallace's re-imagined portrait of Cleveland draws on the city's topographical and architectural history in order to explore the position of his own literary practice, poised between regional and national scales and imbricated in the processes of regionalisation that occur at these intersections. If regionalisation as a form of geographical imagination plays a prominent and long-running role in the spatial culture of the United States, *Broom* – and the 1990s essays that expanded on some of its ideas – reflect on how regional images and identities were being renegotiated amid the material decentring and restructuring of geographical relationships after the 1970s.

This debut novel shows Wallace playfully, but not un-seriously, reflecting on how the Midwest in which he had grown up was imagined; and in turn, it indicates the start of a concern with historically contingent forms of spatial imagination. Leaving aside *Broom*'s more overt philosophical themes allows us to see how the novel incorporates an interest in the histories of built environments; and particularly in architecture as a practice of spatial reconfiguration which provides Wallace with an analogue to his own re-imagining of the heartland city. This interest in the development of built forms and their relation to literary practice would remain a key theme for Wallace in his later novels, as the remaining chapters of this book will explore. On top of this, the exploration of the G.O.D.'s commodified Midwestern nostalgia indicates the beginning of an interest in the intersections between geographical imaginaries and forms of historical consciousness; again, themes which would recur across *Infinite Jest* and *The Pale King*. And, in the play with publishing, textual production, and narrative form in *Broom* and 'Derivative Sport', these concerns also crystallise into a reflexive awareness of the imbrication of Wallace's own literary practice in a decentred and reconfigured material and cultural geography, in which regional narratives and images are negotiated and contested across local and national frames. An engagement with the construction of the Midwest, then, prompted the beginning of a preoccupation with the nature and function of literature as a spatial practice, embedded in both material and cultural geographies – one that I will continue to trace across his subsequent novels. But if the Midwest was the early focus for this concern, in 1989 Wallace was to make a geographical move that would have a profound impact on the direction of his fiction and on the development of his longest and best-known novel. It is to the metropolis of Boston, and to *Infinite Jest*, that I turn in the following chapter.

Notes

1. Giles, *Global Remapping*, p. 175.
2. Quinn, '"Location's Location,"' pp. 87, 104.
3. Josh Roiland, 'Spiritually Midwestern: What Middle America Meant to David Foster Wallace', (7 August 2015), <https://medium.com/just-words/spiritually-midwestern-216d8041f50d> [retrieved 28 February 2022].
4. Daalder, 'Geographic Metafiction', pp. 220, 222–3.
5. Hoberek, 'Wallace and American Literature', pp. 34–5.
6. Cohen, 'Whiteness', p. 235.
7. Hayes-Brady, *Unspeakable Failures*, p. 131.
8. Mark McGurl, 'The Institution of Nothing: David Foster Wallace in the Program', *boundary2*, 41.3 (Fall 2014), 27–54 (pp. 28, 30).
9. Hering, *Fiction and Form*, pp. 44, 41, 47.
10. Ann Markusen, *Regions: The Economics and Politics of Territory* (Totowa, New Jersey: Rowman & Littlefield, 1987), pp. 16–17.
11. Karl Beckson and Arthur Granz, *Literary Terms: A Dictionary*, third edition (London: Andre Deutsch, 1990), p. 227.
12. Mary Austin, 'Regionalism in American Literature', *The English Journal*, 21.2 (February 1932), 97–107 (p. 97, 98, 104–5, 98).
13. David Foster Wallace, review of Michael Martone, *Fort Wayne Is Seventh on Hitler's List: Indiana Stories*, *Harvard Book Review*, 15/16 (Winter/Spring 1990), 12–13 (p. 13).
14. Ibid. p. 13.
15. D. T. Max, *Every Love Story Is a Ghost Story: A Life of David Foster Wallace* (London: Granta, 2012), p. 23.

16. Sergio Perosa, *American Theories of the Novel: 1793–1903* (New York: New York University Press, 1983), p 159
17. Roberto M. Dianotto, *Place in Literature: Regions, Cultures, Communities* (Ithaca: Cornell University Press, 2000), pp. 9 ff.
18. Markusen, *Regions*, p. 17.
19. Edward L. Ayers and Peter S. Onuf, 'Introduction', in Edward L Ayers, Patricia Nelson Limerick, Stephen Nissenbaum and Peter S. Onuf (eds.), *All Over the Map: Rethinking American Regions* (Baltimore: The Johns Hopkins University Press, 1996), pp. 1–10 (p. 5).
20. Williams, *Keywords*, p. 264.
21. Gordon MacLeod and Martin Jones, 'Renewing the Geography of Regions', *Environment and Planning D: Society and Space*, 19 (2001), 669–95 (p. 670).
22. Herb Wylie, Christian Reigel, Karen Overbye and Don Perkins, 'Introduction: Regionalism Revisited', in Christian Riegel and Herb Wylie (eds.), *A Sense of Place: Re-Evaluating Regionalism in Canadian and American Writing* (Edmonton, Alberta: University of Alberta Press, 1998), ix–xiv (x).
23. Judith Fetterley and Marjorie Pryse, *Writing Out of Place: Regionalism, Women, and American Literary Culture* (Urbana: University of Illinois Press, 2003), pp. 2, 6.
24. Tom Lutz, *Cosmopolitan Vistas: American Regionalism and Literary Value* (Ithaca: Cornell University Press, 2004), p. 15.
25. Raymond Williams, 'Region and Class in the Novel', in Douglas Jefferson and Graham Martin (eds.), *The Uses of Fiction: Essays in Honour of Martin Kettle* (Milton Keynes: Open University Press, 1982), pp. 59–68 (p. 61).
26. Hering, *Fiction and Form*, p. 54
27. Fetterley and Pryse, *Writing Out of Place*, p. 7
28. Hsuan L. Hsu, 'New Regionalisms: Literature and Uneven Development', in John T. Matthews (ed.), *A Companion to the Modern American Novel 1900–1950* (Malden, Massachusetts: Blackwell, 2009), pp. 218–39 (p. 223).
29. Hsuan L. Hsu, *Geography and the Production of Space in Nineteenth-Century American Literature* (Cambridge: Cambridge University Press, 2010), pp. 23, 167.
30. Hayes-Brady, *Unspeakable Failures*, p. 45
31. Harvey, *Condition*, pp. 294, 295–6, 303–4.
32. William Issell, *Social Change in the United States, 1945–1983* (Basingstoke, Hampshire: MacMillan, 1985), p. 70.
33. Edward W. Soja, *Postmodern Geographies: The Reassertion of Space in Critical Social Theory* (London: Verso, 1989), pp. 159, 162.
34. Ann R. Markusen and Virginia Carlson, 'Deindustrialization in the American Midwest: Causes and Responses', in Lloyd Rodwin and Hidehiko Sazanami (eds.), *Deindustrialization and Regional Economic*

Transformation: The Experience of the United States (Boston: Unwin Hyman, 1989), pp. 29–59 (p. 34).

35. James T. Patterson, *Restless Giant: The United States from Watergate to Bush v. Gore* (Oxford: Oxford University Press, 2005), p. 79; Robert M. Collins, *Transforming America: Politics and Culture in the Reagan Years* (New York: Columbia University Press, 2007), p. 15.

36. Michael Kowalewksi, 'Writing in Place: The New American Regionalism', *American Literary History*, 6.1 (Spring 1994), 171–83 (p. 171).

37. Lutz, *Cosmopolitan Vistas*, p. 190.

38. Wylie et al., 'Regionalism Revisited', p. xii.

39. Jonathan Franzen, 'Why Bother?' (1996), in *How to Be Alone* (London: Fourth Estate, 2002), p. 69.

40. Wendell Berry, 'Writer and Region', *The Hudson Review*, 40.1 (Spring 1987), 15–30 (p. 22).

41. Jim Wayne Miller, 'Anytime the Ground is Uneven: The Outlook for Regional Studies and What to Look Out For', in Mallory and Simpson-Housley (eds.), *Geography and Literature*, pp. 1–20 (pp. 9, 13).

42. Giles, *Global Remapping*, p. 175.

43. Graham Foster, 'A Blasted Region: David Foster Wallace's Man-Made Landscapes', in Hering (ed.), *Consider*, pp. 37–48 (p. 39).

44. Aisling O'Gara, 'An Understanding of One's Place in the System: An Introduction to *The Broom of the System*', in Coleman (ed.), *Critical Insights*, pp. 97–111 (p. 106).

45. William Alonso, 'Deindustrialization and Regional Policy', in Rodwin and Sazanami (eds.), *Deindustrialization*, pp. 221–40 (p. 228, 230).

46. Robert Goodman, *The Last Entrepreneurs: America's Regional Wars for Jobs and Dollars* (Boston: South End Press, 1983), p. 51.

47. Michael French, *US Economic History since 1945* (Manchester: Manchester University Press, 1997), p. 65.

48. Andrew R. L. Clayton and Susan E. Gray, 'The Story of the Midwest: An Introduction', in Clayton and Gray (eds.), *The Identity of the American Midwest: Essays on Regional History* (Bloomington: Indiana University Press, 2001), pp. 1–26 (p. 23).

49. Dianotto, *Place in Literature*, p. 22.

50. James R. Shortridge, *The Middle West: Its Meaning in American Culture* (Lawrence, Kansas: University Press of Kansas, 1989), pp. 1, 7.

51. Ibid. p. 5.

52. Ibid. pp. 72, 73.

53. See Collins, *Transforming America*, pp. 7 ff.

54. Severs, *Balancing Books*, p. 36

55. Hayes-Brady, *Unspeakable Failures*, p. 68.

56. Ibid. p. 143.

57. John C. Teaford, *Cities of the Heartland: The Rise and Fall of the*

Industrial Midwest (Bloomington: Indiana University Press, 1993), p. 220

58. Hering, *Fiction and Form*, p. 152.
59. Jameson, *Postmodernism*, pp. 20–1.
60. Quinn, '"Location's Location,"' p. 92.
61. Helen Dudar, 'A Whizz Kid and his Wacky First Novel', in Burn (ed.), *Conversations*, pp. 8–10 (p. 10).
62. Mary Shapiro, *Wallace's Dialects* (New York: Bloomsbury, 2020), p. 145
63. Quoted by Thomas F. Campbell, 'Cleveland: The Struggle for Stability', in Richard M. Bernard (ed.), *Snowbelt Cities: Metropolitan Politics in the Northeast and Midwest since World War II* (Bloomington: Indiana University Press, 1990), pp. 109–36 (pp. 114–15).
64. Teaford, *Cities of the Heartland*, pp. 216, 219.
65. Campbell, 'Cleveland', p. 115.
66. David Hering, 'Form as Strategy in *Infinite Jest*', in Coleman (ed.), *Critical Insights*, p. 138.
67. David Anton Spurr, *Architecture and Modern Literature* (Ann Arbor: University of Michigan Press, 2012), p. 3.
68. Teaford, *Cities of the Heartland*, p. 224.
69. Clayton and Gray, 'Story of the Midwest', p. 21.
70. Teaford, *Cities of the Heartland*, p. 147.
71. Frank Lloyd Wright, 'In the Cause of Architecture' (1908), in Hugh S. Donlan and Martin Filler (eds.), *In the Cause of Architecture* (New York: Architectural Record Books, 1975), pp. 53–120 (p. 55).
72. H. Allen Brooks, *The Prairie School: Frank Lloyd Wright and his Midwest Contemporaries* (Toronto: University of Toronto Press, 1972), pp. 3, 5.
73. Teaford, *Cities of the Heartland*, p. 148.
74. Lloyd Wright, 'Cause of Architecture', p. 56.
75. Kenneth Frampton, 'Towards a Critical Regionalism: Six Points for an Architecture of Resistance', in Hal Foster (ed.), *Postmodern Culture* (London: Pluto Press, 1987), pp. 16–30 (p. 21–2).
76. Hering, *Fiction and Form*, p. 53.
77. Teaford, *Cities of the Heartland*, p. 224.
78. Olivia Banner, '"They're Literally Shit": Masculinity and the Work of Art in the Age of Waste Recycling', *Iowa Journal of Cultural Studies*, 10.1 (2009), 74–90 (p. 79).
79. Williams, 'Class and Region', p. 60.
80. Hayes-Brady, *Unspeakable Failures*, p. 68; Severs, *Balancing Books*, p. 42.
81. O'Gara, 'An Understanding', p. 108.
82. Hsu, *Geography*, p. 15.
83. Matthew Luter, '*The Broom of the System* and *Girl with Curious Hair*', in Clare (ed.), *Cambridge Companion*, pp. 67–81 (p. 74).

84. Giles, *Global Remapping*, p. 164.
85. Laura Miller, 'The Salon Interview', in Burn (ed.), *Conversations*, pp. 58–65 (p. 62).
86. Flannery O'Connor, 'The Regional Writer' (1963), in Sally Fitzgerald and Robert Fitzgerald (eds.), *Mystery and Manners: Occasional Prose* (London: Faber, 2014), pp. 56, 58.
87. Gérard Genette, *Narrative Discourse Revisited*, trans. Jane E. Lewin (Ithaca, New York: Cornell University Press, 1988), p. 88.
88. Austin, 'Regionalism', p. 104.
89. Wylie et al., 'Regionalism Revisited', p. xiii.
90. Quinn, '"Location's Location"', pp. 94, 96.
91. Hering, *Fiction and Form*, p. 41.
92. Larry Danielson, 'Tornado Stories in the Breadbasket: Weather and Regional Identity', in Barbara Allen and Thomas J. Schlereth (eds.), *Sense of Place: American Regional Cultures* (Lexington: University of Kentucky Press, 1990), pp. 28–39 (p. 29).
93. Ibid. p. 32.
94. Hones, *Literary Geographies*, esp. p. 130.
95. Soja, *Postmodern Geographies*, p. 172.

Chapter 2

'Abroad in the urban night' (I): Metropolis, 'Postmetropolis' and *Infinite Jest*

Introduction: *Infinite Jest*, Boston and the 'city novel'

If the Midwest, and notions of regional identity, had structured the geographies of *Broom*, Wallace's move to Boston in 1989 entailed a shift in focus: having been concerned with the construction of a regional 'heartland' city in his first novel, he would now set *Infinite Jest* in and around one of America's oldest and largest cities. But the depth of Wallace's engagement with Cleveland and its topographical history in the earlier novel indicates that Boston might well have presented Wallace with more than simply a setting for this next project. How did this city shape Wallace's approach to his novel? Can *Jest* be placed in a particular moment in the history of Boston – and of the American metropolis, and the literary and cultural attitudes associated with it? And what might a reading attentive to this geography tell us about Wallace's relationship to the context of social and economic change in late twentieth-century America?

At first glance, these might seem counterintuitive questions to ask of *Jest*. Description of the cityscape is sparse: there is no direct glimpse of the exterior geography of the city until page 85, when Tiny Ewell makes a brief journey through Watertown by taxi (*Jest* pp. 85–7). Narrative action which takes place in the exterior spaces of the city is also limited to a relatively small number of scenes: of the 981 pages of the novel's main text (excluding endnotes), only around 139 are set in Boston's streets and public spaces. It is not often in this sprawling text that we find ourselves, like Randy Lenz, 'abroad in the urban night' (p. 539). By contrast, the Enfield Tennis Academy ('E.T.A.') and Ennet House – the novel's two dominant institutions – take up a combined total of approximately 507 pages. The novel's long final chapter, meanwhile, is organised around situations of interiority and stasis, with Hal Incandenza and Don Gately in parallel states of horizontal motionlessness within the confines of E.T.A. and St Elizabeth's Hospital; the city almost entirely absent, apart from the occasional glimpse. (I refer, here and in the following chapter, to the parts of the text separated by circular figures as 'chapters'. There are twenty-eight of these, though they are not numbered in the text). This predominance of institutional enclosure leads David Hering to read *Jest* as a novel in which 'the space outside the institution becomes increasingly abstract and effaced', while exterior spaces 'tend to be fundamentally compromised, adulterated or hostile', such that 'the streets of Cambridge ... are plagued with murder, drug abuse and violent crime'. In response, Hering maintains, the novel performs a 'retreat' away from the city and 'into institutional spaces'.[1]

The relatively small amount of page space devoted to the cityscape might account for a relative lack of close attention to its role in the novel in existing critical responses. Those critics who have examined this role have tended to see urban space as a secondary reflection of apparently more central thematic concerns. In an earlier reading, Hering maps thematically significant shapes onto the movements of characters through the city to illustrate a 'geographically concise dramatization' of key thematic and formal elements.[2] Similarly, Stephen J. Burn discusses Wallace's weaving of suggestive place names into a 'philosophical topography of the novel's landscape'.[3] Heather Houser, meanwhile, reads the relative positions of E.T.A. and Ennet House within the city in terms of how they 'express and enforce many of the ethical and social concerns that give *Infinite Jest* its thematic heft'.[4] These readings suggest that the importance of urban geography might run deeper in the novel's DNA than the relatively limited amount of direct description suggests. Each shares an assumption, though, that the topographies of Boston are backdrops onto which purportedly more primary thematic aspects can be mapped. Jeffrey Severs encapsulates this tendency when, having proposed to 'enter into this book's philosophical conundrums by first mapping the ground', he moves almost immediately from the latter to the former: thus (he argues) Wallace shows 'Enfield to be grounded not in space but the *Tractatus*esque "little facts that make up ... idea[s]"'.[5] In this reading, the geography of the city itself seems to dissipate into philosophical abstraction.

I want to complement these readings by proceeding in the opposite direction: rethinking urban space not as constituted by thematic and formal concerns but as constitutive of them. This line of reading has been suggested, in fact, in a number of extra-academic responses to the novel which have attempted to map the connections between Wallace's text and the real Boston it describes. It first appeared in a *Boston Globe* article by Danielle Drellinger and Javier Zarracina, published shortly after Wallace's death, lamenting that Boston had lost 'one of the most imaginative chroniclers of the city'. Illustrated with a map incorporating both real and fictionalised elements of the city as it appears in *Jest*, the article emphasised the layering of Bostonian detail in the novel, and the role of this fidelity to the fabric of the city in constructing 'the book's intense verisimilitude'.[6] This thinking was taken up in a Flikr.com account belonging to Tim Bean and titled 'Infinite Jest Tour of Boston', which compiled photographs of Boston locations featured in the novel.[7] It was a blog project by William Beutler, though, that developed this idea most fully: the result, titled 'Infinite Boston', is described as an attempt to 'say something interesting about the role a given location plays in the story, how it appears in the present day, and what it was like to visit', and includes numerous photographs.[8] The project was expanded in Beutler's subsequent development of 'Infinite Atlas', an interactive map of Boston that plots significant locations in *Jest* – its goal to 'identify, place, and describe every cartographic point I could find in the novel'.[9] This trend of reading the novel alongside the geography of Boston has been continued by Bill Lattanzi, who wonders at the extent to which Wallace's novel engages with the minutiae of Boston: 'it's weird. Wallace only lived here for three years, but you might think he was an Allston-Brighton lifer from all the geographical shout-outs in *Infinite Jest*'. For Lattanzi, tracing *Jest*'s origins in the geography of Boston helps us 'to better understand [Wallace], to walk where he walked in some sort of strange, secular Haj'.[10]

This assertion that *Jest* – and Wallace's literary practice – might be better understood by tracing a path from the city to the text has been more recently echoed by Andrew Hoberek, who notes *Jest*'s 'commitment to describing Boston and its environs in the late 1980s and early 1990s' as well as its 'interest in mapping the social terrain of Boston'.[11] Adam Kelly, too, has explored this idea in an article in which he describes the experience of taking students on the Boston tour first compiled by Beutler. Kelly admits that he had until then 'lacked . . . an appreciation of the rootedness of [Wallace's] work in a specific geography'. Having toured the city, he relates how he came to see that 'Wallace's vision . . . is significantly rooted in the vagaries and possibilities of place'.[12] This suggests a markedly different conception of the city's role in the novel to that of a hostile counter-point to a primary institutional focus. It is very different, too, from the idea of the city as a backdrop onto which more primary themes are projected. In fact, though, Kelly himself has not taken forward the key implication of his article – that the city might have exerted a generative influence on the novel's construction. Instead, his sub-sequent reading prefigures Hering's, suggesting that 'the point made consistently throughout *Infinite Jest* is that the world outside institutions is inhospitable to the contemporary individual'.[13]

This incomplete critical turn towards the city suggests that there is room for a deeper reading of its role in the novel; of the social and spatial encounters that the city occasioned for Wallace, and their connections to the wider economic and social shifts taking place in America during the latter decades of the twentieth century. On a basic level, and despite the apparent reluctance of *Jest* to shine its spotlight on the cityscape, the extent of the geographical detail that 'Infinite Boston' and 'Infinite Atlas' bring into focus is sufficient to demonstrate the closeness of Wallace's engagement with the minu-tiae of Boston's geography at the turn of the 1990s. Umberto Eco characterised mappings of this kind as 'episodes of literary fanship – which is a pleasant activity, and moving at times, but different from the reading of texts'.[14] But more recent work in literary geography has highlighted the critical work that these mappings can do: as David Cooper and Gary Priestnall point out, they provoke a move 'away from metaphorical mapping' and prompt us 'to reflect upon the relationship between textual and mapped space'.[15] In this sense, by mapping the connections between city and text, these readings do some of the work of reframing *Jest* as a novel firmly embedded in the city.

To take this further, I want to use as a starting point the critical idea of the 'city novel'. This interpretive category has a long history, stretching at least to Blanche Housman Gelfant's 1954 analysis of a type of fiction predicated upon a close relationship between 'a social vision of the city and the aesthetics of the novel'.[16] For Gelfant, a city novelist is one for whom the 'formal elements in their work – style, plot, tone, theme, and structure – give literary expression to their specific attitude towards the city as a place, an atmosphere, and a way of life'.[17] This is the central principle around which the criti-cal category of the city novel has developed: Burton Pike describes fiction in which the city forms 'a presence and not simply a setting', and in which 'the process by which the writer evokes the city appears to parallel the process by which the citizen seeks to encompass his experience of it'.[18] Similarly, Richard Lehan talks of a 'symbiosis between literary and urban text',[19] while Raymond Williams, speaking of Charles Dickens's novels, remarks that 'the experience of the city is the fictional method; or the fictional method is the experience of the city'.[20] The essential approach is perhaps best summarised by Diane Wolfe Levy: the city novel is one in which 'the role of the city shifts from that of a symbolic setting for the action to that of an active component of the action. The city ultimately imposes its shape on the fiction'.[21] This is the interpretive framework in which I want to read *Jest*, in order to approach the question of how not only the novel's themes but also its form might be tied to Wallace's experience of Boston between 1989 and 1992, and how this experience connects his composition of the novel with changes affecting the material and imaginative organisation of American geographies.

Metropolis and 'Postmetropolis': Wallace, Boston and the American City

It needs to be borne in mind that all three of Wallace's novels are set in cities. To distinguish *Jest*'s Boston from the regional Cleveland of *Broom* and the 'postindustrial' Peoria of *Pale King* (discussed in Chapters 4 and 5), my keyword for reading Wallace's second novel is 'metropolitan': a city distinguished by its size and its economic and political significance, but also by a particular social and cultural identity. To be 'metropolitan', according to the *Oxford English Dictionary*, is to be 'characteristic of or influenced by the metropolis, its way of life . . . urbane, sophisticated, excitingly varied, cosmopolitan'.[22] Wallace wasn't new to big cities: the modest success of *Broom* had brought him into contact with the literary and cultural industries of New York in particular. But the immersion in Boston's metropolitan environment seems, as D. T. Max's biography indicates, to have proved exciting and stimulating, a marked and refreshing contrast to the familiar landscapes of the Midwest. He described his new neighbourhood of Somerville in almost giddy terms: 'It's lovely and crowded and ethnic and a far cry from flat black land straight to the world's curve.' To his agent Bonnie Nadell, he wrote simply: 'Boston is *fun*'.[23] A metropolitan environment and way of life had imprinted itself on his consciousness.

That this environment played a major role in the development of *Jest* is indicated by accounts of its compositional history. Wallace had begun work on the novel much earlier: as early as 1986, in

Max's account, when he already had the title and seems to have been developing a plotline involving Canadian terrorists.[24] But though he had worked on 'something like' *Jest* in that year before returning to it in 1988 and 1989 (as he later wrote to Marshall Boswell), 'none of it worked, or was alive' – until 'in '91–'92 all of a sudden it did'.[25] Wallace's time in Boston coincided with the resuscitation of a floundering compositional process; and Max suggests that Wallace was throwing out 'piles' of manuscripts in June 1990, perhaps rejecting old material that didn't fit with the new direction his novel was taking.[26] Stephen Moore's account of the draft of the novel he received from Wallace in Autumn 1993 seems to bear this out: according to him, sections set outside the city – including the series of dialogues between Hugh Steeply and Remy Marathe on the Arizona hilltop – were not included in this draft and were presumably added later, suggesting that Wallace's geographical focus during the period of 'alive' writing from 1991 to 1992 was trained more strongly on Boston's geography than the final novel might at first glance suggest.[27]

But how does my 'metropolitan' keyword connect Wallace's new urban sensibility, and *Jest*'s revived composition, to the historical context of the city in the early 1990s? As Raymond Williams points out in his own *Keywords*, the emergence of 'the city as a really distinctive order of settlement, implying a whole different way of life' belongs historically to the maturation of industrial capitalism at the end of the nineteenth century; the development of capitalism and the sense of a metropolitan way of life are closely connected.[28] For Williams, 'there are decisive links between the practices and ideas of the avant-garde movements of the twentieth century and the specific conditions and relationships of the twentieth-century metropolis' – but by the end of the century, 'the cultural conditions of the metropolis have decisively changed'.[29] The historical conjunction of a distinctive metropolitan sensibility, a set of cultural practices and ideas, and the material conditions of capitalist development indicates how this keyword links Wallace's novel with the transitional history of American capitalism at the end of the twentieth century. Like the 'region', the metropolis forms a category through which the profound social, spatial and economic transitions of the late twentieth century were registered; the construction and expression of metropolitan identity operate in dynamic relation to the material geography of the city. Through this and the following chapter, I read *Jest*'s vision of the 'vital North American metropolis' of Boston (*Jest* p. 30), and the thematic concerns and formal strategies that this

vision engenders, as an expression of the sociospatial organisation of
late twentieth-century urban capitalism.

As David M. Gordon suggests, the topography of the metropolis
is deeply inscribed with the structures of the capitalist economy:
'city growth has not flowed from hidden exogenous sources but
has been shaped instead by the logic of the underlying economic
system' – 'American capitalism has bred the American city'.[30] And
the Boston of the late 1980s and 1990s was a city shaped by the transition to a flexible, post-Fordist economy. Edward L. Glaeser spells
out, in triumphant tones, 'Boston's transformation from a dying
factory town to a thriving information city', led by the turn from
an economy grounded in manufacturing to one dominated by 'high
technology, higher education, and financial services' – a transition
that was (at least in Glaeser's account) the salvation of a city that in
the early 1980s had 'resembled many of the industrial hulks dotting
the northeast and Midwest'.[31] Glaeser is not alone in this interpretation: by the late 1980s, when Wallace moved to the city, Boston's
transformation was widely lauded as a 'Massachusetts miracle'.[32]
For David Harvey, indeed, the city is the space in which the late
twentieth-century transformation of capitalist structures was made
most legible, the flexibility and decentralisation of post-Fordism
becoming the principles upon which the 'postmodernist' topographical and architectural reorganisation of the metropolis were carried
out. But what this context produced, in Harvey's account, was not
so much a miracle as 'a conception of the urban fabric as necessarily fragmented . . . shaped according to aesthetic aims and principles
which have nothing necessarily to do with any overarching social
objective'.[33] For Harvey, the kind of transition which imparted a
new economic dynamism to Boston also entailed a decomposition
of social and topographical metropolitan identity, producing a fragmentary and kaleidoscopic urban geography.

Harvey's argument is borne out in the architectural history of
Boston in the late twentieth century. The city had been a centre
for innovative architecture across the twentieth century: Douglass
Shand-Tucci, a historian of Boston architecture, notes that 'the modernist century – at least insofar as architecture is concerned – has
nowhere been more Modern than in Boston'.[34] But, as Shand-Tucci
outlines, the period between the 1970s and mid-1980s in particular
was characterised by architectural and topographical development
so rapid that 'by the eighties the acceleration was dizzying'.[35] Under
the mayoralty of Kevin White (1968–1984) the city saw, as Lawrence
W. Kennedy notes, 'a period of unrestrained development, a building

frenzy' during which 'the transformation of downtown Boston . . . was nothing less than staggering'.[36] And in Boston, the postmodernist architectural design characteristic of the post-Fordist city formed an extension of the architectural experimentation strongly associated (as Shand-Tucci establishes) with the elite academic institutions that now played a leading role in the city's reconfigured economy.[37] Shaken by the shifts in the economy that underpinned it, the Bostonian metropolis that Wallace discovered in 1989 was one left dazed by a period of intense and sustained upheaval in its physical form.

The effects on the city's social and cultural identity were profound. Writing around the time Wallace arrived in the city, Naomi Miller and Keith Morgan described Boston's shift from architectural modernism to postmodernism in terms of a rise of 'pluralism and eclecticism' that reflected 'the consumer society of the eighties and the growth of international capitalism'.[38] This kind of eclecticism was defended by one of the major adherents of architectural postmodernism, Charles Jencks: the postmodernist endeavour to 'cut across the spectrum of tastes with a variety of styles' required, for Jencks, a 'radical eclecticism' valorised as 'the natural evolution of a culture with choice'.[39] By the 1980s and 1990s, though, postmodern eclecticism was generating unease as well as enthusiasm: the geographer Edward Relph decried 'urban landscapes which are a chiaroscuro of increasingly flashy, unrelated and pointless patches, a post-modern . . . monotony-in-variety' – and warned that postmodernism's 'diverse landscapes and decorated buildings' might be a 'disguise for continuing corporatisation'.[40] Kevin Roberts went further, suggesting that the 'return to difference and particularity' had generated 'a very real crisis of urbanity itself' in which notions of civic identity were undermined and 'the very idea of the city itself is now thrown into doubt'.[41] Boston, then, was a centre for an architectural trend that raised questions about the fundamental nature and identity of the metropolis.

These architectural and topographical consequences of Boston's transition are inextricably linked with the social history of the city in this period, as Kennedy maintains: 'change in Boston was not limited to physical construction downtown' but also incorporated the 'momentous social changes [that] rocked America' during this period.[42] And for Boston historian Michael Holleran, these changes were generally for the worse: 'identification of individual interests with the community broke down . . . as a new politics of polarization turned the environment into a battleground of class and ethnic conflict'.[43] This sense of social as well as topographical breakdown in Boston reflects a more general 'urban crisis' that, as Thomas J. Sugrue outlined in 1996, was endemic to many of America's cities: 'scenes of devastation and poverty' had come to feel 'disturbingly familiar to anyone who has travelled through the streets' of America's urban centres. And this was a state of affairs that Sugrue understood to be rooted in the decline of the old industrial economy, the result of which was that 'central-city residence, race, joblessness, and poverty' had become 'inextricably entwined in postindustrial urban America'.[44]

The sense of a metropolitan way of life that had emerged with the maturation of industrial capitalism was challenged, then, by the economic transformations that reshaped the physical and social geography of the city in the last decades of the twentieth century. This challenge engendered a new context that Edward W. Soja labelled 'postmetropolis': the 'product of an era of intensive restructuring as profound in its impact on every facet of our lives as any other period in at least the past two centuries – that is, since the origins of the industrial capitalist city'. 'Postmetropolis' was, for Soja, the result of 'a selective deconstruction and still evolving reconstitution of the modern metropolis': an urban environment 'increasingly unmoored from its spatial specificity, from the city as a fixed point of collective reference, memory, and identity'.[45] Just as Wallace was absorbed into the metropolitan way of life he found in Boston, this sense of urban identity and tradition was being uprooted by the economic transitions that inscribed themselves into the city's social and physical geography.

The impact of this moment in Boston's history on Wallace's sense of the city comes into focus in Wallace and Mark Costello's co-authored *Signifying Rappers*. Aside from its account of the aesthetics of rap music, this text offers an important record of Wallace's initial encounter with Boston in the summer of 1989, as well as a suggestion of some of the thematic concerns that coalesced around this experience (Samuel Cohen describes it as 'the report of a journey into the dark heart of Boston', while Tara Morrissey and Lucas Thompson read it as 'an oblique primer on many of the themes and preoccupations of Wallace's subsequent career').[46] These geographical and thematic concerns coincide in a passage in which Wallace unpacks the social tensions embedded in the city's environment: 'the actual quality of life in poor urban communities declined further just while all around them, in the manicured neighborhoods west and north ... lifestyles of luxury, freedom, power, consumption, and display ... were actually being whitely *flaunted*' (*Signifying* p. 142, original emphasis). These antagonisms are manifested in what, elsewhere in *Signifying*, Wallace calls the 'chasm we feel glad if liberal-guilty is there – some *space* between our own lawned split-level world and whatever it is that lends authenticity to rap' (p. 33, original emphasis): economic and social divisions are inscribed in the space of the city itself, its topography forming an expression of its fractured community.

This fragmentation of the city also leaves its mark on the structure of *Signifying* – with its arrangement of juxtaposed segments attributed individually to either Wallace or Costello, rather than a merged co-authorial voice – in a way that provides an initial hint of the influence of Boston's sociospatial form on Wallace's approach to textual composition. Costello's later preface to *Signifying* suggests that 'the structure ... was a Dave idea ... which gave the book a tense and teeming ambience, appropriately urban, like a mad apartment tower full of pissed-off, squabbling paragraphs who all want war with the landlord' (*Signifying* p. xvi). And this approach extends into *Jest*, where a similar effect is produced by the frequent text breaks that effect sudden transitions between plotlines, settings and chronologies – 'signal[ling] to the reader that the novel is about to shift between narrative lines, or between locations, or to move forward or backward in time', as Stephen J. Burn puts it.[47] The majority of these sections are fewer than ten pages long, and the frequency with which the novel enacts these shifts contributes to the dispersed, fractured feel that is re-emphasised by the complexity of the narrative structure, as plotlines are abandoned and revisited, loop back or jump forward, run parallel or overlap without conjoining. Though three narrative threads come to dominate the bulk of the novel – the E.T.A. and Ennet House plotlines, and the Steeply/Marathe dialogues – these sequences are broken up and dispersed; the novel consistently disrupts any spatial and textual unity it invokes.

Critics have linked this form with the novel's context: Kiki Benzon argues that the novel's structure forms 'a mimetic – if multitudinous and turbulent – depiction of contemporary life in America', and Greg Carlisle suggests that Wallace's strategy of 'purposefully shifting time, location, and point of view' enables him to 'better mirror our frenetic culture'.[48] To this I would add that the enclosure of narrative threads within discrete sections, visually separated on the page by breaks and headers, forms a structural embodiment of the sociospatial 'chasms' of Boston that Wallace had described in *Signifying*. The sequestering of these plotlines in their own separate narrative spaces

as well as in textually discrete sections figures the architectural and
social fragmentation of the post-Fordist city – the dissolution of collective metropolitan experience and identity. Reflecting on the form
of the late twentieth-century city, the architect Alejandro Zaera-Polo
remarked that 'through [the] growing disorganisation of the composition of capital, the contemporary city tends to constitute itself as a
non-organic and *complex* structure without a hierarchical structure
nor a linear organisation' – a description that resonates strikingly
with *Jest*'s form.[49] And Wallace's own comments on the novel's
structure suggest something of this: he remarked that 'the image I
had in my mind . . . was that this book was really a very pretty pane
of glass that had been dropped off the twentieth story of a building'.[50] Invoking a skyscraper – and by implication a metropolitan
setting – for his act of fracturing the novel form, Wallace indicates
a link between his own experience of a fragmented Boston and the
formal arrangement of his novel.

Severs warns against the assumption that Wallace made a 'sudden
leap into mature themes' in 1989; but my suggestion is that this
breakdown of metropolitan community and space, directly experienced in Boston, was a key generative influence on Wallace's newly
prominent concern with a loss of community in late twentieth-
century America.[51] *Signifying* places explicitly in the space of the city
a concern that Wallace highlighted in more general terms, and in
relation to *Jest*, in an interview with Boston's WBUR radio in 1996:
'I think one of the difficulties of my generation is that there's a great
amount of atomism and anomie, and there doesn't feel like a whole
lot of a community.'[52] If Andrew Warren sees a 'general breakdown
of community' as 'the novel's central theme', I read this concern as a
response to the fragmented and fraught urban environment in which
Jest was shaped.[53] In this and the following chapter, I explore how
Wallace's practice responded to this context, and how his composition of the novel represents both an expression of the problems of
American society and community that were starkly illuminated in
Boston, and an exploration of the possibilities for fiction as a means
of addressing this context.

Architecture and Alienation: The Case of A. Y. 'Vector Field' Rickey

If the elite education and high-technology industries that dominated
Boston's late twentieth-century economy were associated with a

radical aesthetic eclecticism that left the city with 'some of the most dramatic examples of modern architecture to be found anywhere' (as Whitehall and Kennedy establish), but also with little sense of collective identity, then Wallace's awareness of this context is suggested by his invention of the fictional architect 'A. Y. ("Vector-Field") Rickey', first introduced in an endnote as the designer of the E.T.A. campus and the 'topology world's closed-curve-mapping-Übermensch' (*Jest* p. 983 n. 3).[54] Through this invented figure, we again encounter the real-world figure of I. M. Pei, architect of Cleveland's controversial Erieview Plaza development which featured in *Broom*: in a brief aside we hear that, through Rickey's work, 'institutional architecture has come a long ways since I. M. Pei' (p. 184). Pei was indeed a key figure in Boston's late twentieth-century architectural transformations; though brief, the reference is enough to indicate that Wallace was not just aware of the city's recent architectural history and its institutional associations, but actively linking this awareness with the topographical reconfigurations he performed in *Jest* via Rickey's fictional buildings. Through this figure, the association between the dizzyingly eclectic development of Boston and the power of its elite education and research industries begins to register in the novel.

The association between Rickey and E.T.A. is certainly significant: this is the institutional space that dominates the early sections of the novel and displaces the city itself to the margins of the text's initial frame of vision – of the first 200 pages of the text, roughly 147 are set directly within the Academy. And E.T.A., in line with the eclecticism of Boston's postmodernist form, is a distinctly idiosyncratic space: the first full description of its layout is studded with strange architectural terminology, from 'spherocubular' to 'proto-Georgian' to (confusingly) 'neo-Georgian' (*Jest* p. 51). The dense technicality of the language intensifies in the endnote that introduces Rickey himself, where we hear that the campus is composed of 'inward-facing buildings convexly rounded at the back and sides to give a cardioid's curve . . . that still wouldn't have been truly cardioid if the buildings themselves didn't have their convex bulges all derived from arcs of the same r' (p. 983 n. 3). This is an architecture couched from the start in obscure registers, and annotations to a typescript draft highlight Wallace's attention to this kind of language: one marginal note records the definition of 'Aventurine – glossy flecked stone', while Wallace added the architectural term 'pargeted' (in 'a pargeted tunnel' [p. 51]) in both a superscript annotation and a marginal note (HRC 16.3). Wallace's compositional process in this section was focused on developing the effect described by Finn

Fordham, in which 'the reader moves through all these signs at two defamiliarising levels: through the signifiers, arranged in complex syntactic structures, and through the signifieds of weird architectural structures'.[55] Even readers versed in architectural terminology will stumble over the 'dendriurethane' material of the academy's inflatable 'Lung' (p. 52), since this appears to be Wallace's invention – a futuristic-sounding material that recalls Miller and Morgan's account of Bostonian postmodernism's uses of architectural materials: 'more frequently veneer than natural, their usage artificial rather than logical, just as public spaces are often privately operated'.[56] As much as its layout, E.T.A.'s very materiality seems confounding, a challenge to the metropolis as public space.

The alienating technicality of the Academy's architecture, and the embodiment of this technicality in the descriptive language that frames its topography, have the effect of thwarting the reader's imaginative entry to the space. This ostentatious architectural strangeness is also a kind of fortification, a complement to the 'portcullis' at E.T.A.'s entrance (*Jest* p. 171): this is architectural form as a paranoid defence against the messy social geography of the city beyond. As such, this physical form dovetails with the valorisation of institutional interiority expressed by Gerhardt Schtitt, 'Head Coach and Athletic Director' and 'dispenser of abstractions . . . a philosopher rather than a king' (p. 79). Tennis, for Schtitt, is 'beautiful because *in*foliating, *contained*' – unlike US society and culture at large, where there is 'Nothing to contain and give meaning . . . *Verstiegenheit*' (pp. 82, 83, original emphases). The word '*Verstiegenheit*' proves an intriguing detail: it is appended with an endnote, which volunteers 'Low Bavarian for something like "wandering alone in blasted disorienting territory beyond all chartered limits and orienting markers," supposedly' (p. 994 n. 36). At once florid and tentative, the note seems curious, especially since the subsequent note on the same page gives a simple, unadorned translation from French ('Wheelchair' [p. 994 n. 37]). The endnote's implied author evidently knows enough German to associate the word with *versteigen* – to become lost. In fact, for *verstiegenheit* the *Oxford German Dictionary* gives 'extravagance' or 'fantastic idea/remark'; Schtitt's exclamation is perhaps a simple expression of disdain.[57] But Severs is right to note that 'etymological links are always worth pursuing with the dictionary-reading Wallace', and if we follow the Latin roots of the English 'extravagance', we come full circle back to the apparently erroneous sense of the endnote: *extra* (outside), *vagari* (to wander, the root of 'vagrancy') – the spatial association with wandering and boundary crossing is not effaced but redoubled.[58] Rickey's architecture and Schtitt's theory are complementary expressions of a turn away from the city as a public space – both form reflections of the eclecticism and social atomisation that had come to dominate Boston as the high-tech and elite education sectors took their place at its economic centre.

The fullest extension of Rickey's weird and alienating aesthetic, though, comes when the novel turns to his '*summum opus*': the 'great hollow brain-frame' of the Massachusetts Institute of Technology (MIT) Student Union building, 'an endowed memorial to the North American seat of Very High Tech' (*Jest* p. 186). Initially, we encounter this structure through a student engineer's entry from the street outside, followed by his traversal of its interior – another suggestion of the turn away from the public space of the metropolis. And as with E.T.A., this inward turn is accompanied by a proliferation of obscure terminology, this time not just architectural but also medical: 'he skips the front entrances and comes in through the south side's acoustic meatus . . . then descends creaky back wooden stairs from the Massa Intermedia's Reading Room down to about the Infundibular Recess . . .' (p. 182). The profusion of Latin terms is not explained for another two pages, when the form of the 'enormous cerebral cortex of reinforced concrete and polymer compounds' is made more explicit; then, after another two pages, the passage moves into a full exterior description of the bizarre facade, largely relayed in a single 26-line sentence that ends in a pile-up of detail:

> even the worst latex slip-and-slide off the steeply curved cerebrum's edge would mean a fall of only a few meters to the broad butylene platform, from which a venous-blue emergency ladder can be detached and lowered to extend down past the superior temporal gyrus and Pons and abducent to hook up with the polyurethane basilar-system artery and allow a safe shimmy down to the good old oblongata just outside the rubberized meatus at ground zero. (p. 186)

A bravura piece of unfathomable description, the passage finally abandons any attempt at punctuation, ending with an uninterrupted stream of architectural materials ('butylene', 'polyurethane') and medical terminology. Like E.T.A., the Union building turns to the novel's reader – as to the city around it – an impenetrable, barely-comprehensible facade. An absurd extension of the postmodernist eclecticism that shaped the topography of 1980s Boston, these 'Rickeyite' architectures self-consciously mark themselves out from the city through both their technical virtuosity and their conspicuous weirdness. In fact, the irony of the MIT building is that – as we hear earlier in the same long sentence – it is the product of an architectural practice that is intended to be 'pro-mimetic' (p. 186). The effect of its description, though, is precisely the opposite: a proliferation of baffling language whose effect is to evade its reader's comprehension, derailing the process of mimetic representation. The conjunction of architectural form with the novel's language produces a conspicuous representational failure; the building's mimetic intent is undone by its sheer materiality, and its description is overwhelmed by its hyper-abundant textuality.

Henri Lefebvre provides some useful reflection on the role of textuality in the production of late-capitalist 'abstract space', squeezing out the organic and lived qualities of 'representational spaces':

> the place of social space as a whole has been usurped by a part of that space endowed with an illusory special status – namely, the part which is concerned with writing and imagery, underpinned by the written text (journalism, literature) . . . [and] that amounts to abstraction wielding awesome reductionistic force vis-a-vis 'lived' experience.[59]

Rickey's textually overloaded architecture produces something like this abstract space. Inscribing urban form with the exclusive technical discourses that belong to the dominant education and technology industries, these buildings squeeze out the lived, social space of the metropolis – and Wallace's style itself seems calculated to engender a failure of textual communication that is entwined with this architectural and social fragmentation. The city novel tradition draws on the idea of the metropolis as a space uniquely capable of disclosing social meaning, and of working in symbiotic tandem with the representational and symbolic structures of the novel to engender a larger cohesive form – but *Jest*'s Rickeyite architectures are focal points for a simultaneous failure of the city as a social form and the novel as a system of signification. If Wallace inherited this tradition, then, he did so not as a ready model but a deep and historically embedded literary problem: a form in which, as Hana Wirth-Nesher puts it, 'the urban setting is the locus for the tensions and contradictions in the novel and in the historical moment, both inscribed into the cityscape'.[60]

But there is also an important counter current that works through the MIT building section. Though Severs has argued that 'the key movement in *Infinite Jest* is always inward', the student engineer's initial interior trajectory is in fact reversed as the section progresses:

we find him climbing 'all the little-used many-staired neurofoam way up to the artery-red fire door of the Union's rooftop' before emerging onto the building's roof (*Jest* p. 185).[61] And the obtuse 26-line sentence describing the facade itself incorporates a complementary directionality – this time downwards, dramatising an escape via the 'venous-blue emergency ladder' to street level, and concluding with the 'rubberized meatus at ground zero' (p. 186) – ending there with a full stop that provides the first piece of punctuation for five lines to bring the spiral of alienating language to a welcome halt. Notably, comparison between handwritten and typescript drafts and the published version shows Wallace layering in additional Latinate vocabulary at each stage, and significantly expanding and complicating his sentences – but both the turn outward towards the roof and the movement down towards the street are included in the passage from the handwritten version (HRC 15.7, 16.4): the directional reversal was a core basis of the section, an underlying structure around which Wallace arranged his confusing excess of language. Even as he was incorporating the alienation of late twentieth-century Boston into his language of space, a fundamental aspect of the section was the suggestion of a turn back outward, towards the city.

The turning point itself is the radio broadcast made by Joelle van Dyne in the guise of 'Madame Psychosis': it is towards the 'windowless laryngeal studio' (*Jest* p. 183) that the engineer makes his initial inward way, and it is once the broadcast has begun that he emerges back out onto the roof. And in fact, it is the progression of the broadcast signal itself that initiates the reversal of direction:

> the engineer flicks a lever and pumps the music up the coaxial medulla and through the amps and boosters packed into the crawl-spaces above the high false ceiling of the corpus callosum's idle tennis courts and up and out the aerial that protrudes from the gray and bulbous surface of the Union's roof. (pp. 183–4)

It is worth comparing this with the typescript draft version of the scene, in which the sentence is much shorter and simpler: 'the engineer pumps the music up the aerial that protrudes from the gray bulbous surface of the Union's convoluted roof' (HRC 16.4). Wallace considerably embellished this earlier version, complicating the syntax and adding some of the obscure medical terminology that characterises the rest of the building's description. But at the same time, the resulting obstructions to the flow of the sentence are counterbalanced by the introduction of a sequence of conjunctions that culminates in the rapid 'and up and out', a burst of connections and directionalities that coincides with the signal's final escape from the building's roof. The signal penetrates the baffling facade of the building – and the density of Wallace's descriptive language – from the inside, inaugurating a tentative move towards the city beyond. It is no coincidence that, immediately after this outward burst, the passage provides a concrete placement of the building itself within the geography of the city: 'off the corner of Ames and Memorial Dr., East Cambridge' (p. 184). The progress of the signal produces an opening onto the wider topography of the metropolis.

Although 'Obstructed on all sides by the tall buildings of East Cambridge and Commercial Drive and serious Downtown' (*Jest* p. 184), Joelle's signal continues its tentative excursion into the city, and continues to draw Boston's topography into the text:

> a couple thin pie-slices of signal escape M.I.T. proper, e.g. . . . between the Philology and Low-Temp Physics complexes on Mem. Dr. and then across the florid-purple nighttime breadth of the historic Charles River, then through the heavy flow of traffic on Storrow Dr. on the Chuck's other side . . . (p. 184)

Again, this passage is worth comparing with the typescript draft version:

> through the P.E.-gap of little-used soccer fields and tennis courts between the Philology and Physics complexes, then across the purple nighttime breadth of the historic Charles River, to bathe Brighton and Enfield, on the river's other shore . . .' (HRC 16.4)

As he developed the scene, Wallace built up its geographical detail, adding references to 'Mem. Dr.' and 'Storrow Dr.' – expanding the sense of the geography through which the signal makes its way. At the same time, the published version counters the rather formal initial mention of 'the historic Charles River' with the colloquial 'the Chuck', introducing a hint of Boston's geography as the subject of a shared vernacular language, a collectively lived environment. As well as a clearer view of the city's material topography, the text begins to introduce a subtle suggestion of language as a function of the shared inhabiting of the metropolis as public space.

This sense of connection with a shared metropolitan environment is also embedded on a structural level, as the progression of Joelle's signal initiates a rare transition between different narrative strands and spaces within a section of the novel (rather than in a text break): the signal finds its way to the living room of Headmaster's House at E.T.A., where Mario Incandenza sits 'right up close to one of the speakers with his head cocked dog-like, listening' (*Jest* p. 189). The weird and alienating facades of these spaces are punctured, metropolitan topography becoming the zone through which their seclusion is broken – and the section follows suit, using the content of Joelle's broadcast as a segue to switch seamlessly to E.T.A. and the Incandenza family's plotline (pp. 187 ff.). Her signal becomes a force that momentarily reverses the general fragmentation of the novel's narrative structure. Robert Chodat identifies Joelle's broadcasts as 'the most exemplary artworks of *Infinite Jest*'; and if the broadcast is a model for the possibilities of a communicative linguistic art, then the signal's tentative progress into the city is central to this function.[62] Where the descriptions of Rickey's buildings themselves create a conflation of architectural and literary alienation, reproducing abstract space in the textual form of the novel, the broadcast suggests a practice of language that engenders spatial, narrative and interpersonal connections across the otherwise fractured urban environment – one that might reconstruct the city as a shared social space.

Into the City: Joelle van Dyne, *flâneuse*?

The role of Joelle's broadcast in opening the text onto the city is extended in the novel's seventeenth chapter, as she herself comes into the centre of the narrative focus. As she sits in Molly Notkin's apartment and prepares to intentionally overdose on crack cocaine, she recalls her walk through the Back Bay district and across Boston Common – providing one of the first extended sequences in which we closely follow a character's movement beyond the institutional interiors that dominate the opening sections and through the external space of the city. Indeed, in typescript drafts the walk sequence follows directly from the MIT section, confirming the continuity of their composition; this walk is a direct extension of the initial turn towards the city that began with the outward progress of Joelle's signal (HRC 16.4). The prospect of a communicative artistic practice transcending the alienating space of the institution leads the text here: to a character inhabiting the streets of the city. And this outward turn is reflected in the style of the passage, as Joelle reflects on her walk:

> undeniably pretty, the overall walk toward her last hour was, on this last day before the great O.N.A.N.ite Interdependence Day revel. East Charles to the Back Bay today is a route full of rained-on siennaglazed streets and upscale businesses with awnings and wooden signs hung with cute Colonial script, and people looking at her like you

look at the blind, not knowing she could see everything at all times. She likes the wet walk for this . . . the brick sidewalks of Charles St. unchipped and impersonally crowded, her legs on autopilot, and she a perceptual engine . . . (*Jest* p. 221)

The conspicuous shift from past to present tenses between the first and second sentences suggests the promise of immersion in the direct and immediate experience of the space of the city. And indeed, Joelle's role as a 'perceptual engine' is confirmed as the passage opens out into two lengthy sentences whose form provides a counterpoint to the unpunctuated mass of obscure language in the MIT building description: these sentences are evenly punctuated and divided into clauses that are mostly moderate in length – invoking the steady pace of Joelle's walking – so that their length produces not an alienating excess of text but a feeling of expansive openness. This is a meandering and digressive form, a textual expression of Joelle's immersion in the geography of Boston as she makes her way through its streets. And as they unfurl, these sentences become increasingly evocative, their language sensual and onomatopoeic:

[Joelle] can hear the rain's *thup* on tight umbrellas and hear it hiss in the street . . . cars sheening by with the special lonely sound of cars in rain . . . and the little cataract of rainwater off the edge of each dumpster's red annex's downsloping side and hitting refrigerator boxes' tops with a rhythmless thappathappappathap; somebody going *Pssssst* from an alley's lip . . . (p. 221)

The experiential and impressionistic quality of this description presents a distinct contrast to the technical registers that accompany Rickey's buildings; here, a receptiveness to the city as a phenomenal environment is inscribed in the language of the text. Through this stylistic turn, Joelle's walk reframes the metropolis as a lived space, produced through an embodied and sensual form of inhabitation.

This sense of an opening up to the experiences of metropolitan space connects with a long tradition of urban writing; we can trace it back to Charles Baudelaire's 'painter of modern life', a 'kaleidoscope endowed with consciousness' who 'gazes at the landscape of the great city' in order to extract from the fleeting and transient impressions of urban life 'the poetry that resides in its historical envelope'.[63] This is walking as *flânerie*, one of the major literary and theoretical traditions of metropolitan space, in which the walker collects and arranges the disparate impressions of urban life in poetic form; Joelle's walk not only continues the function of her broadcast in reconnecting the text with the city, but also links *Jest* with the long literary tradition of the metropolis. Where the symbiotic connection of text and city as meaningful forms seemed to have collapsed in the descriptions of Rickey's buildings, Joelle's progress through the streets begins to suggest a possible reunion of novelistic and urban forms. It is unsurprising, then, that Joelle's walk is shortly followed by a detailed description of the fictional district of Enfield, 'a kind of arm-shape extending north from Commonwealth Avenue and separating Brighton into Upper and Lower, its elbow nudging East Newton's ribs and its fist sunk into Allston' (*Jest* p. 240); as her signal prompted the placing of the MIT building in the topography of Boston, so her walk brings an expanded sense of the city's wider geography into the text.

This opening up to the city is also connected with an extension of the association between Joelle's signal and the possibility of narrative connectivity. As it suggests a receptiveness to the phenomenology of the city, her walk also provides a nexus of subtle connections between some of the disparate plot strands that have been developing in these early stages of the text: through the walk, Joelle's story is brought into contact with James Incandenza's filmmaking (*Jest* p. 222); with the E.T.A. students (via her recollection of the 'husks of Lemon Pledge that the school's players used to keep the sun off' (pp. 223, c.f. pp. 99–100); and with the Quebecois terrorism plot (through the cardboard display of a wheelchaired figure offering a blank cartridge, which Joelle interprets as 'some kind of anti-ad' [p. 224]). Attentive readers will also notice subtler linkages: Lady Delphina, from whom Joelle buys the cocaine with which she intends to overdose, is also a sometime dealer to Poor Tony Krause (whose story I will discuss in Chapter 3) (p. 300). If the novel's fractured structure reflects the atomised 'postmetropolis', Joelle's walk begins to suggest the possibility of a connectivity still latent in metropolitan space. This suggestion of narrative convergence is expanded on another level as the walk is intercut with the chronology of 'subsidized time' that appears on page 223: a simple and unadorned list of named years, this segment provides crucial clues about the novel's overall temporal scheme. Placing it here, of all places, redoubles the connection between the city street on the one hand and temporal and narrative cohesion on the other: the reader organises and traverses narrative scales at the same time as Joelle negotiates the streets of the city. Metropolitan topography, temporal patterning, and narrative development begin to interweave in the space of the city street.

Joelle's recuperated *flânerie*, then, provides the crux for an expanded point of connection between the lived space of the city and the developing form of the text. Establishing Joelle as *flâneuse*, though, also brings Wallace's depiction of her relationship to the metropolis into an ambivalent relationship to the historical gendering of urban space. The possibility of female *flânerie* is a contentious topic: in 1985, Janet Wolff argued that *flânerie* should be understood as a category that reflects the exclusion of women from the public space of the metropolis, resting on 'a freedom to move about in the city, observing and being observed' that is denied to women through the traditional gendered division of public and private space. Thus for Wolff '[t]here is no question of inventing the *Flâneuse*: the essential point is that such a character was rendered impossible by the sexual divisions of the nineteenth century'.[64] But if this rigid gendering was part of the established structure of the old industrial metropolis, then the transition to a decentred and malleable post-Fordist urban form also brought upheaval to these old divisions, as the urban theorist Leslie Kern has suggested: 'As global north cities have transitioned away from economies based on manufacturing to economies based on knowledge and service work . . . the more masculinized features of cities have changed.'[65] Joelle's walk, perhaps, emerges from this loosening of the gendered segregation of the metropolis: the possibility of her *flânerie* itself is a reflection of the historical transitions in the socioeconomic structures of late twentieth-century capitalism.

Certainly, Joelle provides a welcome counterpoint to the novel's presentation of Avril Incandenza, introduced early in the novel when Hal eats a piece of mould in the Incandenzas' 'first home, in the suburb of Weston' – prompting an episode of 'adult hysteria' in which Avril runs 'around and around the garden's rectangle', neurotically tracing and re-tracing the boundaries of the domestic space: 'even in hysterical trauma her flight-lines were plumb . . . her turns, inside the ideogram of string, crisp and martial' (*Jest* p. 11). Obsessively re-establishing the border between the private space of the home and the public space beyond, Avril's 'hysteria' is a distinctly gendered manifestation of the rejection of the social space of the city expressed in theoretical terms by Gerhard Schtitt; in the novel's present, Hal describes Avril as 'an *agoraphobic* workaholic and obsessive-compulsive' who 'never goes anywhere anymore . . . never leaves the grounds' (p. 42, original emphasis). This agoraphobia (from *agora*, the meeting place in the ancient Greek city – the public space of social encounter and interaction) reinscribes the traditional association between femininity and the private sphere in a pathologised form.

Initially at least, Joelle's walk provides an alternative to this rather uncomfortable portrait, instead placing a female figure at the centre of the novel's move outward into the city. But Joelle's immersion in the public space of the metropolis turns out to be temporary: her expansive walking leads her first to 'all four mirrors of her little room's walls', then to Molly Notkin's bathroom, where she locks herself in and prepares to overdose (*Jest* p. 223, pp. 234–40). These domestic confinements mark a withdrawal from the exterior spaces of the city; we later find her ensconced in Ennet House and 'finding she just liked to clean', which she does obsessively over two segments of the text (p. 736). For Lauren Elkin, the *flâneuse* ought to be understood 'not merely [as] a female *flâneur*, but a figure to be reckoned with, and inspired by, all on her own', and as such her remit is to '[force] us to confront the ways in which words like *home* and *belonging* are used against women'.[66] Performing a rather disheartening reversion to a portrait of neurotic domesticity – reminiscent of Avril's 'violent phobic thing about ... facility hygiene' (*Jest* p. 671) – the trajectory of Joelle's narrative hardly fulfils this function. Instead, it reinstates the traditional confinement of women to a private domestic sphere, imagined to be separate from the public space of the metropolis at large.

While Joelle's broadcast and her walk are suggestive of an artistic and literary practice that might recover the lived space of the city, the gendering of her relationship to the metropolis begins to indicate how this idea intersects with the politics and ideology of urban space in the wake of the economic changes that had reshaped urban America. Indeed, this gendering works on another level, too: the feminist geographer Gillian Rose has explored how assumptions about spatial knowledge and its production are tied at a deep level to notions of differently gendered subjectivities and their relationships to geographical space. For Rose, the normative epistemology that underpins the production of geographical knowledge, as it 'aims to be exhaustive' and 'assumes that, in principle, the world can be fully known and understood', implies an implicitly male subject – 'just that rational, objective gaze at the world which so many feminists have associated with dominant masculinities'. In Rose's account, this masculine-coded form of knowledge requires an excluded feminine opposite: 'while men assumed that their knowledge depended only on the abstract thought of the mind, they argued that women were ruled by the passions of their bodies'.[67] Perhaps *flânerie*, even as an exclusively male category, has always involved a romanticised adoption of this excluded feminine relationship with space; its embrace of the fleeting impressions of the metropolis a valorisation of the sensual and the partial over the dominant rational and totalising epistemology.

In any case, Rose's account suggests another way of reading Joelle's sensual and embodied relationship to urban space: as much as it allows for an alternative to the abstract and technical space of Rickey's buildings and the alienation of postmetropolitan Boston, it also forms an expression of a traditionally gendered assumption about the kind of geographical understanding that women produce – less the opposite than the complementary flip side of Avril's neurosis. For Rose, moreover, the dominance of this gendered epistemology ensures that 'women have been and continue to be marginalized as producers of geographical knowledge'.[68] And indeed, Joelle's embodied connection with the metropolis produces an itinerary through Boston's geography that, while ostensibly organised around various street names and landmarks that are scattered through the section (Charles Street, Boylston Street, the 'black-bronze equestrian statue of Boston's Colonel Shaw' [*Jest* p. 223], Boston Common), in fact bears only a loose and confused correspondence to the real topography of the city – as William Beutler discovered when he tried to map the walk for 'Infinite Boston'.[69] Joelle's impressionistic and sensual relationship to her environment, even as it opens the text onto the lived space of the city, allows for only a partial and limited sense of Boston's material space: just as her own association with the exterior spaces of the city is temporary, the traditionally feminine form of spatial knowledge that Joelle brings to the text produces only a loose and fleeting mimetic correspondence between the novel and the metropolis.

This is not only true of Joelle's perception of the physical topography of the city. *Flânerie* in its classical form posited the urban walker as a figure whose movement through the city could provide a tangible sense of convergence with the city as a legible social form – an idea embodied in the category of the 'crowd'. For Baudelaire, 'the crowd is [the *flâneur*'s] domain, just as the air is the bird's, and water that of the fish. His passion and his profession is to merge with the crowd'.[70] If the crowd here is a figure for the massed urban society resulting from the concentration of labour in the industrial cities of the nineteenth century, an element of the original idea of a distinct metropolitan way of life, then *flânerie* is a means of imagining a poetic relationship with this potentially challenging totality: as Walter Benjamin suggested in his reading of Baudelaire, the purpose of *flânerie* is to 'endow this crowd with a soul', and hence the industrial metropolis 'for the first time . . . becomes the subject of lyric poetry'.[71] In the classical literary tradition of the city, walking and social connection are combined through the mobile gaze of the *flâneur*. In Joelle's walk, though, this sense of emergent social and aesthetic coherence is replaced by a far more diffuse series of encounters. Other figures appear to her only as disembodied parts – 'the rustle and jut of limbs from dumpsters . . . other people's blue shoeless limbs extending in coronal rays from refrigerator boxes . . . ghastly-white or blotched faces declaiming to thin air' – or as fleeting impressions: 'the receding staccato of brittle women's high heels on brick' (*Jest* p. 221). If the crowd was a figure for the massed social totality in the industrial city, one through which lyric poetry could conjoin the space of the street with a renewed form of social engagement, all that remain in Joelle's picture of the late twentieth-century metropolis are fragments and receding traces.

In fact, examination of the typescript drafts of this section reveals that the absence of the crowd is not simply an omission, but the result of a deliberate process of elision. Between these typescripts and the published version of the novel, Wallace cut a substantial description of figures passing as Joelle walks:

> damaged people and intact people on those streets, those with shoes pointed at valid destinations and those without shoes or ~~homes~~ places to be, wet and weaving, ranting, or else mute and over-careful as ~~if~~ are the shoeless around broken glass, young undeformed women in ~~sharp~~ snappy rainwear and running sneakers, the creative locomotion of amputees, simple Sunday afternoon drunks moving between bars with closed red window-shades . . . men who work near the water and smell of it, those fat-billed wool ~~skullcap~~ Donegal berets seen only in U.S. Boston, several Hassidim in no hurry, attorneys jogging in the near-fluorescent jogging clothes attorneys favour, a pot-bellied cop eating a red ice cream cone. . . (HRC 16.4)

This passage bears a much closer resemblance to a classic crowd scene, a visible social typology manifest in the public space of the city. This suggestion of a tangible social form is underscored in a further sentence, also cut:

> the sidewalks themselves like highways only better, choreographed, that sense of near-jostle . . . opposed coaxials of northbound and southbound slithering in and out of each other with the frictionless suggestion of melt, twining, in the cold and hanging spatter. . . . (HRC 16.4)

Here there is a sense of confluence with the crowd, an absorption into the city as a convergent social space; a reflection of Wallace's initial excitement on discovering the crowded and bustling spaces of the metropolis. Tim Groenland has established that this scene was revised late in the editing process and under some duress from Wallace's editor Michael Pietsch, but the choice of material to remove is nonetheless significant: cutting these details, Wallace worked from an initially strong sense of social relationality to a disordered series of impressions.[72] The result of this compositional process is that the tentative and limited correspondence between the text and the physical geography of the city produced by Joelle's walk is also reflected in her relationship with the social space of Boston; the impressionism of her walk, its gendered embodiment and sensuality, produces a subjective and partial view of the city that underscores the loss of a sense of coherent social space in the late twentieth-century metropolis.

This sense of social diffusion is particularly notable considering that Joelle's walk brings her to Boston Common, among the most prominent and historically significant of the city's public spaces: 'the screen' upon which Bostonians 'project their images of stability', as Michael Holleran puts it.[73] As Joelle approaches it, though, the Common is reframed as a conspicuous space of absence that is also configured in noticeably gendered terms: 'a lush hole Boston's built itself around' (*Jest* p. 222). Joelle's walk is not the only section of the novel that concerns Boston Common – and indeed, the typescript draft of the walk also includes a marginal note at the point where Joelle reaches the Common itself: 'c.f. Public Gardens – pond chapter' (HRC 16.4). Presumably, this refers to the section later in the novel in which the student engineer (who facilitated Joelle's earlier broadcast) is kidnapped while sunbathing on the Common; a section that begins with a more explicit gesture to the idea of the metropolitan crowd, as spectators gather to watch the draining of the pond in the adjacent Public Gardens, attracted by 'the priceless chance to be part of a live crowd, watching' (p. 620). The draft note indicates that Joelle's walk is compositionally connected with this potential reappearance of the crowd, and the urban collectivity that it represents.

But, as in the walk, this prospect of participation in a shared social experience of the city turns out to be fleeting. The crowd that attaches to the spectacle of the pond cleaning is marked with a sense of immateriality and diffuseness: 'crowds brought together now so quickly, too quickly even to see them, a kind of visual inversion of watching something melt' (*Jest* p. 621). And, though the crowd 'thickens in a dense ring' as the passage continues (p. 621), by the time the brief section reaches its conclusion it is 'largely-dispersed-already' (p. 625). Contingent and temporary, the crowd is a transient assemblage of individuals rather than a genuine convergence; at its heart is not a concrete or stable social relation but a point of fleeting interest. And in the wake of its dispersal, we are given a description of the homeless figures that surround the engineer: 'roughly three dozen human forms scattered over the steep slope, a human collection without pattern or cohesion or anything to bind them, looking rather like firewood before it's been gathered' (p. 623). Having been coded as a feminine space of emptiness through Joelle's walk, the Common comes to embody the fragmentation of the city's social environment.

Notably, this absence of social convergence is again the product of an active process of elision. Much like Joelle's walk, a handwritten draft of this scene includes a much longer and fuller description of the gathering crowd, with extensive additions and revisions showing the depth of Wallace's attention to the details that signify various social types and their differentiations:

> lovers crossing the pond's wooden bridges, people ^{in officewear} who commute to work and are walking briskly through. ^{Shoppers of Newbury} ^{with bags with string handles.} ~~Brittle-haired women in~~ ^{Brittly coiffed women with} hard faces and soft coats. Men in Burberry coats, ~~holding cellular phones~~ ^{the bulge of phones at their belt,} briefcases they seem handcuffed to. You can see wheeling gulls in the reflection off some of the shoes ^{of the men with cases.} ^{The shoes are that well-shined}. Unopened umbrella-carriers. Students ~~with~~ ^{whose} backpacks ~~not on~~ ^{aren't on} their backs. ^{Knit-capped} joggers with new ^{Goretex} gloves who try to trot in place for a while, ^{watching the pond ~~sink~~ twirl and sink.} Day-care ladies with kids strung out behind them holding hands in long lines . . . Panhandlers work the crowd with respectful whispers, saying ^{thanks and} God Bless before they even ~~ask~~ stem you. ^{Skittish knit-capped} pamphleteers proffer without hawking. (HRC 15.6)

This kind of social typology is an effort to render stable and legible the complex social and economic structures that underlie the metropolis – its removal is a deliberate turn back towards the atomisation of the post-Fordist city. As in Joelle's walk, the lack of the crowd is not simply an absence but the result of a process: first building up and then stripping away a detailed image of the city's social scene. The dissolving fragments that are presented in the published text are the shadow that remains from this process – a compositional procedure that replicates the dissolution of the 'postmetropolis'.

Joelle stands in the early part of this text as a figure for a connective artistic practice whose efficacy is closely connected to its embeddedness in the geography of the city, and her walk gestures to the tradition of *flânerie* in order to suggest a recuperation of the genera-

tive relationship between literary and urban forms that is central to
the city novel tradition. As it does so, though, it also entwines *Jest*
with the gendering of metropolitan space: the sociospatial sense of
the city that emerges through Joelle's walk is limited by the subjective and partial form of knowledge that is attributed to her, so that
the prospects of spatial and narrative coherence that are suggested in
this chapter can only stand as latent reminders of what is lost in the
fragmented postmetropolitan city. The connection between walking
and the prospect of connectivity that appears in this chapter remains
an important idea as the text progresses, and in the following chapter
I will explore how this suggestion is extended when the practice of
walking is taken up by some of the novel's male characters, moving
beyond the gendered limitations ascribed to Joelle. But, constrained
by the gendered form to which the text consigns it, Joelle's own
experience of the city cannot reconstitute it as the legible sociospatial
environment that is central to the city novel tradition. Her excursion
itself ultimately serves not to transcend but to reinscribe the absence
of concrete and permanent relationships with the physical and social
space of the post-Fordist city.

History, Collectivity, Nostalgia: Don Gately and the Citgo Sign

If for Rose the gendering of spatial epistemology acts to displace
women as producers of geographical knowledge, it is notable that
Joelle's confinement to Ennet House is also the event that prompts
a male character to take up the mantle of moving out into the city –
obliging Don Gately to 'blast down to the Purity Supreme down in
Allston and pick up some eggs and peppers' (*Jest* p. 475). Gately's
drive, appearing towards the end of the twenty-fourth chapter, forms
a second extended excursion through the streets of the city; if Joelle's
gendered relationship to the city limits her capacity to reconstitute
it as a coherent environment, might Gately have better luck? As he
drives, a shift in the gendered mode of movement through the city is
certainly evident: where Joelle's meandering walk weaves a peripatetic image of the metropolis, Gately drives 'basically like a lunatic:
ignoring lights, cutting people off, scoffing at One-Ways, veering
wildly in and out, making pedestrians drop things and lunge kerb-
ward' (p. 475). Speed and aggression mark his movement through
the city, and his driving is given a clear gendered inflection when we
hear that 'He likes to . . . open *her* up down the serpentine tree-lined

boulevard of the Ave.' (p. 476, my emphasis) – a handwritten draft gives simply 'open it up' (HRC 15.7), the tweak adding an aggressively masculine resonance to Gately's manic driving.

And as he speeds past the cityscape outside, the material of the city registers not as a collage of sensual impressions as in Joelle's walk, but as a body of visual, empirical data:

> He passes the Unexamined Life club, where he no longer goes, at 1800h. already throbbing with voices and bass under its ceaseless neon bottle, and then the great gray numbered towers of the Brighton Projects, where he definitely no longer goes. Scenery starts to blur and distend at 70kph. Comm. Ave. splits Enfield-Brighton-Allston from the downscale edge of North Brookline on the right. He passes the meat-colored facades of anonymous Brookline tenements, Father & Son Market, a dumpster-nest, Burger Kings, Blanchard's liquors, an InterLace outlet, a land-barge alongside another dumpster-nest, corner bars and clubs – Play It Again Sam's, Harper's Ferry, Bunratty's, Rathskeller, Father's First I and II – a CVS, two InterLace outlets right next to each other, the ELLIS THE RIM MAN sign, the Marty's Liquors that they rebuilt like ants the week after it burnt down. (*Jest* p. 476)

Neither the alienating technicality of Rickey's buildings nor the sensual and digressive mode of Joelle's walk is at work here – instead, Gately's drive brings a concentrated point of direct geographical referentiality, an accumulation of concrete fact. As Heather Houser puts it, this passage presents a 'strategy of description by enumeration' that forms 'part of the information-generating machinery that has earned [*Jest*] a prominent place among encyclopedic novels'.[74] Indeed, as Beutler established while researching 'Infinite Boston', the details assembled in this passage have a strong correspondence to real landmarks along Commonwealth Avenue in 1989–1992, in contrast with the loose correspondence between Joelle's walk and the real topography of Boston; and if these real-world landmarks are interspersed with invented ones (the fictional 'InterLace' outlets), this blend of fact and fiction also suggests a close meshing of real and imagined geographies through the descriptive form of the text.[75] Where Joelle was immersed in the sensual environment of the metropolis, Gately gazes from behind the window of his car, accumulating an abundance of geographical fact suggestive of the exhaustive, totalising form of spatial knowledge that Rose associates with dominant masculinity.

If Fredric Jameson had called for a singular 'aesthetic of *cognitive mapping*' in response to the social fragmentation of post-Fordist capitalism, *Jest*'s excursions into the city are a reminder that different

kinds and degrees of mapping are bound up in the gendered construction of urban space.[76] There is a gendered politics of mappabil-
ity at work in the literary expression of the metropolis, a politics that
frames the available aesthetic responses to the spatial upheavals of
the late twentieth century. But if Gately's empirical and exhaustive
view of the city suggests the re-inscription of a dominant masculine
form of knowledge, things are not quite so simple here. The form of
the sentences that convey these details registers a sense of an almost
overwhelming volume of data: with multiplying topographical referents, proliferating nested clauses, and an accelerating pace that
reflects Gately's manic driving, both the sentence and the space it
describes prove tricky to navigate. The string of full stops in 'Scenery
starts to blur and distend at 70kph. Comm. Ave. splits ..'. serves to
blend abbreviations together and obscure the full stop marking the
end of the sentence, so that the passage seems to perform the blurring and distending it describes; Wallace's syntax seems momentarily
unable to contain and control the geographical material that it collects. If Gately's drive displaces Joelle's walk with a masculine relationship to the city, the epistemological dominance associated with
this relationship seems to be on the point of breaking down amid the
fragments of post-Fordist urban space.

Importantly, though, these distending sentences are also
bookended with references to another real Boston landmark whose
appearance plays a key role in the form of the passage. Immediately
before these sentences, we hear that Gately is driving 'past Boston
U. and toward the big triangular CITGO neon sign and the Back
Bay' (*Jest* p. 476). As this sentence helps to embed the mass of geographical references within an overall trajectory across the city, it
introduces the real-world Citgo sign in Kenmore Square – and this
landmark reappears when the spiralling series of topographical referents is followed by two progressively shorter sentences that wind
the sentence down and lead us out of the maze of the city (and of
Wallace's confusing syntax), bringing us gently in to land again at
the Citgo sign: 'He passes the hideous Riley's Roast Beef where the
Allston Group gathers to pound coffee before commitments. The
giant distant CITGO sign's like a triangular star to steer by' (p. 476).
Structuring the passage in this way, Wallace winds Gately's vision of
Boston around the sign, the passage itself seeming to steer by this 'triangular star' just as Gately does. Through this formal construction,
the sign's presence gathers the depiction of the city into coherence,
organising and containing the otherwise unwieldy material of the
post-Fordist metropolis.

As well as a physical orientating marker, the sign's presence also makes itself felt in another important way: through the complex vocal arrangement of this section of the text. For the most part, the passage is focalized through Gately, using free indirect speech – though moments of distance are introduced to complicate this perspective: 'what he imagines is a Rebel Yell' (*Jest* p. 476). This ambiguity continues as the passage unfolds and Gately races a subway train:

> He likes to match a Green Line train all the way down Commonwealth's integral ς and see how close he can cut beating it across the tracks at the Brighton Ave. split. It's a vestige. He'd admit it's like a dark vestige of his old low-self-esteem suicidal-thrill behaviours. He doesn't have a license, it's not his car, it's a priceless art-object car, it's his boss's car, who he owes his life to and sort of maybe loves, he's on a vegetable run for shattered husks of newcomers just out of detox whose eyes are rolling around in their heads. Has anybody mentioned Gately's head is square? (p. 476)

Here, things get more complex. The invocation of the mathematical symbol ς is surely not the high school dropout Gately's voice, while 'he likes to' and 'he'd admit' stand as further markers of the gap between narrative voice and character. But the subsequent rush of 'what-am-I-doing' self-consciousness seems to shift us much closer to him – only to end in the unexpected interruption of a previously unacknowledged narrator in the final sentence. There is a jostling vocal multiplicity at work in the passage as Gately makes his way through the city under the star of the Citgo sign; at the same time as this sign frames the passage's description of the physical geography of the city, Gately's drive draws us towards a sense of intersecting and overlapping voices lying beneath the surface of the text.

Crucially, the intrusion of this narrator seems to gesture towards a community of voices in the form of the 'anybody' who might have conveyed the story of Gately's square head. In Houser's reading of this interruption, 'the text calls in another narrator from the wings suggesting that data is so superabundant that the labor of presenting it must be shared'.[77] What is central to my reading is the way in which this division of labour – and the collective effort it suggests – emerges through the process of moving through the city itself, with the Citgo sign as a guiding marker: Gately's negotiation of the physical space of the metropolis opens the novel onto a tangible sense of social space incorporated into its vocal structure. Where Joelle's feminised relation to the metropolis constrained her to a subjectivity that precludes the perception of the city as a coherent social environment, Gately's drive points to a sociospatial epistemology in which the geography of the city, the prospect of community, and the form of the novel are integrally linked. And the culmination of this unfolding communality comes as the passage again approaches the Citgo sign:

> The CITGO sign's still off in the distance. You have to go a shocking long way to actually get to the big sign, which everybody says is hollow and you can get up inside there and stick your head out in a pulsing neon sea but nobody's ever personally been up there. (*Jest* p. 477)

The individuating 'anybody' evoked earlier in the passage becomes an inclusive 'everybody', the urban legend operating in the shared realm between individual experiences. It also becomes a 'nobody' – and Severs has suggested that Wallace's habit of marking handwritten drafts with the word 'nobody' might be interpreted as 'the signature of the anonymous collective . . . that coauthors this commonwealth text'.[78] The collective voice that appears at the Citgo sign points to a surviving sense of collective identity, embodied in a reservoir of rumours and urban legends whose subjects are the recognisable points in the topography of the metropolis.

This function is also connected with the status of the real-world Citgo sign as 'an important relic of America's industrial heyday' (in the words of Robert Campbell and Peter Vanderwarker) – a fragment of the old industrial Boston that had been displaced by the fractured topography of the city's post-Fordist configuration.[79] If the sign's appearance enables a moment of both physical and social coherence in the form of the city, it also represents a surviving trace of the old urban form that had been overturned by the economic transition of the late twentieth century – in fact, the early 1980s had seen an unsuccessful attempt to have it designated an official historical landmark.[80] This function of the sign is emphasised by its role in providing a pre-emptive counterpoint to the appearance of a second monumental sign a little later in the novel: the 'Brighton Best Savings Bank's rooftop digital Time and Temperature display'. This sign is encountered via Randy Lenz's retelling of Doony Glynn's nightmarish hallucination that turns the Boston sky into a 'flat square coldly Euclidean grid with black axes and a thread-fine reseau of lines creating grid-type coordinates . . . with the DOW ticker running up one side of the grid and the NIKEI index running down the other' (*Jest* p. 542). This vision reflects the prominent role of the finance and insurance industries in the topographical reconfiguration of Boston in the 1970s and 1980s: by the time Wallace moved to the city, as Walter Muir Whitehall and Lawrence W. Kennedy have established, 'the city's banks had erected massive monuments to themselves', with 'massive towers proclaiming financial might' coming to '[domi-nate] Boston's image'.[81] This monumentalism is a complement to the alienating architectural eclecticism associated with Rickey's build-ings and with the power of academic and technology industries in the city; framing the cityscape in its entirety through the Dow (US) and Nikkei (Japanese) stock markets (neither of which ought to be capitalised, their stylisation as such reflecting their literally inflating status in the Bostonian and American economies of the late twentieth century), this vision produces another form of alienating abstract space, this time associated with the sociospatial power of interna-tional finance.

The Citgo sign possesses a very different form of monumentality: a relic of the old industrial city that has been displaced by the new topography of globalised and high-tech finance, it allows Wallace to thread together the history of Boston's form, the consequences of its 1970s and 1980s restructuring, and his own near-future pro-jection. Acting as a spatial point in the city's topography around which not just the cityscape but also the complex vocal system of the novel is gathered, the Citgo sign produces something like the form of monumentality advocated by Italian architect and urban theorist Aldo Rossi – who, although he worked mainly in Italy, declared the American city to be 'the decisive confirmation' of his ideas.[82] For Rossi, monuments 'offer themselves as primary elements, fixed points in the urban dynamic'; they form 'persistences' in the fabric of the city, points that connect metropolitan topographies both to their unfolding histories and to the communities that inhabit them. They allow the city to become both 'a repository of history' and a 'synthesis of values' that, constituted as such, 'concerns the collective imagination'.[83] As such a monument, the Citgo sign is a counterpoint to the 'lush hole' of Boston Common and the sociospatial dissolu-tion it signifies in Joelle's walk. And this suggestion of connectivity also has a structural component, as the sequence leads into a mid-sentence transition to the Antitoi brothers' shop and the novel's ter-rorist plotline:

> one piece of the debris Gately's raised and set spinning behind him, a thick flattened M.F. cup, caught by a sudden gust as it falls, twirl-ing, is caught at some auerodyne's angle and blown spinning all the

way to the storefront of one 'Antitoi Entertainent' [sic] on the street's
east side, and hits . . . with a sound for all the world like the rap of a
knuckle . . . (*Jest* p. 479, square brackets original)

Re-confirming her displacement as the representative of an artistic
connectivity rooted in the city, this sentence takes up the mantle of
Joelle's earlier broadcast, providing another rare moment of actualised narrative connection in the form of a seamless switch between
plotlines that works against the prevailing fragmentation of the text
– and that is again placed in the exterior space of the metropolis.
Where Joelle's temporary relationship to the city was constrained to
a solitary sense of impressionistic subjectivity, Gately's drive – as it
brings the Citgo sign into view – allows for the emergence of both
social and historical consciousness embedded in the geography of
the city.

But the Citgo sign is also marked distinctively as a monument
to a remembered past, rather than to a present reality or a possible
future. In his Boston radio interview in 1996, Wallace noted that
'one of the things that I think my generation misses is that real sense
of unity and community in the sixties' – and it seems uncoincidental
that the Citgo sign was built in 1965, forming a spatial reminder of
the community whose loss Wallace saw as a profound factor in the
culture and society of the 1990s.[84] If the sign is a monument that
fulfils Rossi's ideal of 'the *locus* of the collective memory', enabling
us to see history 'as the relationship of the collective to its place',
this nostalgic element also underscores the distance between postwar
industrial society and the metropolis that emerged from the transition of the 1980s and 1990s.[85] Here I diverge from Severs's argument
that Wallace's writing 'resurrects' older economic and social values
'in reaction to financial capital's excess in the 1980s and 1990s':
though a previous economic and social geography plays an important role, the collectivity that attaches to the remnants of this geography is also attached to a receding past, felt in fragments and traces.[86]

Though resting in part on a retrospective fantasy that ignores long
histories of class and racial conflict in the industrial city, this nostalgia formed a common response to the profound changes of the 1980s
and 1990s: what Soja calls 'postmetropolitan nostalgia'.[87] And this
nostalgia itself is also bound up in the gendering of urban space at
the end of the twentieth century: in a critical review of Harvey's
Condition of Postmodernity, Rose notes how Harvey 'describes,
almost with nostalgia, Fordism after the Second World War'; while
'The modern is heroic, rational, progressive . . . Harvey seems to be

able to make sense of postmodernism only as a feminine Other, and hence his fear, his fascination, and his rejection'.[88] If the sociospatial dissolution of the city is associated with Joelle's gendered form of knowledge, the nostalgia for the stable and knowable social form of the industrial metropolis that accrues to the Citgo sign is also connected with this nostalgia for the control and domination that are discursively connected with a masculine epistemology. Between Joelle's walk and Gately's drive, *Jest* draws on the traditional gendering of geographical knowledge in its effort to give further shape to the problem of metropolitan literary form at the end of the twentieth century; a problem whose expression in the form of the text is built around a dynamic of absence and nostalgia. This, then, is the structure of feeling associated with the American city in transition, framed by the gendering of spatial practice and geographical knowledge: to move through the space of the metropolis at the end of the twentieth century is to inhabit a topography of loss.

Conclusion

Boston, with its promise of a 'metropolitan' way of life, was the environment that revived Wallace's failing composition of *Jest*; and it animated the novel with a sense of the social and spatial fragmentation of urban space produced by the late twentieth-century's transitional form of capitalist economy – a sense that made itself felt in the fabric of his description and in the formal arrangement of his narrative. *Jest* is a city novel, then: not in the sense of a novel in which urban geography is a straightforward point of reference, but a novel in which the post-Fordist city's sociospatial form represents a rich representational problem to be worked out in the form and language of the text. Joelle's walk and Gately's drive are excursions that dramatise the effort to reconnect the novel with the metropolis, moving beyond the alienating abstract space produced by the dominant academic and financial sectors that had displaced the old industrial city. As they do so, they also reflect established gendered assumptions about space and geographical knowledge: problematic insofar as it reproduces the attribution of limited and limiting forms of knowledge to women and re-enacts their displacement as producers of urban space, this gendering forms part of the prism through which Wallace attempted to re-orient the novel in relation to the geography of the late twentieth century city. The result of these excursions – and their differently gendered outcomes – is a dynamic of absence and nostalgia that reflects the structure of feeling produced by the deep upheavals in the urban geography of 1980s and 1990s America. As such, it was Boston that provided Wallace with a new focus for the problem of realigning his practice with the social world – a problem that is inscribed deeply into the form of the novel. The question that arises, then, is how this form could go beyond registering the challenge of the 'postmetropolis', moving past the limited excursions of the opening half of the text in order to take up the initial promise of Joelle's signal: that an artistic practice embedded in the city could reconnect its fractured spaces and isolated inhabitants. This is the question to which I will turn in the next chapter.

Notes

1. Hering, *Fiction and Form*, pp. 45, 63.
2. Hering, 'Triangles', pp. 95–6.
3. Stephen J. Burn, *David Foster Wallace's* Infinite Jest: *A Reader's Guide*, second edition (London: Continuum, 2012), p. 71.
4. Houser, 'Environmental Case', p. 119.
5. Severs, *Balancing Books*, pp. 93–4.
6. Danielle Drellinger and Javier Zarracina, 'Boston's Infinite Jest: A David Foster Wallace Memorial Tour', *Boston Globe* (undated), <http://www.boston.com/bostonglobe/ideas/graphics/092108_infinite _jest/> [retrieved 28 February 2022].
7. Tim Bean, 'Infinite Jest Tour of Boston: A Tour of the Boston Locations Mentioned in Infinite Jest', Flikr.com account (undated), <https://www .flickr.com/photos/25383051@N05/sets/72157612365092520/with /3182231319/> [retrieved 28 February 2022].
8. William Beutler, 'Infinite Boston' (July–September 2012), <http://www .infiniteboston.com/> [retrieved 28 February 2022].
9. William Beutler, 'Infinite Atlas', <http://www.infiniteatlas.com/> [retrieved 28 February 2022]. For Beutler's description of the project, see 'Infinite Boston'.
10. Bill Lattanzi, 'Messing with Maps: Walking David Foster Wallace's Boston', *Los Angeles Review of Books* (6 February 2015), <https:// lareviewofbooks.org/article/messing-maps-walking-david-foster -wallaces-boston/> [retrieved 28 February 2022].
11. Hoberek, 'Wallace and American Literature', p. 44; 'Novel After David Foster Wallace', p. 222.
12. Adam Kelly, 'The Map and the Territory: Infinite Boston', *The Millions* (13 August 2013), <https://themillions.com/2013/08/the-map-and-the -territory-infinite-boston.html> [retrieved 28 February 2022].
13. Adam Kelly, 'Dialectic of Sincerity: Lionel Trilling and David Foster

Wallace', *Post-45* (17 October 2014), <http://post45.research.yale.edu/2014/10/dialectic-of-sincerity-lionel-trilling-and-david-foster-wallace/> [retrieved 28 February 2022].

14. Umberto Eco, *Six Walks in the Fictional Woods* (Cambridge, Massachusetts: Harvard University Press, 1994), p. 84.
15. David Cooper and Gary Priestnall, 'The Processural Intertextuality of Literary Cartographies: Critical and Digital Practices', *The Cartographic Journal*, 48.4 (2011), 250–62 (p. 250).
16. Blanche Housman Gelfant, *The American City Novel* (1954), second edition (Norman: University of Oklahoma Press, 1970), p. vii.
17. Ibid, p. 10.
18. Burton Pike, *The Image of the City in Modern Literature* (Princeton: Princeton University Press, 1981), pp. 8, 12.
19. Richard Lehan, *The City in Literature: An Intellectual and Cultural History* (Berkeley: University of California Press, 1998), p. xv.
20. Raymond Williams, *The Country and the City* (1973) (London: Hogarth Press, 1993), p. 154.
21. Diane Wolfe Levy, 'City Signs: Toward a Definition of Urban Literature', *Modern Fiction Studies* 24.1 (Spring 1978), 65–73 (p. 70).
22. 'Metropolitan, n. and adj', *OED Online* (Oxford: Oxford University Press) (December 2018), <http://www.oed.com.ezproxy01.rhul.ac.uk/view/Entry/117705?redirectedFrom=metropolitan#eid> [retrieved 28 February 2022].
23. Quoted by Max, *Every Love Story*, p. 123, original emphasis.
24. Max, *Every Love Story*, p. 159, 123.
25. Quoted in Marshall Boswell, 'Preface: David Foster Wallace and "The Long Thing"', in Marshall Boswell (ed.), *David Foster Wallace and 'The Long Thing': New Essays on the Novels* (New York: Bloomsbury, 2014), pp. vi–xii (p. vii).
26. Max, *Every Love Story*, p. 146.
27. Steven Moore, 'The First Draft Version of *Infinite Jest*', *The Howling Fantods* (2003), <http://www.thehowlingfantods.com/ij_first.htm> [retrieved 28 February 2022].
28. Williams, *Keywords*, p. 56.
29. Raymond Williams, 'Metropolitan Perceptions and the Emergence of Modernism', in Williams, *The Politics of Modernism* (ed. Toney Pinkey) (London: Verso, 1989), p. 37.
30. David M. Gordon, 'Capitalist Development and the History of American Cities', in William K. Tabb and Larry Sawers (eds.), *Marxism and the Metropolis: New Perspectives in Urban Political Economy* (New York: Oxford University Press, 1984), pp. 21–53 (pp. 22–3).
31. Edward L. Glaeser, 'Reinventing Boston: 1630–2003', *Journal of Economic Geography*, 5.2 (2005), 119–53 (p. 120, 144, 151).
32. Fox Butterfield, 'What You See is What You Get', *New York Times*

(1 May 1988), <https://www.nytimes.com/1988/05/01/books/what-you-see-is-what-you-get.html> [retrieved 28 February 2022].

33. Harvey, *Condition*, p. 66.
34. Douglass Shand-Tucci, *Built in Boston: City and Suburb 1800–2000: Revised and Expanded Edition* (Amherst: University of Massachusetts Press, 1999), pp. 235, 300.
35. Ibid. p. 316.
36. Lawrence W. Kennedy, *Planning the City upon a Hill: Boston since 1630* (Amherst: University of Massachusetts Press, 1992), pp. 195, 202.
37. Shand-Tucci, *Built in Boston*, pp. 265 ff.
38. Naomi Miller and Keith Morgan, *Boston Architecture 1975–1990* (Munich: Prestel-Verlag, 1990), p. 14.
39. Charles Jencks, *The Language of Postmodern Architecture*, sixth edition (London: Academy Editions, 1977), pp. 13, 105.
40. Edward Relph, *The Modern Urban Landscape* (London: Croom Helm, 1987), pp. 237, 215.
41. Kevin Roberts, 'Prisoners of the City: Whatever Could a Postmodern City Be?', in Erica Carter, James Donald and Judith Squires (eds.), *Space and Place: Theories of Identity and Location* (London: Lawrence and Wishart, 1993), pp. 303–30 (p. 303, 314).
42. Kennedy, *Planning*, p. 214.
43. Michael Holleran, *Boston's 'Changeful Times': Origins of Preservation & Planning in America* (Baltimore: John Hopkins University Press, 1998), p. 10.
44. Thomas J. Sugrue, *Origins of the Urban Crisis: Race and Inequality in Postwar Detroit* (Princeton, New Jersey: Princeton University Press, 1996), p. 3.
45. Edward W. Soja, *Postmetropolis: Critical Studies of Cities and Regions* (Oxford: Blackwell, 2000), pp. 148, 150.
46. Morrissey and Thompson, 'Rare White', p. 88, 86; Cohen, 'Whiteness', p. 235.
47. Burn, *Reader's Guide*, p. 36.
48. Kiki Benzon, '"Yet Another Example of the Porousness of Certain Borders": Chaos and Realism in *Infinite Jest*', in Hering (ed.), *Consider*, pp. 101–12 (pp. 101–2); Greg Carlisle, 'Introduction: Consider David Foster Wallace Studies', in Hering (ed.), *Consider*, pp. 12–23 (p. 17).
49. Quoted by Douglas Spencer, *The Architecture of Neoliberalism: How Contemporary Architecture Became a Tool of Control and Compliance* (London: Bloomsbury, 2016), p. 64, original emphasis.
50. Mark Caro, 'The Next Big Thing: Can a Downstate Author Withstand the Sensation over His 1,079-page Novel?', in Burn (ed.), *Conversations*, pp. 53–7 (p. 57).
51. Severs, *Balancing Books*, p. 5.
52. Kunal Jasty, 'Lost 1996 Interview'.

53. Andrew Warren, 'Modelling Community and Narrative in Infinite Jest and The Pale King', in Boswell (ed.), *Long Thing*, pp. 61–84 (p. 68).
54. Walter Muir Whitehall and Lawrence W. Kennedy, *Boston: A Topographical History*, third edition (Cambridge, MA: Belknap Press/Harvard University Press, 2000), p. 241.
55. Finn Fordham, 'Katabasis in Danielewski's *House of Leaves* and two other recent American novels', in Joe Brady and Alison Gibbons (eds.), *Mark Z. Danielewski* (Manchester: Manchester University Press, 2011), pp. 33–51 (p. 40–1).
56. Miller and Morgan, *Boston Architecture*, p. 14.
57. 'Verstiegenheit', in M. Clark and O. Thyen (eds.), *Oxford German Dictionary*, third edition (Oxford: Oxford University Press, 2008), p. 775, original italics.
58. Severs, *Balancing Books*, p. 177.
59. Lefebvre, *Production of Space*, p. 52.
60. Hana Wirth-Nesher, *City Codes: Reading the Modern Urban Novel* (Cambridge: Cambridge University Press, 1996), p. 3.
61. Jeffrey Severs, '"We've been inside what we wanted all along": David Foster Wallace's Immanent Structures', in Brynnar Swenson (ed.), *Literature and the Encounter with Immanence* (Leiden: Brill Rodopi, 2017), pp. 8–29 (p. 18).
62. Robert Chodat, *The Matter of High Words: Naturalism, Normativity, and the Postwar Sage* (Oxford: Oxford University Press, 2017), p. 251.
63. Charles Baudelaire, 'The Painter of Modern Life' (1863), trans. P. E. Charvet (1972), in *The Painter of Modern Life* (London: Penguin, 2010), pp. 13, 14, 16.
64. Janet Wolff, 'The Invisible Flâneuse: Women and the Literature of Modernity', *Theory, Culture & Society*, 2.3 (1985), 37–46 (p. 40, 45).
65. Leslie Kern, *Feminist City* (London: Verso, 2020), p. 103.
66. Lauren Elkin, *Flâneuse: Women Walk the City in Paris, New York, Tokyo, Venice and London* (London: Chatto & Windus, 2016), pp. 22–3.
67. Gillian Rose, *Feminism and Geography: The Limits of Geographical Knowledge* (Cambridge: Polity Press, 1993), pp. 7, 9.
68. Ibid. p. 2.
69. Beutler, 'Joelle's Walk to "The Very Last Party,"' in 'Infinite Boston', <http://www.infiniteboston.com/post/31520104130/joelle-charles -back-bay> [retrieved 28 February 2022].
70. Baudelaire, 'Painter', p. 12.
71. Walter Benjamin, 'On Some Motifs in Baudelaire' (1940), in *The Writer of Modern Life: Essays on Baudelaire*, ed. Michael W. Jennings, trans. Howard Eiland, Edmund Jephcott, Rodney Livingston and Harry Zohn (Cambridge, Massachusetts: Belknap Press, 2006), p. 278 n. 26; Benjamin, 'Paris, Capital of the Nineteenth Century', in *Writer of Modern Life*, p. 40.

72. Groenland, *Art of Editing*, p. 131.
73. Holleran, *Changeful Times*, p. 275.
74. Heather Houser, 'Managing Information and Materiality in *Infinite Jest* and Running the Numbers', *American Literary History*, 2.4 (Winter 2014), 742–64 (pp. 746–7).
75. Beutler, 'Infinite Boston'.
76. Jameson, *Postmodernism*, p. 51, original emphasis.
77. Houser, 'Managing Information', p. 749.
78. Severs, *Balancing Books*, p. 133.
79. Robert Campbell and Peter Vanderwarker, *Cityscapes of Boston: An American City Through Time* (Boston: Houghton Mifflin Company, 1992), p. 185
80. Jess Bidgood, 'Boston Takes Step to Elevate Citgo Sign From LED Beacon to Landmark', *New York Times* (13 July 2016), <https://www.nytimes.com/2016/07/14/us/boston-citgo-sign-landmark.html> [retrieved 28 February 2022].
81. Whitehall and Kennedy, *Boston*, pp. 247, 241, 273.
82. Aldo Rossi, *The Architecture of the City* (Cambridge, Massachusetts: MIT Press, 1982), p. 13.
83. Ibid. pp. 127–8.
84. Jasty, 'Lost 1996 Interview'.
85. Rossi, *Architecture*, pp. 130–1.
86. Severs, *Balancing Books*, p. 24.
87. Soja, *Postmetropolis*, p. 246.
88. Gillian Rose, review of Edward W. Soja, *Postmodern Geographies: The Reassertion of Space in Critical Social Theory*, and David Harvey, *The Condition of Postmodernity: An Enquiry into the Origins of Cultural Change. Journal of Historical Geography*, 17.1 (1991), 118–21 (p. 120).

Chapter 3

'Abroad in the urban night' (II): Empathy, Community and the Image of the City in *Infinite Jest*

Introduction: Encountering the Metropolis

Wallace's move to Boston had, as the previous chapter has shown, entailed a reframing of the question of how his literary practice could align with the social conditions that had emerged from the socioeconomic upheavals at the end of the twentieth century: a question that was now intimately bound up with the deep formal and representational problems that the 'postmetropolitan' city posed for the novel. The city appears in the early stages of *Infinite Jest* as a space of fragmentation, loss and nostalgia; but Joelle van Dyne's broadcast had also signalled the prospect of a connective artistic practice embedded in the metropolis. Is this possibility a dead end for *Jest*, one that dissipates along with the crowd whose elision from the text reflects the social atomisation of the city? Despite the dominant sense of dissolution, the tentative urban excursions of Joelle and Don Gately in the opening half of the text also contain latent suggestions that a renewed juncture between city and novel might yet revive the metropolis as a shared environment, a lived social space. How the novel builds on this suggestion despite the predominance of fragmentation, and how it locates possibilities of community in the very metropolis that seems so inimical to collective life, is the question I explore in this chapter. And as a starting point, I want to return to Wallace's own encounter with the social scene of Boston.

In Chapter 2, I emphasised the excitement Wallace expressed on first moving to the city in the summer of 1989; but this excitement proved short-lived, as a serious mental health crisis saw him hospitalised in late 1989 and 1991, before gradually returning to city life through Boston's addiction recovery network and halfway house facilities. This experience perhaps explains his later reflection that 'I don't do well in big cities', a sentiment that might seem to justify the view that Wallace's attitude to metropolitan environments was essentially a negative one.[1] But even this crisis, on closer inspection, took on a generative role in *Jest*'s development. Wallace's own comments on the role of his experiences of the city in the writing of his novel are limited, but when asked about this role in his WBUR Radio interview in 1996, he focused specifically on the encounters with a sense of social alterity that took place there:

> I was raised in an academic environment and in a pretty middle-class one. I'd never really seen how a lot of other people lived. My chance to see that was here in Boston, and a lot of it was in the halfway houses for this book.[2]

In Boston and through recovery, Wallace experienced for the first time 'the finding of yourself next door to alterity' that, for Doreen Massey, constitutes the 'surprise of space'.[3]

The encounter with the social reality of the city that recovery entailed seems to have been particularly important to the revival of *Jest*'s composition: the period immediately after Wallace's hospitalisation, as he returned tentatively to city life via Boston's halfway houses, appears to have been the point at which his previously drafted material found newly compelling form. The suspicion that the parts of the novel that deal with Ennet House are modelled on Wallace's own experience in the Granada House facility is confirmed by a handwritten draft of the description of the Enfield Marine Hospital, dated '4/23/1990', in which the building that became Ennet House is in fact named 'Granada House' (HRC 15.7; c.f. *Jest* p. 193). In D. T. Max's account, Wallace left Granada House in June 1990, meaning that this draft must have been written while Wallace was still living there – placing the origins of this new material firmly in Boston's geographical networks of recovery.[4] Elsewhere, Wallace labelled a May 1991 draft of the scene that recounts Don Gately's 'dream duty' interactions with Ennet House residents (*Jest* pp. 563–5) as 'embryonic' (HRC 15.7). This is a striking designation to append to a draft for a novel that had already been underway for at least five years; it indicates that Wallace envisioned an entirely new beginning for his novel as he processed the experiences of recovery.

The importance of this context is suggested in the appearance of Ennet House itself in the novel. Well before the facility is mapped from above as part of Enfield Marine Hospital (*Jest* pp. 193–8), it is approached at street level by Tiny Ewell:

The early November day is foggy and colorless. The sky and street are the same color. The trees look skeletal. There is bright wet wadded litter all along the seams of street and curb. The houses are skinny three-deckers, mashed together, wharf-grey w/ salt-white trim, madonnas in the yards, bowlegged dogs hurling themselves against the fencing. Some schoolboys in knee-pads and skallycaps are playing street hockey on a passing school's cement playground ... (*Jest* p. 86)

Here the plethora of grim urban detail, and the sense of concreteness imparted by the short and matter-of-fact sentences, impart a mate-rial immediacy to the space of the street – a pronounced contrast to the weird facades of E.T.A. and the MIT building that dominate this early part of the novel. Ennet House is introduced as a place defined by its concrete geographical context, prefaced by its connection to the material of the city. This is underscored by the later description of the House's 'huge protruding bay windows that yield a view of ravine-weeds and the unpleasant stretch of Commonwealth Ave' – and that, despite this apparently 'unpleasant' situation, form 'the House's single attractive feature' (p. 197). Considerably later, this point is redoubled: 'the downhill view from the bay window ... was like the only spectacular thing about Ennet House' (p. 464). As Ennet House establishes the prospect of connectedness to the social and spatial reality of the city, the markedly changed terms in which this connectedness is couched – from 'unpleasant' to 'spectacular' – suggest a developing attitude to the city as the novel progresses. Bill Lattanzi suggests that, having encountered 'a whole other Boston ... invisible to the express lane of American success that he'd been traveling', Wallace proceeded to 'pour his new knowledge of the democracy of pain into *Infinite Jest*, marking it out on the streets as if its invisible stories were burned on the sidewalks, every dumpster a monument'.[5] In this chapter, I explore how *Jest*'s formal strategies and its celebrated themes of empathy and community unfurled from this shaping encounter with Boston's underside.

Fiction and the Urban Encounter: William T. Vollmann and 'Yrstrly'

Wallace had already come across some models for the fictional pos-sibilities contained in urban social encounters in some of the works of fiction that he read with enthusiasm shortly before his move to Boston. Jonathan Franzen's *The Twenty-Seventh City* (1988), a novel of St Louis municipal politics, 'showed a familiarity with its chosen city that Wallace could only marvel at' – so much so that reading it '"depressed" him', according to D. T. Max.[6] William T. Vollmann's collection *The Rainbow Stories* (1989), meanwhile, engaged closely with the social scene of 1980s San Francisco; Wallace read it repeatedly and avidly when he received a proof copy early in 1989.[7] Of the pieces in Vollmann's collection, Wallace particularly admired the novella 'The Blue Yonder', a story set among the marginalised population of San Francisco, and that follows the activities of an itinerant serial killer with a double personality (The Zombie/The Other) who murders homeless people by forcing them to drink Drano drain cleaner. Wallace wrote to Franzen that the piece 'simply separates sock from pod',[8] and according to Mark Costello it was still a 'fave' that summer, as the two began working on *Signifying* in Boston (*Signifying* p. vi) – this fictional expression of the city's challenging social contexts was foremost in Wallace's reading as he turned to the prospect of writing the city.

If 'The Blue Yonder' is a possible model for Wallace's approach to the social alterity he had found in Boston recovery, one particularly interesting feature is its use of voice. The story is presented in a mode resembling reportage, establishing a detached, pseudo-documentary narrative voice. Formal, verbose and opinionated, this voice dominates the early part of the novella, frequently breaking the chain of narration with interjections: 'some people think that the worst part of life is knowing that they must lose everything. Those people are all rich!'[9] But, describing the death of the first of The Zombie's victims, the narrator retreats, allowing the voice of a halfway house resident to present a sustained account (complete with typographical renderings of his pronunciation): 'Two firemen . . . came in with a re-*soos*-itator, to see if he was breathing, you know. They didn't so much as apply their re-*soos*-itator to him. They just said he was dead.'[10] Another voice, emanating from the city's social fabric, stages a narrative interruption.

This displacement of the controlling documentary voice is complemented later in the piece as the narrative follows The Zombie towards an ultimately suicidal crisis. A crucial long section opens with a close description of the cityscape, in which an interplay of light and darkness is suggestive of a concern with the knowability of the city: cars 'passed through tunnels of light' past 'the black water', 'none knowing that beneath them was a long hollow darkness'. As these cars speed 'past the Transamerica Pyramid and the radiant necklaces of the Bay Bridge', we hear that they are 'headed for Emeryville and Berkeley and thence who knows where' – specific geographical references trailing off into indistinction, a process that continues as the passage ends with a move from the illuminated surface of the freeway into the 'hollow darkness' beneath: 'That was where the Other was'.[11] As the story continues, this interplay of dark and light frames an unsettling convergence of Vollmann's detached voice and The Zombie's consciousness, enacted through a subtle shift towards free indirect speech: 'yes, he was fenced in now;' 'yes, it was light, too, that he feared, not for itself, but for what it revealed to the night'.[12] Drifting uneasily between detached observation and close rendering of The Zombie's internal voice precisely as it describes an anxiety over the illumination of darkened city space, Vollmann's story disrupts the implied distinction between detached external observer and subject that underlies the documentary mode. A new and ambivalent relationship between the observing writerly consciousness and its social subject emerges against the backdrop of a darkened and disorientating city space; epistemological failure and social revelation are entwined here, a double process inextricable from its metropolitan frame. The darkened spaces in the city's map and territory are the points at which troubling new encounters with social alterity arise.

The clearest point of contact between 'Blue Yonder' and *Jest*'s portrait of Boston comes in the 'Yrstrly' monologue that bursts unexpectedly into Wallace's novel after 128 pages, puncturing the early dominance of E.T.A. as the novel's primary space (we later learn that this is Ennet House resident Emil Minty [*Jest* p. 300]). Indeed, a connection with Vollmann's story is suggested in what appears to be a direct reference towards the end of the Yrstrly passage, when Bobby C's graphic death is attributed to a 'Hotshot' laced with 'Drano with the blue like glittershit and everything like that taken out' (*Jest* p. 134), just as The Zombie used Drano as a murder weapon in 'Blue Yonder'. And, recalling Vollmann's story, the interruption of Yrstrly's monologue entails a striking departure from the third-person voice into which *Jest*'s narrative has settled after Hal's first-person opening. Against this dominant voice, the strong dialect and typographical idiosyncrasies of Yrstrly's monologue are a stark contrast: 'The AM were wicked bright and us a bit sick however we scored our wake ups boosting some items at a sidewalk sale in Harvard Squar where it was warm upping and the snow coming off the onnings . . .' (p. 128). Recalling Vollmann's use of typographical form to register the interruption of a voice from the city's social scene, Yrstrly's sudden appearance brings a stark and jarring lexical

otherness to the early part of the novel; Mary Shapiro notes that
the section 'contains Wallace's only extended use of "eye dialect" –
misspellings that trigger strong awareness of incorrectness'.[13] If the
excess of obscure textuality in the descriptions of Rickey's buildings
produces an alienating form of abstract space, here Wallace's use of
text registers a very different challenge: an unsettling incursion of the
messy social material of the city into the linguistic fabric of the novel.
And while Joelle and Gately trace tentative moves outward into the
metropolis, Yrstrly's interjection signals a complementary opposite:
a sudden inward intrusion of the city's social scene into the language
of the text.

Yrstrly's monologue is not just a sudden interruption of a markedly different voice; by contrast with the strongly bounded space
of E.T.A., this section also leaves the reader adrift in Boston's
geography, with no sort of narrative map to guide them. There are
place names aplenty in Yrstrly's account, but nothing to link them
to one another or anchor them to any organising sense of the city's
cartography:

> We go down to the Brighton projects to cop . . . and we go down to
> the library at Copley where we stash our personnel works . . . And
> back we go to the Harvard Squar however on arrival Poor Tony
> wanted we should hang for lunch time with his red leather fags in the
> Bow&Arrow . . . and yrstrly and C said fuck this shit and we screwed
> out and go up to the Central Squar . . . (*Jest* p. 129)

Providing no description and no narrative account of the journeys
Yrstrly's crew make between these named places, the section leaves
us without means of grasping the geography it invokes. And disorientation occurs at the level of the sentence too, as the crew arrive at
Central Square and spatial relations proliferate at baffling, unpunctuated speed: 'we come up and run into Kely Vinoy that was working
her corner *by the* dumster *by* Cheap-O records *in the* Squar *by the*
email place . . .' (p. 129, emphases added). The dislocation produced
by this section, and its culmination in the unpleasant death of Bobby
C, might seem to justify the assumption that the city in *Jest* figures
primarily as a space of fear and violence. But Yrstrly also provides
us with a vision of exactly the 'extravagant' wandering across the
borders of the metropolis that Gerhard Schtitt and E.T.A. are so
keen to preclude; there is a vibrant energy to his narration, and his
interruption produces the potentially generative form of disorientation that comes with crossing lines of division in the city's physical
and spatial topography. The Yrstrly section represents an encounter

with the city couched in terms of a challenging and exciting interruption of spatial and social alterity – one that re-enacts the generative intrusion of urban social difference into the composition of the novel in 1991.

Wallace's attention to this interruption of urban alterity is perhaps unsurprising given the prevalence in the popular American imagination of what Robert M. Collins calls the 'specter of an American underclass' in the 1980s. This spectre emerged, according to Collins, from 'a seemingly recent phenomenon in the nation's urban ghettos: the rise of a debilitating complex of persistent poverty in conjunction with sustained unemployment and welfare dependency, family breakdown, school failure, rampant drug use, escalating and increasingly violent crime'.[14] This was a discourse fuelled by the displacement of former industrial workers as the metropolis underwent the economic transition of the 1980s, and by the endemic poverty this displacement produced. And the spectre of the 'underclass' was bound up especially with an epidemic of homelessness, especially prevalent in larger cities, which became 'a national scandal' as the decade took its course – and which is reflected in the focus on itinerant urban communities in both Vollmann's *Rainbow Stories* and *Jest*'s Yrstrly section.[15] Wallace's own encounter with the social scene of Boston's recovery networks coincided, by way of his reading of Vollmann, with this wider preoccupation with the social difference bound up in perceptions of urban space – a preoccupation that intersected with a longer-running literary and cultural construction of the 'urban underworld' as 'an imaginative space that middle-class residents have sought to enter . . . a space in which to fantasize about other ways of living and being', as Thomas Heise puts it.[16] The idea of an expanding underclass, and the prospect of encounters with it, frames the fascination with the city and its social challenges that is expressed in both Vollmann's novella and Yrstrly's monologue.

What is at work here recalls Raymond Williams's idea of the 'knowable community': the range of social vision rendered in a work of fiction, which is also 'part of a traditional method – an underlying stance and approach – that the novelist offers to show people and their relationships in essentially knowable and communicable ways'. In Williams's account, it is in the metropolis in particular that, across the history of modern writing, this knowable community is frequently discovered in crisis: 'in the experience of the city', he says (speaking of Charles Dickens), 'so much that was important, and even decisive, could not be simply known or simply communicated, but had . . . to be forced into consciousness'.[17] This last phrase suggests that this kind of metropolitan fiction should be seen not just as a passive reflection on spatial encounters with alterity, but an active effort to bring these encounters into full imaginative expression – force them into consciousness – through the practice of writing: the social experience of the metropolis is what compels the novel form to reckon with 'unknown and unacknowledged relationships, profound and decisive connections'.[18] For Wallace (as for Vollmann), this effort gained new impetus against the backdrop of the late twentieth-century city that had been so profoundly shaken by the changes of the previous decades. Transposing the social encounter that recovery had entailed into a literary interruption through Yrstrly, *Jest* frames the geography of Boston as a focal point for the question of how to use the language and form of fiction to effect this forcing into consciousness of the social relationships that characterised the post-Fordist metropolis.

From Encounter to Empathy: The Subway and Poor Tony

That Wallace was interested in a form that could make something of the encounter with the city is suggested in notes for his review of Joseph Frank's biography of Fyodor Dostoevsky, published the year before *Jest*: 'D[ostoevsky] able to distil "haunting Baudelairian poetry" out of "sordid Petersburg slums" – like Dickens' London, Balzac's Paris' (HRC 4.12). Wallace was apparently interested in a metropolitan literary tradition in which urban social context provided the basis for fictional form – but a footnote in the review itself strikes a somewhat critical note on Dostoevsky's *Poor Folk* in particular: 'a standard-issue "social novel" . . . with depictions of urban poverty sufficiently ghastly to elicit the approval of the socialist left' (*Consider* 266 n. 17). The raw social material of the city was important to Wallace's project, but he was looking for a kind of fiction that would move beyond the sheer spectacle of social difference: a fiction in which the sociospatial environment of the city appears not as mere content to be neatly packaged and presented to the reader, but as a deeper influence on the form and practice of the novel.

A connection between the encounter with the city and the need for a renewed conception of literary practice runs through Vollmann's reflections on the status and purpose of late twentieth-century fiction. He explained the move from the postmodern surrealism of his first novel *You Bright and Risen Angels* (1987) to the documentary style of *Rainbow Stories* in terms of the need for a form that could 'create a context so that people in these different worlds could see each other'.[19] Asked about the impetus for this transition, he pointed more specifically to his meeting with the San Francisco street photographer Ken Miller, and Miller's connections with the city's social underside, placing Vollmann's idea of making different worlds visible (itself reminiscent of the practice of street photography) in the streets of the metropolis.[20] And he followed *Rainbow Stories* with a 'diagnosis' of American literature that insisted – in terms that echo Wallace's own famous advocation of fiction that provides 'imaginative access to other selves'[21] – on writing that 'takes us inside other minds' and 'treat[s] Self and Other as equal partners'.[22] Tracing the arc from provoking new dialogue between the social worlds of *Rainbow Stories* into the more generalised terminology of 'Self' and 'Other' in the 'diagnosis', we can see how a theorised notion of fiction's purpose unfolds from the specific urban encounters Vollmann dramatises in *Rainbow Stories*. The fascination with urban underworlds that shapes Vollmann's and Wallace's depictions of the city, and the more generalised and theoretical appeals to sincerity and empathy prominent in these writers' manifestos, can both be linked to the structure of feeling that is also expressed in the 'underclass' discourse of the 1980s: a sense of essentially divided urban communities encountering each other across deep ruptures in the late twentieth-century cityscape.

To see how this connection is at work in *Jest* – how Wallace's well-known appeals to 'single-entendre principles' (*Supposedly* p. 81) and fiction as 'deep conversation'[23] are related to the challenge of urban alterity that kick-started his novel in Boston – I will start with a return to *Signifying Rappers*. Wallace's sections of this book focus on rap's significance in terms that echo his later reflection on the importance of Boston's social scene and its sudden appearance in his range of vision: rap's attraction, he suggests, lies in its ability to 'afford white listeners genuine, horse's-mouth access to the life-and-death plight and mood of an American community . . . we've been heretofore conditioned to avoid, remand to the margins, not even *see* except through certain careful abstract, attenuating filters' (*Signifying* p. 35, original emphasis). What Wallace values in rap's aesthetic is its capacity to enact a social encounter that in turn forces a necessary realignment of the social epistemology of white, affluent America.

This renewed perception of urban space as an arena of social alterity is most fully developed in section 2C, in which Wallace invokes the experience of subway travel in metropolitan America, inviting 'those of you who live in like Chicago or NYC' to consider 'how commuters on the train tend to get all quiet and tense when South Side or South Bronx starts to flow past' (*Signifying* p. 75). Wallace suggests that this tension is rooted in 'a kind of rigid fascination with the beauty of ruins in which people live but look or love nothing like you, a horizonful of numbly complex vistas'; 'White people', he notes, 'have always loved to gaze at the "real black world," preferably at a distance and while moving briskly through' (*Signifying* pp. 75–6). But, in a sentence that matches the rhythm of the subway with the excitement that attends the vista of urban otherness, Wallace instead invites his reader to:

> step out, even just for a moment, and it turns out that this time it isn't the train that's moving, it's the gutted landscape of rap itself; and the 'ruins' that are its home and *raison* aren't nearly the static archaeology they seem, they themselves are moving, arranging themselves, becoming something no less bombed-out and dire but now somehow *intended from within*, a hegemony that matters, a self-conscious apposition, moving into expression, into Awareness, . . . so that what had looked from the moving glass to be a place's and people's past-in-present reveals itself now a ruined totem to *total* presence – a separate, unequal, Other place-and-time, exploding outward. (*Signifying* p. 77, original emphases)

In this vision, rather than facilitate a comfortable distance, the subway transports Wallace's reader directly into a vision of an urban space invested with a kinetic energy derived from the encounter with its otherness, instantiated in the long sentence's pulsing rhythm and the hum of clashing registers, from the vernacular 'gutted' and 'bombed-out' to the high-theoretical 'hegemony' and 'apposition'. Even before the experience of recovery framed the revival of *Jest*'s composition, this is a metropolitan space whose description embodies an exciting encounter between the lexis of the academic Wallace and the social materiality of urban geography. A stark sense of social difference charges these spaces and renders them more than backdrops; the privileged white novelist's encounter with the city is simultaneously and inextricably an encounter with this alterity and with the living, dynamic spaces it produces.

The connection with Wallace's conscious turn to renewed social engagement in his fiction can be traced in the continued appearance of the subway space as a motif through Wallace's manifesto 'E Unibus Pluram: Television and US Fiction', and into *Jest* itself. In the former (first published in 1993, but begun as a commissioned piece for *Harper's* in 1990, as Wallace was emerging from recovery in Boston),[24] the subway promises – or threatens – a counterpoint to televisual spectacle, a potentially uncomfortable real-world encounter between living individuals for which television claims to prepare us: 'further viewing begins to seem almost like required research, lessons in the blank, bored, too-wise expression that . . . [we] must learn how to wear for tomorrow's excruciating ride on the brightly lit subway' (*Supposedly* p. 63). For Blanche Housman Gelfant, the subway is a key motif in the city novel tradition because 'subway life in a way epitomizes city life: in the daily life situation within the subway are the collective physical conditions and psychological tensions that give rise to a manner of life defined as urbanism'.[25] For Wallace, this typically metropolitan space is the venue in which we deploy practised cosmopolitan aloofness in order to evade social encounters; but as such, it seems by implication to form the site in which such encounters might happen, if only the passengers were to venture out from behind their masks.

The fruition of the subway motif as an urban site of direct interpersonal contact emerges in the section of *Jest* that deals with Yrstrly crewmate Poor Tony Krause's seizure on a Boston subway train, picking up the itinerant addicts' subplot introduced to such disorientating effect in the Yrstrly section. If Yrstrly had heralded a stark challenge to the sociospatial epistemology of the text, though, this section opens with a contrasting sense of geographical clarity: 'Poor Tony Krause had a seizure on the T. It happened on a Gray Line train from Watertown to Inman Square, Cambridge' (*Jest* p. 299). The provision of the full name and the careful placing of the scene within the city's topography underline the fact that, in contrast to the Yrstrly passage, this sequence is to be related by a strong, organising narrative voice. What follows is a grittier reconfiguration of the subway car from 'E Unibus Pluram', as Poor Tony finds he has become 'one of those loathsome urban specimens that respectable persons on T-trains slide and drift quietly away from without even seeming to notice they're even there' (p. 304). What in 'E Unibus Pluram' was an innocuous everyday avoidance of social encounters becomes infused with pathos, as Poor Tony 'wept silently in shame and pain at the passage of each brightly lit public second's edge . . . sat all alone at one end of the car, feeling each slow second take its cut' (p. 304).

If the introduction of this section's objective organising voice allows for a firm geographical placement of the scene, it also serves to set up a crucial shift in perspective. While Poor Tony's fellow pas-

sengers, recalling those of 'E Unibus Pluram', become 'terribly interested in the floor tiles between their feet' (*Jest* pp. 304–5), Wallace's
narrative denies us the familiar luxury of flinching from the scene,
shifting away from the initial detached point of view and taking us
inside Poor Tony's head as 'the floor of the subway car became the
ceiling of the subway car' (p. 305) and the seizure descends. What
follows is an extended depiction of the experience of the seizure from
Poor Tony's point of view, during which we bear direct witness to
his re-lived traumas: first referring back to the Yrstrly section as 'he
saw Bobby ('C') C's blood misting upward in the hot wind of the
Copley blower', and then allowing a glimpse into the pain and shame
of his familial past, as 'His father knelt beside him on the ceiling in a
well-rended sleeveless tee-, extolling the Red Sox of Rice and Lynn'
and then 'his last worry was that red-handed poppa could see up his
dress, what was hidden' (pp. 305–6). The decentring of a detached
and objective narrative voice is again associated with the space of the
city; but here, this shift produces not a turn to disorientation but a
moment of shared interiority, a glimpse of pathos and empathy. This
move serves to actualise the latent relationality located in the social
space of the subway in 'E Unibus Pluram': through this forced act of
witnessing on the reader's part, the passage establishes the carriage
as a metropolitan space that generates a formal attempt at forcing
into consciousness a social relationship we might prefer to ignore.

In the move from Yrstrly's challenging interruption to Poor
Tony's seizure, the novel traces a progression from the disorientating spectacle of the urban encounter to the realisation of this kind of
felt connection; a progression that is deeply rooted in the experience
of the city. If the excursions of Joelle and Gately combine to give a
sense of absence and nostalgia in the metropolis, the prospect of a
type of empathetic connection enacted through the novel's language
presents a counterpoint to this 'postmetropolitan' structure of feeling
– it is perhaps not coincidental that Wallace's later reminiscence
on Boston and its significance in *Jest* would gravitate towards the
city's subway: 'I'll go back at some point. Sure. Ride the B Line'.[26]
Empathy begins in the city: it was the combination of fear and sympathy that coloured the discourse of an urban 'underclass', with
roots in the fractious relations of class and race characteristic of the
post-Fordist metropolis, that also provided Wallace with a motivat-
ing framework for a turn to direct engagement.

From Empathy to Community: Randy Lenz, Bruce Green and the Practice of Walking

Appearing in the first half of *Jest* alongside Joelle's walk and Gately's drive, Yrstrly's monologue and Poor Tony's seizure suggest an alternative approach to the city: one focused neither on fragmentation nor nostalgia, but on the metropolis itself as the foundation for a realignment with the social world enacted in and through the novel. And in the second half of the text, the city's spaces begin to grow in prominence; a growth that accompanies the movement of more characters out into the streets, primarily on foot. This is perhaps not surprising given the importance of walking in Wallace's initial experience of Boston in 1989: in his later preface to *Signifying*, Mark Costello reflects that 'in 1989, humanity lacked the great and hungry search tools of today, Google, Yahoo, YouTube, Bing. But on mild Friday nights in dense-packed urban areas, we did possess another life-enlarging search engine. It was called walking' (*Signifying* p. viii). If recovery was Wallace's window onto Boston's social other, it was prefigured and complemented by these 'life-enlarging' excursions on foot into the metropolis. In the previous chapter I explored how Joelle's walk begins to trace a tentative and incomplete turn towards the city; and while Joelle's own association with the public space of the city is short-lived, the practice of walking that she introduces does not end with her withdrawal into Ennet House. How, then, is the peripatetic experience of the city translated into fictional form in *Jest* – and what role does walking play in extending the prospects for empathetic connection with the city's social scene?

It is in the twenty-sixth chapter that walking moves further into the centre of the frame, as we find Randy Lenz and Bruce Green 'abroad in the urban night' (*Jest* p. 539): walks that comprise only four of the sixteen sections in this chapter, but that take up far more page space (approximately 35 of 93 pages) than any of its other threads. Where Joelle's walk and Gately's drive both formed isolated excursions into the city, in this chapter movement through urban space becomes a more consistent narrative focus. Bill Lattanzi has proposed a particular connection between Wallace's own Boston walks and these sections of the novel: 'I think he walked the streets of Allston/Brighton relentlessly. I think the rambles of Lenz and Green were built on streets he'd walk.'[27] And indeed, it is as we find Lenz 'apparently strolling' (p. 539) that the topography of the city again begins to imprint itself on the text:

> He's mastered the streets' cockeyed grid around Enfield-Brighton-Allston. South Cambridge and East Newton and North Brookline and the hideous Spur. He takes side-streets home from meetings, mostly. Low-rent dumpster-strewn residential streets and Projects' driveways that become alleys, gritty passages behind stores and dumpsters and warehouses and loading docks and Empire Waste Displacement's mongo hangars, etc. (p. 539)

Here, Lenz's mastery of the city's geography is translated into the flow of the passage itself. After the first sentence establishes the organising frame of the urban 'grid', the subsequent fragment gives only a bare sequence of topographical references. But this string of place names opens out onto a longer, flowing sentence that collects descriptive details, harnessing socially significant observations ('low-rent' streets, housing Projects, 'gritty' alleyways) to the initial set of geographical nouns. The sequence of unpunctuated conjunctions in this sentence's second clause might indicate an abundance of available detail emanating from Lenz's progress through the streets – but the comma leading into the closing 'etc.' suggests a calm and controlled handling of this profusion. The vision of the city accompanying Joelle's walk had been constrained by the attribution of a gendered type of embodied and subjective experience, and the material of the city had threatened to overwhelm the form of the text in Gately's drive; but here, the city begins to emerge as a fully realised environment, directly communicable in the language of the novel.

Walking, then, becomes an expansive process that is translated into the formal progression of the passage, opening the text onto the city. And this process is evident in the composition as well as the content of the passage: for the first two sentences, a handwritten draft gives more simply 'Lenz has mastered the ~~grids~~ streets' grid around Enfield. He takes side streets, mostly' (HRC 15.6). A typescript version shows the addition of the second sentence containing the string of place names (HRC 16.6), while 'and the hideous Spur' was added between this typed draft and the published version. At each stage between handwritten and typed drafts and the published text, Wallace layered in additional topographical references; Lenz's walking through the grid of streets was the focal point for the development of a thickening map of the metropolis. If walking the streets of Boston with Costello had been a key part of Wallace's initial connection with the city, this process was reproduced in the composition of this walking-focused chapter; walking becomes the practice through which text and topography are enmeshed. Michel de Certeau says of urban pedestrians that 'their intertwined paths give

their shape to spaces' and 'weave places together', and thus 'They are
not localized; it is rather that they spatialize' – and if Joelle's walk
ultimately failed to concretely place the text in the city, Lenz's strolling begins to take on a spatialising function.[28]

This process continues as Lenz is joined by Green, and the concretisation of the city in these sections is given particular focus in two
montage sequences. In the first, a paragraph opens with a focus on
the soundscape of the metropolis:

> The night noises of the metro night: harbor-wind skirling on angled
> cement, the shush and sheen of overpass traffic, TP's laughter in interior rooms, the yowl of unresolved cat-life. Horns blatting off in the
> harbor. Receding sirens. Confused inland gulls' cries. Broken glass
> from far away. Car horns in gridlock, arguments in languages, more
> broken glass, running shoes, a woman's either laugh or scream from
> who can tell how far, coming off the grid. (*Jest* p. 556)

The opening sentence here, with its colon followed by a neatly punctuated list of details, indicates a careful cataloguing of impressions
that attends the act of walking. The attention to a sensual aspect of
the city partly recalls Joelle's embodied relationship to the streets she
walks; but the impressionistic quality of her walk is countered by
the simplicity and staccato brevity of the sentences and clauses here,
producing a much more concrete, empiricist feel. Where the embodied nature of the act of walking was a limiting factor for Joelle, this
passage returns once again to the 'grid' whose mastery is enabled by
Lenz's itinerary. It is walking – when it is associated with these male
characters, at least – that engenders the text's response to the representational problem that Boston's fragmentary post-Fordist form
presented to the novel: walking is a practice that produces the city,
first as topographical fact, then as an increasingly coherent social
and phenomenal environment.

At the same time, this walk also plays a connected and vital role
that picks up the idea of urban space as a venue for empathetic interpersonal engagement introduced in Poor Tony's seizure; one that is
most clearly visible in a handwritten draft of this montage of 'night
noises'. In this draft, the soundscape sequence leads directly, in the
following sentence, into a mention of Lenz's 'huge hydrolystic compulsion to tell Green . . . pretty much every experience or idea that
streaks across his ~~head~~ mind's horizon' (HRC 15.6). In the published
text, this line is moved to the next paragraph, where it appears as a
need 'to share with Green or any compliant ear pretty much every
experience and thought he's ever had, to give each datum of the case

of R. Lenz shape and visible breath' (*Jest* p. 557). But despite the expanded gap, the transition from the spatialising function of the montage to this narrative 'compulsion' suggests that walking, as it acts to produce a concrete sense of the city, is also closely connected to the act of storytelling; the montage of 'night noises' itself is the kernel out of which Lenz's (increasingly improbable) tales emerge. Indeed, even if Lenz's compulsion is explained by 'maybe five lines total hoovered in a totally purposive medicinal nonrecreational spirit' (p. 557), his storytelling is linked with the pair's progression through the streets: he 'breathes about every third or fourth fact, ergo about once a block' (p. 557). This association continues as Lenz's tall tales are interspersed with lines that place their telling precisely in the topography through which the pair are walking, and that form a refrain threaded through the passage: 'On the 400 block of W. Beacon . . .'; 'Under a streetlamp on Faneuil St. off W. Beacon . . .'; 'In a dumpster-lined easement between Faneuil St. and Brighton Ave., Brighton . . .' (pp. 558, 559, 561). Lenz's need to narrate may be chemical in origin, and the tales it produces may be absurd, but his compulsive narration plays out in a way that conjoins the spatialising function of his walking with the act of storytelling.

This emergence of spatially situated narrative acts out of an urban montage sequence is repeated later in the chapter, as a second sequence of urban impressions appears:

> The city of metro Boston at night. The ding and trundle of the B and C Greenie trains heading up Comm. Ave'.s hill, west. Street-drunks sitting with their backs to sooted walls, seeming to study their laps, even the mist of their breath discolored. The complex hiss of bus-brakes. The jagged shadows distending with headlights' passage. Latin music drifting through the Spur's Projects, twined around some 5/4 'shine stuff from a boombox over off Feeny Park, and in between these a haunting plasm of Hawaiian-type music that sounds at once top-volume and far far away. (*Jest* p. 577)

Again, the simplicity of the syntax, the short sentences, and the concreteness of the descriptive style combine to produce a strong impression of the city. Here, though, it is the Hawaiian music which closes the sequence of impressions that is particularly significant, as we hear that 'The zithery drifting Polynesian strains make Bruce Green's face spread in a mask of psychic pain he doesn't even feel is there' (p. 577). The text uncovers the significance of Green's reaction on the following page: even as we hear that 'The searing facts of Bruce Green's natural parents' deaths' are 'deeply repressed inside Green' (p. 578), the same sentence moves seamlessly into an extended account, beginning with his mother's heart attack upon unwrapping a novelty 'can of Polynesian Mauna Loa-brand macadamia nuts' that in fact contains 'a coiled snake with an ejaculatory spring' (pp. 578, 580). Again, the montage of urban impressions that emerges from the process of walking provides the seed from which narrative unfurls; and where Green himself is unable to vocalise his own experience, the novel's narrative voice steps in to provide the necessary storytelling act. As in Poor Tony's subway seizure, the text takes metropolitan space as a venue in which to enact a link between private trauma and public expression: the practice of walking, as it produces a concrete sense of the city, simultaneously prompts acts of narration that work to convert individual psychopathology into shared experience. If Joelle's walk was associated with a gendered sense of atomisation and isolation, for these male wanderers the process of walking is tied to the prospect of the social.

This association recurs as, alongside the rambling of Lenz and Green, the twenty-sixth chapter introduces a parallel walk taken by Mario Incandenza, the earlier recipient of Joelle's broadcast from the MIT building. We have heard earlier in the novel that, despite Mario's 'physical challenges' (*Jest* p. 313), he is something of a walker: 'the most prodigious walker-and-recorder in three districts', he 'hit the unsheltered [Enfield] area streets daily at a very slow pace, a halting constitutional' (p. 316). In the twenty-sixth chapter, Mario walks not into Enfield but, in an important moment of spatial connection, between E.T.A.'s grounds and Ennet House – two adjacent but until this point almost entirely separate spaces. As he 'totters past on the broken sidewalk', Mario observes Ennet House from the outside and hears, from an upstairs window, 'the quiet but unmistakable sound of a broadcast of "Sixty Minutes More or Less with Madame Psychosis"' (p. 591); a reprisal of this initial figure for an artistic practice that faces outward into the metropolis. Mario cannot know that Joelle herself is inside the house that he observes as he walks: poignantly, the scene leaves this to stand as a moment of unrecognised near-convergence. Still, the passage ends with a different affirmation of connectivity that is carefully situated in the cityscape. As he continues to walk back in the direction of E.T.A., Mario observes:

> in the big protruding window of Ennet's House's Headmistress's office that the window overlooks the Avenue and the train tracks and the Ngs' clean Father and Son Grocery . . . the last thing Mario can

see, before the hillside's trees close behind him and reduce the Ennet House to shattered yellow lighting, is a wide square-headed boy bent over something he's writing. (*Jest* pp. 592–3)

The Ennet House window, whose view onto the city signals the connection between the experience of recovery and the encounter with the city, reappears here; and the closing glimpse of the 'square-headed' Gately in this window marks the novel's only directly narra-tivised point of connection between him and the living Incandenzas.

Where Poor Tony's seizure established urban space as the scene for an individual moment of empathetic connection, walking is the process that entwines a larger sense of the city with the prospect of a more systematic acknowledgement of its human relationships: it is the act through which the experience of empathy develops into the possibility of community. In this respect, it is intriguing to note that – following the decades of rapid and uncoordinated development whose influence on *Jest* I explored in the previous chapter – Boston's municipal politics had recently shifted as Wallace worked on the novel. As Lawrence W. Kennedy's account explains, the election of Raymond Flynn as mayor in 1984 brought a slowing of the earlier flurry of construction and the beginning of a remedial effort in the city's municipal politics. Flynn, 'an earnest advocate for binding the city together across racial and neighbourhood lines', introduced the Interim Planning Overlay District strategy – known as 'linkage' – that required developers to pledge investment in under-developed neighbourhoods in order to be considered for sought-after down-town space.[29] The programme was prominent in the city's municipal rhetoric in 1991, as *Jest* revived in the wake of Wallace's encounter with the city: it represented, according to an official source of that year, 'a new social contract to build lasting bridges of economic opportunity between those areas of the city experiencing rapid growth and the people in Boston neighbourhoods who, historically, have not shared in the benefits of that growth'.[30]

Here there is an emphasis on the connection between the geo-graphical, architectural and social forms of the city, with building projects tied explicitly to the idea of a renewed 'social contract'; as Naomi Miller and Keith Morgan put it in 1990, 'urban values seem once again to be taking priority over strictly architectural ones'.[31] Against the turmoil of capitalist reorganisation and its fragmentary sociospatial effects, the contours of a revived metropolitan com-munity were becoming discernible. How far Wallace was aware of these municipal specifics can only be guessed, but it is a striking coincidence that one of the first neighbourhoods to be incorporated into the linkage scheme was Brighton-Allston – the narrative centre of *Jest*, and site of the Granada House facility that was home to Wallace from late 1989 to June 1990.[32] At the same time that Wallace was walking the city with Costello, and the gap between his privileged middle-class experience and 'other people' was closing, Boston was taking steps to overcome the rifts in its topography; and this 'linkage' finds an expression in his novel, as the practice of walking produces both an increasingly coherent sense of the city's topography and a series of moments of narrative connectivity.

Walking is central to *Jest*'s own project of 'linkage', reflecting the one at work in Boston itself; as the second half of the novel unfolds, the walks of Lenz, Green and Mario take up the movement into the city that the excursions of Joelle and Gately tentatively began, and the sense of absence and nostalgia that accompanied those excursions is displaced by an emerging network of present relationships. And despite the fractured tendency of the novel, this process is not confined within these discrete sections; walking sequences are also linked to one another and to other strands of the novel through a network of references that emerges as they unfold. Andrew Warren has argued that *Jest* builds a model of community in part around scattered references to the 'Storrow 500' – a Boston argot for the major thoroughfare of Storrow Drive. Warren notes that this colloquial geographical reference reappears across the novel, focalised through different characters, in a thread through which – in contrast to the stark linguistic otherness of Yrstrly's interruption – 'the reader is . . . slowly drawn into the novel's language community'.[33] Warren's argument centres on a general idea of linguistic community, but his use of the particular example of the 'Storrow 500' also points to the importance of the city itself as a point of collective reference that sits at the core of this formal approach. Indeed, this is only one of several topographical references that repeat across different sections and between different characters' perspectives: the Charles River, Commonwealth Avenue and Memorial Drive all frequently recur, often rendered in colloquial or abbreviated forms ('Chuck', 'Comm. Ave'., 'Mem. Dr'.), which imply familiarity and demand that the reader work to keep up, so that the mapping out of the city's topography and a feeling of active participation in a linguistic community are consistently intertwined.

If the city initially appears as a scene of challenging lexical alterity in Yrstrly's monologue, the construction of this network of references across the text works to draw its reader into a sense of the metropolis as a shared environment. This process is not limited to place names: as Lenz and Green walk, subtle but discernible echoes link the phenomenal impressions and experiences of the city in these sections with Joelle's earlier tentative excursion, and other segments in the novel. The sound of traffic, for example, provides a spatial detail that recurs between Joelle's walk ('cars sheening by with the special lonely sound of cars in rain') and that of Lenz and Green ('the shush and sheen of overpass traffic'; 'the big Ssshhh of a whole city's vehicular traffic') – and takes us back to Hal, waiting to be loaded onto the ambulance in Tucson in the novel's opening sequence: 'the street's passing traffic is constant and seems to go "Hush, hush, hush"' (*Jest* pp. 221, 556, 542, 16). Another echo is less directly connected to the impressions of the city, but produces a striking connection between the figures who move through its space: as Lenz walks with Green, he refers (via free indirect speech) to 'where yrstrly and Green strolled through the urban grid' – taking up the moniker associated with the initial interruption of the metropolis in the Yrstrly section, complete with its distinctive typographical styling (p. 562). The migration of this moniker suggests a shared identity that emerges through the vernacular language associated with the city, again engendered through the practice of Lenz's walking. Through these connections, the novel reflects the way in which – as de Certeau puts it – 'the figures of pedestrian rhetoric' can work to produce 'a story jerry-built out of elements taken from common sayings, an allusive and fragmentary story whose gaps mesh with the social practices it symbolizes'.[34] Despite the fractured form of *Jest*, urban impressions come to represent shared experiences expressed in a common language, constructing a tangible sense of the metropolis as a collectively lived space.

One of these echoes is especially significant: recalling James Incandenza's skill at hailing improbable taxis, Joelle recalls 'the oncoming taxi undergoing a sort of parallax as it bore down over tumbleweed streets' (*Jest* p. 225) – and later, with Lenz and Green, we hear of 'the noises parallaxing in from out over the city's winking grid, at night'. (p. 556). Wallace marked the word 'parallax' in pen on a typescript draft of Joelle's walk, suggesting that the double appearance of this unusual piece of spatial and perspectival terminology was a deliberate decision, producing another thread that draws the separate walks of these different characters together (HRC 16.4). At the same time, as Dominic Steinhilber has shown, the repeated appearance of this term also forms a reference to James Joyce's *Ulysses* (1922), a classic city novel in which the idea of parallax – the shift in the apparent position of an object when viewed from differ-ent perspectives – forms a key structural concept: as Steinhilber sum-marises, 'The fragmenting, constantly shifting perspectives of *Ulysses* can only be unified and thus made meaningful by readers aware of parallax'.[35] By deploying the term itself as a point of overlap between the perspectives of these different characters, *Jest* performs a reprisal of this structural principle: the different perspectives generated by these urban walks intersecting at a structural level to produce a sense of larger convergence.

The linking action engendered by these threads woven through the novel's geography produces an emergent sense of the city as a collec-tive environment, progressively pieced together around these charac-ters' itineraries as the text is negotiated by its reader. As such, urban walking forms not just a focal point for Wallace's composition of a portrait of Boston, but also an analogue for the kind of reading that the novel is intended to engender. Wallace remarked that he aimed for a novel in which 'some of the narrative arrangement has got to be done by the reader . . . the reader has to do the work of connecting [sections] to each other and the narrative'.[36] His critics have taken this up: for Frank Louis Cioffi, the novel casts its reader as 'a kind of performer of . . . the narrative',[37] while Joseph M. Conte places Wallace among a set of literary 'disruptors' whose texts 'should be treated as open systems that require the input of energy and infor-mation from the reader to be fully realized as works of art'.[38] Toon Staes echoes this reading when he notes that 'the many unspecified actions and textual gaps in *Infinite Jest* indicate that it is up to the reader to reorganize the seemingly unrelated narrative strands into a meaningful whole'.[39] *Jest* is a novel that requires explorative reading, a careful negotiation of its fragmented narrative and textual topog-raphy. In the previous chapter, I suggested that the fractured form of the novel reflects a sense of dissolution in the 'postmetropolitan' city; the walking sequences, in their association with narrative and convergence, provide a figure for the kind of connective readerly work that this form demands in response. Thus, walking forms both the occasion and the model for a process of negotiating *Jest*'s formal fractures that serves to 'reconnect, in imaginative ways, the reader to the text and the world', as Ira B. Nadel puts it (speaking particularly of the novel's endnotes).[40] The frequent gaps that fracture the novel's text, even as they reflect the experience of urban space produced by the economic upheavals of the late twentieth century, are there to be bridged – much like gaps between neighbourhoods and communities in the Boston of the 1980s and 1990s.

Narratologist Joseph A. Kestner has identified a 'clear nexus of novelistic structure to architectural functional form', suggesting that:

> In the novel ... the elements of word, sentence, and paragraph, of chapter and book, comprise methods by which the novel may become its functional form, the building of an edifice, whether a house or a cathedral, through which the reader may enter, pass through, and exit.[41]

But *Jest* offers a far more challenging space: less a singular edifice to be inhabited by the reader than a jarring and disorganised mass of forms between which they must find their way. The reader does not inhabit this novel as they would a house or a cathedral; they walk it as they would a city. Walking, as Lauren Elkin puts it, 'is mapping with your feet. It helps you piece a city together, connecting up neighbourhoods that might otherwise have remained discrete entities' – and in this respect, she suggests, 'it's like reading'.[42] If both *Jest* and the late twentieth-century metropolis present atomised forms, then walking and reading are parallel processes that promise to reconstitute a sense of sociospatial coherence allowing for a vision of urban community.

Rebecca Solnit has remarked that, while 'many people nowadays live in a series of interiors – home, car, gym, office, shops – disconnected from each other', walking provides an alternative form of being: 'on foot everything stays connected ... one lives in the whole world rather than in interiors built up against it'.[43] Requiring us to negotiate the gaps between narrative spaces, plotlines and text sections, the reading of the novel engenders a transcendence of the alienating architectural structures that dominate its initial sections, shifting the emphasis from the fortified enclosure of the institutional facade onto the breaks – white spaces in the text, exterior spaces in the city – which through reading and walking become sites of renewed connectivity. These twinned acts are crucial to the process David Hering describes, in which 'the form of *Infinite Jest*, which first appears fragmentary and "closed," becomes strategically unified and "open" through the very process of being read' – and this opening up of the form of the text is closely connected with the opening up of the novel's knowable community, the gradual emergence in the reader's consciousness of a system of social relationships that makes up the metropolis.[44] If Poor Tony's subway seizure signalled the prospect of translating the city's challenging social alterity into an empathetic and ethically engaged literary form, it is walking that extends this process onto a structural level as the novel progresses, opening up the connected prospects of the city as a collective space and the text as a coherent narrative structure.

The 'Inman' Chapter and the Image of the City

If the twenty-sixth chapter of *Jest* moves Green's and Lenz's walking towards the centre of the narrative frame, the subsequent chapter develops this further still, as characters drawn from different narrative strands make interspersed appearances, each moving on foot through the streets around Inman Square in Cambridge. First, Poor Tony – discharged from hospital after his seizure – finds himself 'just an eight-block stroll east on Cambridge St. and then south on Prospect, through mentholated autumn air, through Inman Square and up to Antitoi Entertainment' (*Jest* p. 690). As he walks, he begins 'debating with himself about whether to have a go at the purses of the two young and unstriking women walking just a few steps ahead' (p. 691) – who shortly turn out to be Ennet House residents 'Ruth van Cleve ... walking alongside a psychotically depressed Kate Gompert on Prospect just south of Inman Square' (p. 698). This intersection of itineraries and plotlines is framed by the window through which Matty Pemulis – Poor Tony's 'old former crewmate' (p. 691) and brother of E.T.A. student Michael Pemulis, yet more narrative connections – looks out on the square: in the 'Man o' War Grille ... [whose] front windows overlook the heavy foot traffic between Inman and Central Squares', and through which Matty notices first 'two underweight interracial girls moving across the window' (Gompert and van Cleve), then 'a few seconds behind them Poor Tony Krause ... his eyes either on or looking right through the two skinny girls plodding ahead of him' (p. 682–4). Meanwhile, the chapter also follows Randy Lenz, now expelled from Ennet House and heading 'east on Bishop Allen Dr. under Central' before taking 'the turn onto Prospect St. two or a few blocks below Central Square, moving in the direction of Inman Square' (p. 716). As each of these characters walks a closely mapped itinerary through the city, Inman Square emerges as the potential scene for a moment of convergence in the novel's otherwise fractured and multi-directional plot.

The structural importance of this spatial and narrative node in *Jest*'s twenty-seventh chapter is demonstrated by a set of typed drafts that contain not just the walking sequences from this chapter but also much of its other, seemingly unrelated content (including several Ennet House interior scenes and the developing terrorism and lethal cartridge plotline), each labelled with the heading 'Inman', and numbered (HRC 16.7). Only sections numbered three, four and five are present in the archive, so it is impossible to say exactly what and how much material Wallace was grouping under this heading. But since so many disparate scenes are included in these 'Inman' drafts, it seems likely that the entire twenty-seventh chapter was being composed and organised under the 'Inman' designation; I'll therefore refer to this chapter here as the 'Inman' chapter. What is certainly clear from these drafts is that, by this point in the novel, Boston's geography has become not just an influential context but a compositional and structural framework for the text – one around which a wide range of its characters' arcs was organised.

This is not only evident in the 'Inman' drafts themselves: this space also seems to have played a role in Wallace's development of the wider arrangement of the novel. A note appended to a draft of the much earlier (and otherwise not obviously related) E.T.A. 'big buddy' scenes (*Jest* pp. 109–21) reads 'see Inman sect[ion]' (HRC 16.3). Elsewhere, key earlier city-based sections were apparently being tied to this eventual node as Wallace worked out the novel's overall organisation: a typescript draft of Gately's drive includes the marginal note 'Ryle's Jazz Club = Inman Sq – mention' (HRC 16.6), while handwritten drafts of Poor Tony's seizure show Wallace amending Tony's intended destination on the subway from 'the Fenway Community Health Center' to 'Inman Square, for the Antitoi Brothers' (HRC 15.7). Evidently, Wallace saw both this chapter and its central location as important touchstones in the overall unfolding structure of the novel. Inman Square promises a structural fruition of the linkage developed through the novel's walking sequences: drawing together different characters and narrative strands, its role in the chapter's organisation and composition suggests the possibility of a tangible sociospatial relationality that might counter the fragmentary tendency of the late twentieth-century city.

Where Boston Common in Joelle's walk was a (gendered) space of absence and social dissolution, and the Citgo sign in Gately's drive was a nostalgic monument to a lost collectivity associated with the industrial metropolis, Inman Square signifies the possibility of a fully present space of narrative and social confluence. An organising locus for the intersecting trajectories and overlapping perspectives that are threaded through the chapter, the square comes to form the focus of what the urban theorist Kevin Lynch called the 'image of the city'. For Lynch, the traditional top-down perspective of urban planning was a distortion: instead, 'we must consider . . . the city being perceived by its inhabitants'.[45] The resulting images of the city, which provide 'the strategic link' in 'the process of way-finding', are not cartographic abstractions but the dynamic products of lived experience: 'nothing is experienced by itself, but always in relation to its surroundings, the sequences of events leading up to it, the memory of past experiences'.[46] For Lynch, movement is crucial to the formation of the city image, and he identified 'paths' as one of its key elements: 'People observe the city while moving through it, and along these paths the other environmental elements are arranged and related', a function comparable to the spatial and narrative role that walking takes on across the twenty-sixth and twenty-seventh chapters of *Jest*.[47] And the function of 'paths' is also related to Lynch's category of the 'node': 'strategic spots in a city into which an observer can enter, and which are the intensive foci to and from which he is travelling . . . typically the convergence of paths, events on the journey'– a role that Inman Square promises to fulfil as this chapter develops.[48] Crucially, the development of an image of the city also 'plays a social role' in Lynch's analysis: 'It can furnish the raw material for the symbols and collective memories of group communication.'[49] Through the collective construction of the image of the city, coming into view in the 'Inman' chapter, the metropolis emerges as a reservoir of shared experience, bringing into view the overlaps between apparently disparate fields of vision and figuring the possibility of reconstructing a collective sociospatial environment.

But if this thickening image promises to culminate in a convergence at Inman Square, the chapter in fact takes a markedly different turn: instead of a confluence of characters around a central point, we find a dispersal effected as – following separate but parallel purse-snatchings – Poor Tony and Lenz flee away from the linear and ordered streets around Inman Square and into the 'kind of second city' of the alleyways beyond (*Jest* p. 728). Hering traces this reversal, noting that while 'the actions of both Krause and Lenz broadly mirror each other in relation to prospect street . . . this mirroring appears to descend into chaos' in the alleyways as 'Wallace's fairly lucid geographical descriptions break down'.[50] Indeed, this process of spatial dissolution is evident in Wallace's revisions to the scene as he developed it: a handwritten alteration on one typed draft changes 'careered south' to 'careered up Prospect', an alteration retained in the published text (HRC 16.7; *Jest* p. 719) – a small change, but one that actively withdraws objective orientation ('south') as Lenz flees towards the alleyways, replacing it with a relative directional marker ('up'). This dispersal was enacted on a structural level, too:

the segment describing E.T.A. student James Struck's research into the history of Canadian separatism – which contains important plot details as well as providing a subtle link between E.T.A. and Ennet House via Geoffrey Day, an Ennet House resident and the author of the article Struck reads (*Jest* p. 1056 n. 304) – first appeared within the main text of the 'Inman 4' typescript draft (HRC 16.7), before being moved to form endnote 304 in the published text. This structural revision shows Wallace in the process of opening up a textual gap at the same time as he was dissipating the geographical unity that the chapter's move towards confluence had seemed to promise. Wallace may not initially have intended the chapter to end in this centripetal mode: labelling the 'Inman 4' draft, he added the note 'CONCLUSION PLEASE!!!' – suggesting that at one point he had a more convergent ending in mind (HRC 16.7). Ultimately, though, it is the denial of any climactic totality that shapes the direction the chapter takes. In turning away from a centralising 'conclusion' to the chapter, as in the elision of the crowd from Joelle's walk and Boston Common, we can see Wallace not just omitting but actively withdrawing convergence from his portrait of Boston.

The 'Inman' chapter seems, then, to return to the fragmentation and loss of civic identity characteristic of the 'postmetropolis'. In Gelfant's definition, a convergent vision of the metropolis is essential to the city novel: 'the city novelist sees urban life as an organic whole, and he expresses a coherent, organized, and total vision of the city'.[51] This argument channels the traditional preference for rational and exhaustive forms of knowledge associated with masculine geographical and epistemological dominance (and Gelfant's gendering of the city novelist is perhaps not coincidental). But Gelfant's account also describes the city novel at an earlier historical moment: that of the industrial metropolis of the nineteenth and early twentieth centuries, to which the Citgo sign is *Jest*'s nostalgic monument. The post-Fordist city that informed Wallace's novel, shaped by the transition to a decentralised economy, and from the landscape of manufacturing to a new spatial form dominated by elite education, technology and finance, necessitated a different kind of urban fiction. It is important to note that the lack of a total, cartographic view of the city in *Jest* is not simply an absence; the failure of final convergence is actively dramatised in the centrifugal dispersal of the 'Inman' chapter. This active disruption of metropolitan cartography seems entirely appropriate to a late twentieth-century city marked by transition, where physical, economic and social geographies were in the process of being deconstructed and reconstituted within the wider changes beginning in the 1970s and 1980s. I diverge, then, from Hering's argument that 'Krause and Lenz . . . move from clearly delineated spaces to more confusing geographical areas . . . through an apparent motif of personal choice – their separate decisions to commit theft'.[52] Instead, I see the confusing geography itself as a foundational influence on both the direction taken by the 'Inman' chapter and the structural composition of the novel as a whole.

Does the refusal of convergence in the Inman chapter therefore amount to a capitulation to postmetropolitan atomisation, a finally pessimistic view of the prospects of community in the city – and in the novel – at the end of the twentieth century? Gately's drive showed the (traditionally masculine) impulse towards exhaustive knowledge on the point of collapse in the post-Fordist city, and there the text fell back on a nostalgia for the sense of collectivity associated with the lost industrial metropolis. But by the time we reach the 'Inman' chapter's dissolution, the second half of the novel has given up the guiding star of the Citgo sign and its nostalgia, instead emphasising the active and unfolding processes of connectivity and linkage that are centred around the act of walking. If total comprehension is no longer possible in the late twentieth-century city, the denial of totality in the 'Inman' chapter serves to shift the emphasis back onto this open and emergent process. On the one hand, the withholding of a final, complete image of the city reflects the fragmentation of post-Fordist urban form. But on the other hand, it is this denial itself that keeps the city image in a state of emergence, a signal of the possible and necessary work of reconstituting sociospatial consciousness in the late twentieth century.

De Certeau opens his account of pedestrian practice with a critique of the instinct towards an exhaustive cartographic view of the city: describing the bird's-eye view from the top of New York's World Trade Center, he acknowledges the giddy excitement and sense of satisfaction attached to such a view, in which the city's 'agitation [is] momentarily arrested by vision'. But this satisfaction is deeply suspect for de Certeau: the viewer's 'elevation transfigures him into a voyeur. It puts him at a distance' – and to maintain this beguiling distance, 'the voyeur-god created by this fiction . . . must disentangle himself from the murky intertwining daily behaviours and make himself alien to them'. In order to counter this alienation from the lived experience of the city, he proposes a return to ground level, where 'the ordinary practitioners of the city live . . . below the thresholds at which visibility begins'.[53] The withdrawal of a final totality in *Jest* serves to keep its image of the city working below this threshold: a process rooted in the lived practice of the metropolis, not a finished object for the reader's passive consumption. Indeed, Lynch also emphasises this emergent and unfinished nature of the city image: 'not a final but an open-ended order, capable of continuous further development'.[54] The image of the city, as it is translated into *Jest*'s formal construction, becomes a fictional strategy that involves the reader in the active and ongoing reconstruction of a knowable community within the altered space of the late twentieth-century metropolis. *Jest* offers no easy compensation for the sociospatial fragmentation of the city; instead, its formal approach answers Doreen Massey's call for a recognition of space as 'the dimension which poses the question of the social'.[55]

This emphasis on a process that is engendered by, but ultimately exceeds, the content of the text accords with Wallace's later comment that *Jest* 'does resolve, but it resolves sort of outside the right-frame of the picture'.[56] Here Wallace seems to be invoking visual art or cinema as his metaphor for resolution beyond the text, but in fact his phrase explicitly recalls the restaurant window through which the near-convergence of the 'Inman' chapter is framed: as Pemulis watches, the 'two Brazilians' disappear suddenly with 'the forward man's sudden charge carrying them both past the window's right frame' – then Gompert, van Cleve and Poor Tony themselves move 'out of the window's right-hand side' (*Jest* pp. 683–4). The move beyond the framed view of the metropolis is the procedure through which Wallace moves from a given to a potential resolution; withholding convergence within the text allows the process of the city image to remain an open one, the beginning of a larger engagement with the world rather than a literary product to be consumed and set aside by its reader.

In *Signifying*, meditating on the position of the outsider in relation to the city, Wallace had remarked: 'for people not in or of it, a community's a *thing*, not a *place*. And it's certainly not an *environment* where separate species in all their differences and complexity mingle and diffract' (*Signifying* p. 39, original emphasis). The shift from map to image, from totality to process, is a strategy for effecting a shift from community as thing – a literary object for straightforward representation and consumption – to community as place and environment, the ongoing diffraction of social trajectories. It is this shift that reworks the effort to enact empathetic connection through the form of the novel, signalled in Poor Tony's seizure, into an ongoing process of engagement: it gives full form to the idea of a literary practice that could go beyond simply representing the social

context of post-transitional America and become an active intervention in this context, a producer of a renewed social consciousness.

Gender, Race and the Limits to the Image of the City

The image of the city is central to Wallace's effort to establish a literary form and practice that would constitute a remedial intervention
against the sociospatial fragmentation of the post-Fordist metropolis
– but this strategy is not without its points of tension, and I want to
end this chapter by examining the ambiguous role of both gender and
race in the novel's image of the city. In this and the previous chapter,
I have noted how *Jest*'s construction of both spatial and social senses
of the city, especially as it occurs through the practice of walking,
rests on gendered constructions of spatial knowledge that centre
male experience to the exclusion of women. This gendered epistemological structure necessarily raises questions around the position of
women in the construction of the image of the city; and, as the practice of walking is taken up by male characters in the second half of
the novel, this question takes on more explicit contours. As Lenz and
Green walk, for example, the latter recalls a joke about the industrial
working-class district of Allston that conjoins the topography of the
city with a distinctly off-colour sexual humour: 'Green takes a gasper
from behind his ear and lights it and puts a fresh one on-deck behind
the ear. Union Square, Allston: Kiss me where it smells, she said, so I
took her to Allston, unquote' (*Jest* p. 578).

This joke has in fact already been related earlier in the novel, in
an aside that recounts Mike Pemulis's Allston origins: 'an old joke
in Enfield-Brighton goes "'kiss me where it smells' she said so I took
her to Allston"' (p. 154). Here, as in other echoes that link Lenz and
Green's walk with different sections of the text, the reader's action
of joining up these dispersed instances produces a moment of narrative connectivity whose activating point of reference is, once again,
the geography of the city itself. And in the later instance, Green's
recollection reframes the joke in free indirect speech and prefaces it
with colloquial expressions ('gasper', 'on-deck'), so that this second
telling occurs in the overlap between the narrative voice and Green's
own, while 'unquote' suggests yet more voices at work somewhere
behind the text; between its two appearances, the joke shifts across
the vocal layers in this distinctively polyvocal novel. Drawing on a
shared repertoire of local Boston humour, the joke's repetition serves
to draw the district into the text's emergent urban community. But

here, the overtly misogynistic content of the joke also marks this instance of linkage as distinctively masculine, while casting the city itself as a crudely feminised point of reference around which this male community is constructed – indeed, Green's recollection of the joke echoes a starker instance of this gendering of the city in the earlier 'night noises' montage, focalised through Lenz: 'You got your faint cuntstink of the wind off the bay' (*Jest* p. 556). The text is ventriloquising rather than endorsing these voices; but even so, the effect is to introduce a thorny question around the gendered terms of participation in the construction of the city image, much as Joelle's confinement within Ennet House poses a question over the participation of women in the novel's emerging sense of urban community.

This question is raised again in the 'Inman' chapter, as the image of the city becomes central to the organisation of the text. Here, a point of connection between the trajectories of the different characters around Inman Square is provided by the appearance of the 'bag-lady-type older female' whom Matty Pemulis sees 'lift her skirts and lower herself to the pavement and move her scaggly old bowels right there in full view of passersby and diners both' (*Jest* p. 683). The results of this act then form a point of reference around which different perspectives of the street revolve: the two Brazilians 'move, each missing the dollop of bowel-movement on the walk', before van Cleve and Gompert pass by, 'neither looking at the shit everyone's stepping around' (p. 683). The moment echoes out beyond this section of text, and through a shift in focalisation, as Poor Tony 'sidestepped an impressive pile of dog-droppings' (p. 691), before recurring in Lenz's concurrent walk as he passes 'a gray-faced woman squatting back between two dumpsters, her multiple skirts hiked up' (p. 718). These grotesque and scatological apparitions of a female body serve to engender a link between these walkers; she is cast as a spectacle that allows for the convergence of their separate paths through the city. I am not convinced by Karl A. Plank's suggestion that this woman's appearance prompts a moment of empathetic reading, provoking an effort to 'understand the woman from her own point of view' that encourages the reader to 'see the woman with empathy'.[57] For me, her reduction to a spectacle conjoining the experiences of the characters around her necessarily positions her outside the text's network of empathetic connections; as such an object, she cannot also be a participant in the sphere of shared experience – the knowable community – that is constructed through the production of the image of the city. Where Joelle's walk generated a sense of the city's nodes as gendered absences – Boston Common as a 'lush hole'

(p. 222) – here the role of the female body is reversed in a no less troubling fashion, becoming itself a node that connects the paths and perceptions of these different characters.

If gender is a point of ambiguity in *Jest*'s image of the city, the issue of race also provokes some difficult questions. Reading the novel, indeed, one might well wonder what happened to the dynamic and energised African American neighbourhoods into which the subway promised to transport the white reader of *Signifying*. Marlon Bain might invite Hugh Steeply to 'take a spin through Boston's [historically Black] Roxbury and Mattapan districts' in order to witness America's 'real armed conflict' (*Jest* p. 1047 n. 269), but the invitation remains purely rhetorical; African American districts figure only on the very margins of the text's vision of Boston. The most prominent example is the 'Brighton Projects', another topographical reference that recurs at different points in the novel – but that, unlike Warren's 'Storrow 500', has a more ambiguous role in the construction of the novel's urban community. These housing projects figure consistently as an elsewhere-space, and in the 'Yrstrly' section they are explicitly racialised: framed through Yrstrly's own racism, their inhabitants are registered as 'Project Nigers' and 'animals' (pp. 129, 131). Again, this is clearly a dramatisation of the racial conflicts inherent in the city rather than an endorsement on the part of the text; but again, as with the gendering of the city image, it introduces a question about who participates in the imaging of the city, and on what terms.

This question remains unresolved as, instead of being counteracted in the novel's connective formal procedures, the othering of the Projects begins to recur in the construction of the text's city image. The occasional glimpses of this space are persistently framed in negative terms: Poor Tony 'hadn't dared show one feather . . . at the Brighton Projects . . . since last Xmas', (*Jest* p. 300) while in Gately's drive they are mentioned only briefly as a place 'where he definitely no longer goes' (p. 476). Where the formal arrangement of other topographical referents draws the novel's reader into a sense of a shared geography, the Brighton Projects indicate a flipside to this process: the construction of the city image's racialised outside, an other-space that begins to define its limits. Tellingly, with their racial otherness established through the Yrstrly section, the Projects go on to play an unsettling role in the passage that maps Enfield's topography: a mention of 'the huge and brooding Brighton Project high-rises' (among other aspects of the impoverished district) leads to a slippage out of the passage's formerly objective and omniscient tone and into a much more uncertain register: 'To I think it must be the southwest . . .' (p. 241). Colson Saylor is right to point out that *Signifying*'s attention to 'the legislative means by which space becomes racialized' does not extend into 'Wallace's conception of empathy as it pertains to a so-called "shared" experience' – but I don't fully agree that this is the result of a tendency to see 'space as a universal experience, rather than one marked by racialized difference'.[58] Rather, the ambiguous position of the Brighton Projects in relation to *Jest*'s image of the city indicates that a conception of racialised space was in fact unsettling Wallace's formal approach to the metropolis: the encounter with this racialised periphery seems to destabilise the novel's efforts to orientate itself in Boston and establish its geographical parameters.

These ambiguities are most fully embodied in a figure in whom the gendered and racialised forms of difference that trouble the novel's city image are combined: Ruth van Cleve. As she appears alongside Kate Gompert in the 'Inman' chapter, van Cleve becomes the first character of colour to be included in the skein of overlapping trajectories that produces the image of the city; but this inclusion is marked as a point of tension from its initial appearance, as Matty Pemulis first spots the two walkers and we hear that this 'interracial' pairing is 'rare and disquieting in metro Boston' (*Jest* p. 691). This sense of disquiet is redoubled as van Cleve is subject to some unflattering and discernibly racialised physical description, focalised through Gompert: her 'hair is a dry tangled cloud, with tiny little eyes and bones and projecting beak underneath' (p. 698). At the same time, she is nonetheless explicitly sexualised – 'even though underweight and dry-haired and kind of haggish, Ruth van Cleve's manner and attire and big hair broadcast that she's all about sexuality and sex' (p. 699) – even before we hear Gompert's characterisation of her as 'slutty' (p. 700): she is marked as other in both racialised and sexual terms. The geographer Katherine McKittrick has traced a long-running tendency within dominant geographical discourse to position African American women as 'ungeographic' subjects: she writes of '[t]he "not-quite" spaces of black femininity' that form 'erased, erasable, hidden, resistant geographies and women that are, due to persistent and public forms of objectification, not readily decipherable'.[59] Thus, for McKittrick, 'the dispossessed black female body is often equated with the ungeographic, and black women's spatial knowledges are rendered either inadequate or impossible'.[60] If this trope of the 'ungeographic' woman of colour runs deep in the ideological construction of American space, then van Cleve's ambivalent appearance within *Jest*'s cast of walkers raises the question of how spatial perspectives and practices that have been posited as unavailable or inadmissible to the sphere of sociospatial knowledge might be incorporated into the novel's image of the city.

In fact, as with the wandering of Lenz and Green, van Cleve's walk with Gompert also forms a point at which '[a]n oral narrative begins to emerge', and we hear, in a relatively brief paragraph, the outline of a story of her abandonment of her new-born baby (*Jest* p. 699); walking seems to draw her, too, into the network of empathetic narrative connections that emerges through walking. But – in contrast to the fluid system of intersecting voices and perspectives that accompanies movement through the city elsewhere – van Cleve's story is kept at a firm remove, parsed through Gompert's response and clearly marked as indirectly reported speech: 'apparently'; 'substances Kate Gompert can only speculate about'; 'what Ruth van Cleves describes several times as . . .' (p. 699). On the other hand, at the same time as she is denied any direct expression in the text, her apparently excessive speech is repeatedly emphasised: she is twice described as 'yammering' (pp. 698, 700), and Gompert complains that she 'talks nonstop into her right ear' (p. 699). This is a figure whose peripatetic acts of speech register as an excess and are placed beyond the vocal range of the text – a distinct and troubling contrast to the connection between walking and storytelling that accompanies the walking of Lenz and Green. As a result, in contrast to the novel's construction of empathy from Poor Tony's seizure to Green's childhood trauma, no room is left for an affective response to van Cleve's story on the reader's part, despite its evidently tragic content. This distancing is sustained through the chapter; at no point is her voice itself rendered outside of Gompert's focalisation, nor is her own point of view shown either directly or indirectly. Despite her apparent inclusion in the network of paths whose intersection produces the thickening image of the city in this chapter, she remains positioned at a point just outside the text's structure of overlapping perspectives.

This ambiguous positioning continues as the 'Inman' chapter progresses. Following Poor Tony's theft of the pair's handbags, Tony takes over as the focaliser and van Cleve becomes 'the black Creature' (*Jest* p. 720); Wallace added 'black' between the typescript draft version and the published text, deliberately working up the racialised aspect of the scene's tension. This shift between Gompert's and Poor Tony's perspectives only serves to underscore the lacuna of van Cleve's own point of view, redoubling the sense that – as both a sexually and racially othered figure – she stands outside the text's range of available perspectives. At the same time, it is telling that it is her movement through the city in pursuit of Poor Tony that actually inaugurates the chapter's turn away from the careful plotting of trajectories and towards the geographical confusion of the alleyways; an association with spatial fragmentation that is redoubled as Poor Tony flees and, although we hear that he is headed for 'a parking alley that cut west off Prospect just before Broadway' (p. 720), this orientating gesture soon gives way to geographical and perceptual dissolution under the pressure of the chase: 'The entrance to the parking alley west was between a Tax Preparer's and something else; it was right around here; . . . tiny rings with opaque centers . . . floated upward through his sight like balloons' (p. 721).

Seeming to confirm McKittrick's critique, it is van Cleve whose movement through this topography, far from contributing to the expanding image of the city, instead marks the text's turn to the 'ungeographic'. Van Cleve's name carries an obvious echo of Joelle van Dyne's; but where Joelle's walk introduced an initial interface between text and city, albeit in a way that carried gendered limitations, van Cleve's chase seems to bring the novel up against a racialised limit to the range of geographical experiences that its form is capable of assimilating: her combination of sexual and racial otherness marks a boundary to its image of the city. Indeed, the final hint of confluence in the 'Inman' chapter comes as, following Lenz, we hear of the 'tiny crash off somewhere south down the network of alleys' that 'was actually Poor Tony Krause rolling the steel wastebarrel that tripped Ruth van Cleve' (*Jest* p. 728): the prospect of convergence now 'tiny' and receding, lost in a geographically indistinct tangle of directionalities ('off somewhere south down . . .'). This final glimpse of van Cleve also constitutes one of the last direct invocations of the metropolis in the novel before the exterior space of the city disappears almost entirely, as the twenty-eighth chapter turns inward into E.T.A. and St. Elizabeth's Hospital; her movement through the city's topography coincides not only with the collapse of geographical coherence but also a decisive turn away from the metropolis itself.

Hovering on the edges of the text, these questions of race and gender seem to unsettle its representational and narrative response to the altered urban landscape of American capitalism. Mary Shapiro, in riposte to some of Wallace's stronger critics, has insisted that his writing evinces a 'belief that it should be possible for white readers to empathize along racial lines' that 'can be read as optimism and confidence in a shared sense of humanity, despite the social structures that continue to keep populations separate'.[61] But the association of van Cleve with the failure of topographical and social convergence raises a question over how women of colour figure in the continuing imaginative work that *Jest* prompts from its readers through the withdrawal of a finished sociospatial totality. The encounter with a class-bound but still white and male alterity in the Yrstrly section marked the start of an unfurling progression to empathy and community, but van Cleve is associated with a disruptive sense of otherness that runs counter to this process – an otherness that is implicitly associated with the fragmentary tendencies of the post-Fordist city against which *Jest* is intended to act. And if the novel uses the emergent image of the city to recruit its reader in the reconstruction of the late twentieth-century city's knowable community, then the combination of gendered and racialised difference that marks van Cleve's presentation in the text also comes to indicate a structural limit to the process: a social border beyond which the reader's action of imaginatively reconstituting the sociospatial environment of the metropolis, insofar as it is engendered by the formal procedures of the text itself, seems doomed to break down into fragmentation and dissolution.

Conclusion

The spaces of *Jest*'s Boston seem at first glance to be crowded out, dwarfed by the closed interiors of the institutions that dominate the novel's page space – but they turn out to be thematically, structurally and narratively crucial. If Boston confronted Wallace with a loss of community felt in the form and social fabric of the city, it was also the place that prompted him to search out formal strategies for a more directly engaged kind of fiction. The alienating postmodern facades of the novel's elite institutions are countered by the journeys of the novel's peripatetic cast of characters who weave together an unfinished image of the metropolis and, at the same time, trace the outlines of possible communities. *Jest*'s formal approach makes the metropolis itself central to its project of a newly engaged literary practice: moving from Yrstrly's interruption of social alterity to the actualised empathy of Poor Tony's seizure in the space of the subway, then to the prospect of community through the urban walking of Lenz and Green, and finally to the structural deployment of the image of the city as the basis for an ongoing reconstruction of the city's possible community, this novel deeply entwines its response to the social context of late twentieth-century America with its portrait of Boston. The structure of feeling that surrounded the metropolis, as it was shaped by the economic transition of the late twentieth century, also framed Wallace's sense of the horizon of fiction's possibilities: its capacity to intervene in a concrete social and cultural moment.

The limits to this strategy – the questions of gender and race that come to suggest boundaries to its efficacy – should be understood as political problems for Wallace's project, but as such they also form part of the close connection between his practice and the urban geography that shaped it in this period; reading *Jest* as a response to the sociospatial conditions of the post-Fordist metropolis also means understanding how Wallace's writing was bound up in the larger ideological systems that produce American spaces and their representations. These limitations, as I will show in Chapter 5, would not end with *Jest* – questions of race and gender would continue to trouble his efforts to respond constructively to the social and spatial conditions of America in his next and final novel project. But if metropolitan space had been crucial to the composition of *Jest*, by the time of its publication Wallace had already left Boston behind him, performing the move out of the big city that is undertaken by Hal at the end of the 'Inman' chapter, as he drives out of Boston and towards 'exurban Natick' (*Jest* p. 798). *The Pale King*, as my next two chapters will show, would focus on a different geography, and be animated by a different set of problems emerging from the economic restructuring of the 1970s and 1980s – problems that would again demand new directions for Wallace's practice.

Notes

1. Patrick Arden, 'David Foster Wallace Warms Up', in Burn (ed.), *Conversations*, pp. 94–100 (p. 96).
2. Jasty, 'Lost 1996 Interview'.
3. Doreen Massey, *For Space* (London: SAGE, 2005), p. 116.
4. Max, *Every Love Story*, p. 145.
5. Lattanzi, 'Messing with Maps'.
6. Max, *Every Love Story*, p. 115. Max is quoting and paraphrasing Wallace in a letter of 1988.
7. Ibid. p. 130.
8. Quoted in Max, *Every Love Story*, p. 130.
9. William T. Vollmann, *The Rainbow Stories* (New York: Penguin, 1992), p. 332.

10. Ibid. p. 344.
11. Ibid. p. 416.
12. Ibid. pp. 418–9.
13. Shapiro, *Wallace's Dialects*, p. 165.
14. Collins, *Transforming America*, p. 124.
15. Ibid. p. 118.
16. Thomas Heise, *Urban Underworlds: A Geography of Twentieth-Century American Literature and Culture* (New Brunswick, New Jersey: Rutgers University Press, 2011), p. 15.
17. Williams, *Country and the City*, p. 165.
18. Ibid. p. 155.
19. Quoted by Larry McCaffrey, 'Moth to the Flame', in Michael Hemmingson (ed.), *William T. Vollmann: A Critical Study and Seven Interviews* (Jefferson, North Carolina: McFarland, 2009), pp. 85–113 (p. 94).
20. AL, 'The Write Stuff ALT-X Interview (1994)', in Hemmingson, *William T. Vollmann*, pp. 114–23 (p. 115).
21. Larry McCaffrey, 'Expanded Interview', pp. 21–2.
22. William T. Vollmann, 'American Writing Today: A Diagnosis of the Disease', *Conjunctions*, 15 (1990), 355–8 (p. 357–8).
23. Laura Miller, 'The Salon Interview', in Burn (ed.), *Conversations*, pp. 58–65 (p. 62).
24. Max, *Every Love Story*, p. 148.
25. Gelfant, *City Novel*, p. 25.
26. Caleb Crain, 'Approaching Infinity', in Burn (ed.), *Conversations*, pp. 121–6 (p. 125).
27. Lattanzi, 'Messing with Maps'.
28. Michel de Certeau, *The Practice of Everyday Life*, trans. Steven Rendall (Berkeley: University of California Press, 1988), p. 97.
29. Kennedy, *Planning*, pp. 225 ff.
30. Quoted by Kennedy, *Planning*, p. 229.
31. Miller and Morgan, *Boston Architecture*, pp. 15–16.
32. See Kennedy, *Planning*, p. 225.
33. Warren, 'Modelling Community', pp. 69–70.
34. De Certeau, *Practice*, p. 102.
35. Dominic Steinhilber, 'Modernist Aims with Postmodern Means: Joycean Parallax and the Doppler Effect in Wallace's *Infinite Jest*', *The Journal of David Foster Wallace Studies*, 1.3 (2020), 41–78 (p. 46).
36. McCaffrey, 'Expanded Interview', p. 33.
37. Frank Louis Cioffi, '"An Anguish Become Thing": Narrative as Performance in David Foster Wallace's "Infinite Jest"', *Narrative*, 8.2 (May 2000), 161–81 (p. 168).
38. Joseph M. Conte, *Design and Debris: A Chaotics of Postmodern American Fiction* (Tuscaloosa: University of Alabama Press, 2002), p. 29.

39. Toon Staes, 'Wallace and Empathy: A Narrative Approach', in Boswell (ed.), *Long Thing*, pp. 23–42 (p. 28).
40. Ira B. Nadel, 'Consider the Footnote', in Cohen and Konstantinou (eds.), *Legacy*, pp. 218–40 (p. 226).
41. Joseph A. Kestner, *The Spatiality of the Novel* (Detroit: Wayne State University Press, 1978), pp. 11, 125.
42. Elkin, *Flâneuse*, p. 21.
43. Rebecca Solnit, *Wanderlust: A History of Walking* (London: Verso, 2002), p. 9.
44. Hering, 'Form as Strategy', p. 142.
45. Kevin Lynch, *The Image of the City* (Cambridge, Massachusetts: MIT Press, 1960), p. 3.
46. Ibid. pp. 7, 1.
47. Ibid. p. 47.
48. Ibid. p. 47.
49. Ibid. p. 4.
50. Hering, 'Triangles', p. 97.
51. Gelfant, *City Novel*, p. 6.
52. Hering, 'Triangles', p. 97.
53. De Certeau, *Practice*, pp. 91–93.
54. Lynch, *Image*, p. 6.
55. Massey, *For Space*, p. 99.
56. Michael Goldfarb, 'The Connection: David Foster Wallace', in Burn (ed.), *Conversations*, pp. 136–51 (p. 145).
57. Karl A. Plank, *The Fact of the Cage: Reading Infinite Jest* (New York: Routledge, 2021), EPUB edition accessed via British Library electronic legal deposit, paragraph 13.8, 15.45.
58. Saylor, 'Loosening the Jar', p. 129.
59. Katherine McKittrick, *Demonic Grounds: Black Women and the Cartographies of Struggle* (Minneapolis: University of Minnesota Press, 2006), p. xv.
60. Ibid. p. 121.
61. Shapiro, *Wallace's Dialects*, p. 78.

Chapter 4

What is Peoria for? (I): Postindustrial Life and the Language of Place in *The Pale King*

Introduction: *The Pale King* and the Changing Geography of Work

What is Peoria for? The question does not appear in the published text of *The Pale King*, compiled by Michael Pietsch from the mass of draft material Wallace left on his death in 2008. But it does appear, with almost obsessive frequency, in the margins of notebooks and drafts from the earliest to the last stages of Wallace's work on the project. The extensive 'Evidence' notebook, whose inside cover is dated '3/96' (a month after the publication of *Jest*), is replete with instances (HRC 43.1). Nearly ten years later, Wallace labelled a zip disk containing draft material 'WPF/PK 05' (according to Pietsch's index of materials, kept in the Harry Ransom Center archive), giving the question of (w)hat (P)eoria is (f)or equal weight alongside the eventual title of the published text (HRC 36.0). In between, numerous drafts and notebooks are headed or annotated with the question. In his extensive treatment of the archival material related to the novel, David Hering identifies a three-stage compositional history: an initial stage running from 1996 to 1999, a second phase from 1999 to 2005, and a third period from 2005 to 2007, with each bookended by a fundamental rethinking of direction.[1] But the persistence of the question of what Peoria is for suggests that this guiding concern with the function of place – in America at the turn of the twenty-first century, and in the novel itself – remained at the centre of Wallace's project throughout this troubled process.

This concern is also signalled in Wallace's conversation with David Lipsky in 1996, where it takes on an explicitly economic inflection. Showing Lipsky around Bloomington-Normal, Illinois

– where he settled in 1993 – Wallace took pains to outline features of the local economy: 'there's a Mitsubishi plant, and then there's a lot of farm-support stuff. There's a lot of firms called like Ro-tech and Anderson Seeds. And State Farm Insurance.'[2] That this material frame was important to Wallace's work on the novel is indicated by his frequent compilation of detailed lists of imagined industries and services with which to populate his version of Peoria: the 'Evidence' notebook contains several notes for invented manufacturing and extractive concerns, like 'Frigid Coal Inc.' and 'Midwest Foam' – a 'place that makes foam insulation, rubber foam' (HRC 43.1). And these ideas are supplemented by imagined service and clerical companies: one note reads 'biz in indust dist. near IRS – Automated package sorting center', while another reads 'A town built on document storage – State Farm, Prudential both have document warehouses there' (HRC 43.1). This attention to service industries is stronger in a list of 'Restaurants/stores/companies in town' in the 'Reward for Return' notebook: here the list is focused on the likes of 'Klick Delivery' and 'All Right Flowers' (HRC 41.1). Similar lists are also appended to several drafts, indicating that they were functioning as conceptual frameworks for the development of particular scenes as well as records of initial ideas. Even more than *Broom* and *Jest*, this was evidently a novel conceived from the start as thoroughly embedded in the economic geography of the late twentieth century.

These sketches show Wallace working towards a space poised between old manufacturing industries and new clerical and service concerns. I have shown in Chapters 2 and 3 how Wallace built the transition from manufacturing to finance, technology and education into his picture of Boston in *Jest*. Here, this transition is focused through a closer attention to the quotidian details of everyday American geographies; rather than the elaborately imagined architectures of *Jest*, these early *Pale King* materials indicate a stronger focus on the immediate reality and material history of late-century spaces. Hering suggests that 'in 1997 Wallace is somewhat archly asking *What is Peoria For?*', while after 2005 'his description of the Midwest has become more attuned to the economic and social problems in the region'.[3] But the close attention to the economic material of geography demonstrated in early notes suggests that a concern with the transition from manufacturing to service industries was central to Wallace's construction of *Pale King*'s geography from its earliest conception. What is at stake in this geography is suggested by his remarks to Lipsky on life in Bloomington:

Today's person spends way more time in front of screens. In fluorescent-lit rooms, in cubicles, being on one end or another of an electronic data transfer. And what is it to be human and alive and exercise your humanity in that kind of exchange? Versus fifty years ago, when the big thing was . . . havin' a house and a garden and driving ten miles to your light industrial job. And livin' and dyin' in the same town that you're in . . . I mean, there's just so much that seems *different*, and the speed with which it gets different is just . . .[4]

The nostalgia for the sociospatial arrangements of an industrial past that had coalesced around *Jest*'s Citgo sign is at work again here. What is new is the attention to work itself. Here Wallace places new kinds of workspace, and experiences of work in service and information industries, at the centre of a change in the textures of everyday spatiality: from the settled geography of work and domestic life centred on a 'light industrial job' to new and potentially dehumanising forms of activity framed by the 'fluorescent-lit rooms' of a service and information economy.

This comment links the economic landscape Wallace was constructing in his notebooks with an experiential focus on the changing nature of work, as forms and patterns of employment altered. The proportion of Americans employed in manufacturing industries declined, according to William Issell, from 42 per cent in 1940 to 33 per cent in 1980, while the rate of employment in professional and clerical sectors increased from 31 per cent to 52 per cent in the same period, marking a profound shift away from early and mid-twentieth-century structures and patterns of labour.[5] In *Pale King*, service work is also capitalised to 'Service' work; clerical occupation tied to the Inland Revenue Service (IRS) in a way that allows Wallace to link labour with the theme of civic duty, well examined in critical responses to the novel.[6] But the focus on government work is also historically apt: a rapid increase in public sector employment was a marked feature of the landscape of work in the late twentieth century, state bureaucracy taking a lead in the move from manufacturing to office-based jobs.[7]

This move was particularly stark in the Midwest – part of the old 'industrial heartland' of the United States – which, from the 1970s, had become 'the loss leader in employment, manufacturing, and population out-migration' (according to Ann R. Markusen and Virginia Carlson).[8] The return to a Midwestern setting recalls the 'regional' dimensions of *Broom*; Hering identifies a 'qualified return to the matter of region' in the late fiction, while Mark McGurl suggests (but ultimately dismisses) the idea of reading *Pale King* as 'a belated work of midwestern regionalism',[9] Jurrit Daalder is less equivocal, arguing that 'the region is an integral part of the novel' [10] And Joseph F. Goeke suggests a connection between region and work, arguing that 'regional association[s] with the Midwest and Peoria as paragons of . . . averageness' help ground Wallace's image of 'a bureaucratic . . . culture destitute of satisfactory existential meaning . . . in a particular place'.[11] Certainly there is a regional dimension to *Pale King*; twice in the published text we hear that the 1980s is 'the era of the region' in the organisational structure of the IRS (*Pale King* pp. 115, 331). But in this chapter I depart from my 'regional' keyword in Chapter 1, to follow Wallace's particular attention to the transitional spatiality of work and its impact on his imaginative geography across the *Pale King* project.

In *Jest*, the topographical alterations of Boston were connected with notions of metropolitan identity and community more than experiences of work itself. Wallace's comments to Lipsky indicate that, as he began to work in earnest on *Pale King*, these experiences were coming into sharper focus; and the representation of work is prominent in critical responses to the novel. Robert Chodat notes that *Pale King* 'shows a deep interest in the arcana of people's labor and institutional life'; James Dorson calls it 'a novel largely about bureaucracy'; Liam Connell places it among 'a body of US novels about service-sector or bureaucratic work'.[12] Luc Herman and Toon Staes wonder if the novel's historical setting might help readers reflect on 'their own situation as dutiful members of an American workforce';[13] for Alice Bennett, it forms 'a critique of the demands of the modern work environment'.[14] Richard Godden and Michael Szalay note how 'Wallace's fictional IRS workers embody the changing nature' of finance in the late twentieth century.[15] Hering explores how *Pale King* 'centralize[s] the world of white-collar office work and workers', dramatising the 'total effacement of personality by the work environment'.[16] For Severs, Wallace's late fiction interrogates 'the degradation of work under neoliberal capitalism'.[17] Nick Levey, in a sustained reading of the roles of work and class in the novel, observes that *Pale King* 'tellingly maps changes in the scene of work' in the late twentieth century.[18]

These accounts orientate *Pale King* in relation to the changing experiences of work that Wallace highlighted in his conversation with Lipsky. But that conversation, together with the notebooks' lists of imagined Peoria companies, suggest that he was specifically interested in the changing 'geography of work' identified by John Ehrman as a prominent feature of the 1980s.[19] The question of what

Peoria is for channels this attention to how a changing economic geography was producing new and unsettling spatial experiences; it indicates an intersection between the questions of what Peoria is for in economic terms and the role that geographies of work play in structuring the ordinary experience of everyday life. Where the experience of work was concerned, the geographies of the post-Fordist transition were – as Wallace had suggested to Lipsky – taking increasingly unfamiliar forms, producing structures of feeling not easily assimilated into older categories like 'regional' and 'metropolitan'. How do we situate Wallace's writing of *Pale King* in relation to these emergent spatial frameworks of industry, work and life? This is the question that links the theme of work with the question of what Peoria is for; as such, it forms the overarching question for this and the following chapter.

Place, Placelessness and 'Postindustrial Life'

This connection between a changing geography of work and the question of Peoria's purpose also links Wallace to a broader trend in American geographical thinking in the last decades of the twentieth century: a renewed attention to the 'sense of place'. This is a concern associated with the rise of humanist geography, with its project of elucidating the affective, sentimental, and existential connections between people and space: what Yi-Fu Tuan called 'topophilia'.[20] But if humanist geographers were keen to promote the value of place, their arguments – particularly by the 1990s – seemed motivated as much by a sense of loss as by a positive affirmation; a sense reflected in titles invoking the 'fate of place' (Edward S. Casey) or the 'geography of nowhere' (James Howard Kunstler), for example.[21] This growing concern for the loss of valued American places extended the notion of a decline from 'place' to 'placelessness', of which Edward Relph had complained in 1976 (in the midst of the post-Fordist upheaval): a condition in which 'it is less and less possible to have a deeply felt sense of place or to create places authentically'.[22] The rise of 'place' in the American geographical lexicon was tied to the perception of a ruptured affective link with the spaces of everyday life.

Still earlier than Relph, Alvin Toffler's 1970 diagnosis of 'future shock' included the complaint that 'we are witnessing a historic decline in the significance of place to human life'.[23] Toffler drew an explicit link with changes in the nature of work that would continue to accelerate through the last decades of the century. For him, it was 'the professional and technical populations' – the growing work-force of the service and information industries – that were 'among the most mobile of all Americans'. These transient workers 'give the society its characteristic flavor, as the denim-clad factory worker did in the past' – though surviving manufacturing-based work was also caught up in the dislocation: 'as technological change roars through the advanced economies, outmoding whole industries and creating new ones almost overnight, millions of unskilled and semi-skilled workers find themselves compelled to relocate'.[24] Toffler's account indicates the connection between economic change and the discourses of placelessness: a connection David Harvey later emphasised when he argued that 'the viability of actual places has been powerfully threatened . . . through the radical reorganization of space relations . . . within capitalist development'.[25] It is unsurprising therefore that the discourse of place began to rise to prominence in the 1970s – the decade in which the transition from Fordist to post-Fordist organisations of industry, society and space began in earnest. This discourse, then, can be understood an expression of the structure of feeling that developed around the changing geography of work in the late twentieth century; a structure of feeling that Wallace evoked when he discussed the unsettled nature of work in the 1990s with Lipsky. Toffler put this succinctly: the new mobility and its resultant placelessness 'grows . . . out of the spread of automation and the new way of life associated with super-industrial society, the way of life of the future'.[26] Toffler's 'super-industrial', though, would shortly be supplanted by the term that forms my keyword for reading *Pale King*: 'postindustrial'.

This term, at a descriptive level, denotes the transition from manufacturing to technological, information and service industries; in this sense, it has already entered the critical lexicon around *Pale King*. Tom McCarthy calls the novel 'a grand parable of postindustrial culture'; while Ralph Clare reads it as 'offering a possible solution to the apparent malaise of post-industrial life'.[27] Levey similarly places it 'in the age generally termed postindustrialism', and goes on to use the term frequently in his reading.[28] Severs, beginning with *Brief Interviews with Hideous Men*, places Wallace's late fiction 'under the sign of the "Postindustrial"'; Jasper Bernes counts Wallace 'among the most skilled chroniclers of . . . the postindustrial world'.[29] In deploying the term as a keyword, though, I want to start by considering its development from its origins in the 1970s – the earliest phase of the post-Fordist transition – to Wallace's writing of *Pale King* between 1996 and 2007. In particular, when coupled with ideas of space and place, shifts in the term's resonances indicate how American geography was understood in relation to historical change.

In 1974, Daniel Bell expanded Toffler's sense of a 'way of life of the future' in his study of *The Coming of Post-industrial Society*. Echoing Toffler's prospective focus, Bell's title framed 'post-industrial society' not as a present condition but a horizon of future development: as he suggests, 'the use of the hyphenated prefix *post-* indicates . . . that sense of living in interstitial time'.[30] Boris Frankel later noted that this futurist tone was widespread in the usage of 'postindustrial' that followed Bell's work, often entailing an 'aggressively optimistic' utopianism: the coming society would liberate the advanced capitalist world from the antagonisms and degradations of industrial labour, and herald an era of creative, humanised work.[31] Brian Jarvis critiques the geographical dimension of Bell's projection as 'a utopian vision of a radically new American landscape, bursting through the husk of its industrial spatial heritage', such that 'postindustrialism . . . manifests itself as a utopian geography'; in order to produce this utopian vision, Jarvis argues, Bell undertakes an 'erasure of the pervasive shaping influence of capital . . . upon the American landscape'.[32] By framing postindustrial society as a radical break with the industrial past, this discourse unhooked geography from history: postindustrial landscapes hover in an imagined future extrapolated from the transitional conditions of the present. But, as William Issell noted in the mid-1980s, it became 'increasingly clear that the . . . growth of professional, clerical and service positions did not imply "a generalized upgrading of work"'.[33] By the first decades of the twenty-first century, the postindustrial utopianism of Bell had morphed into a 'postindustrial blues'; a sense of malaise associated with the precarity, low pay and poor quality of much of the new service work, more recently linked with the 2016 Presidential election of Donald Trump.[34] The imagining of postindustrial futures gave way, around the turn of the millennium, to a coming to terms with the loss of an industrial past.

Wallace was undertaking the composition of *Pale King* at precisely this pivot. I have shown in Chapter 2 how the Citgo sign's monument to industrial space forms the locus for a 'postmetropolitan' nostalgia in *Jest*; Wallace turned to the *Pale King* project in a period in which this retrospective tendency was gaining still more widespread cultural currency. In 1996, as he was moving between the two projects, he remarked that 'the American experience has gotten even sadder – more lost, more afraid, more empty – as . . . our economy is shifting from a manufacturing base to an informational base'.[35] And

Wallace's use of the term 'postindustrial' itself also reflects this shift from future projection to retrospection, connecting with his own approach to fiction and its relation to history. A key earlier instance can be found in Wallace's 1991 review of J. G. Ballard's *War Fever* (1990): here he ascribed to Ballard a 'thoroughly post-industrial phi-losophy of fiction', manifested in near-future settings that enable 'the parodic expansion of some single angst-producing feature of modern social life' – much as Wallace himself had produced near-future visions in *Broom* and *Jest*.[36] But this association of the term with the practice of projecting futures had shifted by the time Wallace composed the opening micro-story in 1999's *Brief Interviews*: 'A Radically Condensed History of Postindustrial Life'. This title itself indicates a shift towards 'postindustrial' fiction as a form concerned with 'history'; a shift that parallels Wallace's initial work on *Pale King*, which is set around 1985 (Wallace's fiction projects having overlapped and cross-pollinated during the late 1990s, as critics working with archival material have established).[37]

The changing temporal association of 'postindustrial' in Wallace's own lexicon signals a move from the parodic extension of contem-porary conditions to an archaeology of their origins. The changing resonances of the 'postindustrial' keyword, then, indicate a general shift from prophecy to retrospection as modes of response to histori-cal change, occurring through the last decade of the century: a shift that forms an important context for Wallace's late historical turn. But this story's content frames this shift in rather problematic terms, especially for the notion of fiction as a means of exploring the purpose of place. This history is indeed 'radically condensed', running to just seven lines in which very little narrative is relayed: two strangers are introduced, each 'hoping to be liked', then 'each drove home alone, staring straight ahead, with the very same twist to their faces' (*Brief Interviews* p. 0). Alongside this diminished narrative – a stark con-trast to *Jest*'s elaborate complexity – another immediately striking feature is the absence of place in the piece; Stephen J. Burn notes that Wallace presents a history 'stripped of individuating local details', and Hering remarks on the story's extreme 'condensation of space'.[38] As such, the story seems markedly at odds with the close attention to geographical detail evident in the *Pale King* notebooks: figured in the absence of setting, placelessness intersects with the newly his-toricised sense of 'postindustrial life' in this piece. At the same time, the story is oddly placed on 'page 0' of the text; a gesture Severs links with 'the absence of meaningful work in postindustrial culture' forming 'a widespread zerohood',[39] but that also seems to indicate a minimisation of the text itself – an elision of literary language and narrative simultaneous with the expunging of place.

Invoking 'postindustrial' as a keyword for reading *Pale King* brings into view the connections between the geography of work, the concern with place and placelessness, and the shift towards fiction as a means of telling a history of the late twentieth-century present. If humanist geographers saw literary texts as producers of place (see Introduction), the stark absence of setting in Wallace's story of 'postindustrial life' points to a deliberate disruption of this process situated explicitly in the postindustrial moment. How, then, can fiction be understood as a practice of 'place' at the end of the twentieth century – and how does this understanding relate to Wallace's increasingly historicist project? In this and the following chapter, I will examine the development of sections of the *Pale King* project in order to approach the unfinished novel as a cross-section of writing *qua* place-making, fundamentally tied to the transitional context in which its composition took place. Hering's detailed account of the overall history of the project is invaluable here – although I will also suggest that he slightly overemphasises the moments of disjuncture in this history, using my focus on geography and place to point out compositional and thematic continuities across Wallace's work from the mid-1990s through to his last writing after 2005. Nevertheless, drawing on Hering's overall chronology, I focus in this chapter on strands from the early and middle periods of Wallace's work on the novel, before shifting focus to the post-2005 reconfiguration of the project – and the reshaping of its spatial and geographical focus – in Chapter 5. Between these two chapters, I explore how Wallace's practice was shaped in this later period of his career by a deep concern over the purpose and possibilities of place during and after the transition of the 1970s and 1980s; as I will show, the question 'what is Peoria for?' cast a long shadow over the project, leading Wallace towards searching questions about the nature and role of literary writing at the turn of the twenty-first century.

Toni Where?

The concern with place in *The Pale King* begins with the section of the published text whose composition can be traced back furthest in the archive: §8, in which Toni Ware and her mother leave their temporary New Mexico trailer park home and head for Peoria, the place of Toni's birth. Wallace started work on this material no later than May 1997, according to the date on one draft (HRC 36.3), and appears to have worked on it as a focused compositional project, a number of drafts having (according to Pietsch's index [HRC 36.0]) been kept together in a folder marked 'electric girl' (an early moniker for Toni). Wallace's developing intentions for these drafts are not entirely clear: Hering notes that the material was at one stage marked for inclusion in *Oblivion: Stories* (2004) alongside other material originally intended for the novel, and the compositional ambiguity is compounded by the fact that Wallace experimented with an explicit link between these drafts and the 'Interview' cycle that forms the core of *Brief Interviews* – in one of the 'electric girl' drafts, he includes the detail: 'title on Inside Page of Journal Girl Keeps . . .: Brief Interviews with Hideous Men', while a sketch of Toni's mother's employment history is marked 'from BRIEF INTERVIEWS WITH HIDEOUS MEN' (HRC 36.3).[40] But the notion of a character who is named after and returns to the place of their birth (as Toni is named after the fictional Peoria suburb of Anthony, Illinois) has origins in the 'Evidence' notebook, where they are conceived as a 'white gangbanger' named 'Peoria' (HRC 43.1). And, significantly, the 'electric girl' drafts are repeatedly labelled 'what is Peoria for?' – linking them both to a larger Peoria-focused project and to the overarching question of place that would continue to link strands of composition until the last stages of *Pale King*. Even if it formed part of an open compositional continuum for much of its development, §8 nonetheless represents some of Wallace's earliest sustained work on the project that became *Pale King*, and the first work that was framed by the question of Peoria's purpose.

If 'Radically Condensed History' gestures to a new concern with the historicisation of postindustrial experience, these 'electric girl' drafts show this concern in fuller development. A number of drafts indicate that Wallace intended to date the different parts of the section, with the departure and journey from New Mexico to Peoria as the 'main body' (the narrative present in this section); the short opening section (*Pale King* pp. 55–6) – which Wallace published separately as 'Peoria (9) "Whispering Pines"' in *TriQuarterly* in 2002[41] – placed in the past and evoking Toni's early childhood; and another section featuring Toni and her friends (not included in the published text) marked as 'future, in Peoria' (HRC 36.3). Wallace seems to have had trouble settling on dates for the sections: on one draft, the opening segment is dated to 1949, while on another (probably later, since it is considerably longer), it takes place in 1986, with the main narrative in 1990 and the 'future' section in 1991 (HRC

36.3). Clearly, Wallace was concerned to place this section historically, but the variation in the dates he was trying out indicates that
he was thinking in terms of a historical range rather than a precise
point in time: specifically, the range between a postwar moment
and the final decade of the century, encompassing the transition of
the 1970s and 1980s as its central point. What is consistent in these
drafts is the structural arrangement of the chronologically differentiated segments: in both handwritten and typed versions, the section
begins with the past 'Whispering Pines' segment, then continues with
the 'future' passage, before moving chronologically backwards into
the 'main body' of the narrative. As he framed his drafts within the
historical span between the middle and end of the century, then, he
also began with a chronological disjuncture that seems appropriate
to this transitional period. Within this scheme, Peoria itself stands
as a marker of both past and future, with the journey that forms
the main narrative forming the present that bridges the two; the
structure of this narrative, it seems, was being developed around the
same sense of Peoria on the cusp between an industrial past and a
still emerging postindustrial present that was being worked through
in the notebooks.

Within this historical framework, ambivalent relationships to
place form a guiding theme in the section. This ambivalence reaches
back beyond the immediate chronological frame, signalled in Toni's
mother's account of her own 'hell on earth ... Peoria girlhood'
during which 'the mother's mother had refused to let her outside
the house over which she had engaged itinerant men to nail found
and abandoned hubcaps', apparently 'in order to deflect the trans-
missions of one Jack Benny, a rich man whom the grandmother
had come to believe ... sought *global thought control*' (*Pale King*
p. 59, original italics). This image of neurotically dysfunctional
domestic space carries an echo of Avril Incandenza's agoraphobia
in *Jest*: again, a gendered conception of spatial pathology is incorporated into Wallace's vision, forming the means through which
degraded relationships with wider social landscapes are expressed.
Here, though – even though its historical placement is vague – this
image is also embellished with details that have clear resonance in
a postindustrial context. The mention of 'itinerant men' suggests
the uprootedness that Toffler had associated with changing patterns
of work, but most striking is the use of discarded hubcaps to effect
the house's fortification – detritus of the Midwestern automobile
industry whose collapse in the latter decades of the century 'symbol-
ized the industrial decline of the United States', according to Haynes

Johnson.[42] One draft, in fact, links the condition of these men more explicitly with the hubcaps themselves: 'found and abandoned hubcaps – found and abandoned men' (HRC 37.1). Deliberately cut off from the Midwestern landscape by the ruins of its industrial heritage, the hubcap house stands as a pointed image of a specifically postindustrial alienation from place. Moreover, rough notes suggest that Wallace considered making the house and its warped relationship with space into Toni's literal inheritance and the motivation for these characters' journey to Peoria: one draft is appended with the note 'G'mother has died? Mother returning home for will/claim house' (HRC 36.3). Intergenerational history combined with signs of industrial decline and a lineage of spatial neurosis form the legacy that brings Toni back to Peoria.

But the hubcap house's paranoid fortification is not simply reducible to alienation; as well as a turn away from exterior geography, it also implies an entrenched and intensified form of habitation, and this ambivalence reappears in a number of ways across the section. It is apparent, for example, in the naming of Toni herself after the fictional Peoria suburb of 'Anthony, Illinois' (*Pale King* p. 59, c.f. p. 62); the co-naming of character and place indicates an entwining of the two, along the lines of the conjunction of people and setting prized by humanist geographers. This is re-echoed when (in one draft version) we hear 'she had herself been born there, Peoria, inc. 1814 – she knew the facts of her history' (HRC 36.3); the material history of place blending with the details of personal experience. But this co-naming also carries opposite gestures: Saint Anthony is traditionally associated with lost objects and people, so Toni's name also carries a shadow of displacement that complicates the surface-level connection with place. And while her first name is also a place name, her surname seems to contain a questioning of location – Ware/where? – that undercuts this identification of character with setting.[43] Through her naming, Toni becomes a focus for the ambiguities of postindustrial place. It is little wonder, then, that in one draft Wallace attributed his key question to her: 'when the mother returned to her she knew it was the moment in which to have their talk about the truck and man and whether the map had been true and why Peoria, [what was Peoria for]' (HRC 36.3, square brackets original).

This ambivalent dynamic of place recurs in other forms through the section. It is present, for example, in the road atlas that 'appeared and lay athwart the counter's medial crack opened to the mother's home state' (*Pale King* p. 57), forming one of the 'auguries and signs' of imminent departure (p. 56). In itself, a road map is a doubled object: as a cartographic text, it reduces space to a static and legible form – but it also functions as an aid to mobility, and thus carries an association with itinerance. In the published text, moreover, we hear that the map's 'representation of [Toni's] place of origin' is marked with 'a spore of dried mucus spindled through with a red thread of blood' (p. 57); a gesture that suggests a violent despoliation of place with bodily effluvia, but in doing so also indicates a visceral form of connection to this cartographic representation of Peoria. The double nature of the gesture is clearer in the draft origins of the sentence: one version has Peoria marked with 'an arrowshot valentine heart of mascara', the clichéd symbol of affection highlighting a sentimental attachment to place, while another version replaces the valentine's heart with 'chocolate prints' – space overlaid by the unique identifying markers of the embodied self (HRC 36.3). Abjection and sentimentality are twinned in Wallace's careful composition of this detail, a combination he worked through in different ways as the section took shape.

Wallace's writing of this section, then, stands in a complex relation to the sense of place privileged by the humanist geographers: while maintaining a thematic concern with existential links between character and place, he was also experimenting with ways of unpicking these connections. To see this process in action, we can compare versions of one sentence from §8. In the published text, this sentence appears as:

> Sometimes at night the sounds of fire carried, or the circling planes, or those of long-haul trucks on 54 for Santa Fe whose tires' plaint had the quality of distant surf's lalation; she lay listening on the pallet and imagined not the sea or the moving trucks but whatever she right then chose. (*Pale King* pp. 61–2)

An annotated typescript draft shows a version of the sentence under construction:

> Sometimes at night the sounds of the fire carried ~~or~~ ^and^ the circling planes, ~~or~~ ^and^ those of longhaul trucks on 54 for Santa Fe whose tires' plaint from a distance had the soothing quality of surf, lalation;[dash instead???] she lay ~~listening~~ ^alert^ on the ~~pallet~~ ^mattress^ and imagined not the road or trucks themselves but the abstract movement [the way to move without loss yet again being <u>simply</u> ^merely^ to wish to (HRC 36.3, square brackets original)

The invocation of the 'long-haul' trucks suggests the itinerance towards which Toni and her mother tend and foreshadows the journey by road to Peoria upon which they are about to depart, while the questioning note about punctuation ('dash instead???') indicates Wallace's effort to incorporate the 'lalation' of the trucks' rhythm, and the mobility it suggests, into the form of the sentence itself. The question this raises is whether the organisation of the sentence around the trucks' sound suggests the action of a strong organising consciousness, actively arranging the sounds into a coherent rhythm, or the conditioning of this consciousness by the transience signalled in the highway's soundscape. Here, the revision of 'or' to 'and' is important: replacing the juxtaposition of differentiated sounds with an integrative gesture, the published version of the sentence moves towards a depiction of Toni assembling the sonic fragments of the landscape into a managed whole.

Still more striking is the change to the latter part of the sentence between the two versions. The draft's invocation of 'the way to move without loss' signals a sadness inherent in the transience evoked by the trucks; its suggestion that the method of averting this loss is 'merely to wish to' (together with the revision of 'listening' to the more active 'alert') indicating the strength of Toni's self-possession against her itinerant condition. But the confusing syntax of the sentence's final clause in the draft version undercuts this invocation of autonomous, emplaced selfhood: loose and vague, it performs a breaking down of meaning and expression that is bound up with the mimicking of the truck's sound (and perhaps suggestive of a drift into sleep, the dissolution of consciousness). In the published version, where the mention of 'loss' is removed, the sentence's end is very different; Toni's ability to choose the subject of her own imagining is embedded in the clarity and strength of the much shorter final clause, which ties up the sentence in an unambiguous closing affirmation of the agency of consciousness, reinforced by the emphatic closing string of monosyllables: 'she right then chose'. The drafting of this sentence illustrates Wallace's use of the process of the text to work through the complex relationships between character and setting, psychological experience and postindustrial place.

This guiding concern with place and its expression is embedded in the opening part of the section (the 'Whispering Pines' passage), which Wallace appears to have first composed as a stand-alone description, since it appears by itself on what seems to be the earliest handwritten draft (dated '5/16/97') (HRC 36.3). In this early version, as Wallace added the 'Whispering Pines' name in a marginal note, he also tried out several versions of the 'defaced name' that appears on the trailer park's sign (*Pale King* p. 55) – 'WHIP RIPE', 'WING PIN', 'RINGS', 'SPEN' (HRC 36.3) – experimenting with the literal degradation of the language of place. This process is embedded in the form of the passage as it appears in the published version, beginning with a sentence that runs for twenty-five lines and deftly combines close attention to the phenomenal details of place – the 'dense copse as yet uncleared for new single-wides', the 'two bottles and bright plastic packet impaled on the mulberry twig', the 'needles and stems of a long winter' – with an embodied and mobile perspective (*Pale King* pp. 55–6). But while these details and the embodied, immediate framing of the description work towards the construction of a concrete sense of the space, this process is complicated somewhat through the formal construction of the sentence; in particular, through the repeated 'and' conjunctions around which – in the almost total absence of punctuation – it is organised:

> Under the sign erected every May above the outer highway reading IT'S SPRING, THINK FARM SAFETY and through the north ingress with its own defaced name and signs addressed to soliciting and speed and universal glyph for children at play and down the blacktop's gauntlet of double-wide showpieces past the rottweiler humping at nothing in crazed spasms at chain's end and the sound of frying through the kitchenette window of the trailer at the hairpin right and then hard left along the length of a speed bump into the dense copse as yet uncleared for single-wides and the sound of dry things snapping . . . (*Pale King* p. 55)

As these conjunctions link the sentence's multiplying clauses, they often abruptly change its sense: the first 'and' indicates motion – 'and through the north ingress'– and helps place the scene, but this is followed by a string of conjunctions that articulate a list of road signs and their subjects (p. 55). This in turn is followed by yet another 'and', this time returning to movement: 'and down the blacktop's gauntlet' (p. 55). But another of these movements ('and then hard left . . .' [p. 55]) is followed by a conjunction effecting a shift to description: 'and the sound of dry things snapping' (p. 55). At each of these conjunctions – switching between movements in space, lists and descriptive clauses – the unfolding sentence turns unpredictably, much like the turns in the road being followed ('hairpin right . . . hard left'). The result is that the language itself feels unsettled, its sense as mobile and transient as Toni and her mother themselves – in a revealing slip of the pen, Wallace initially wrote 'hairpin write' for 'hairpin right' on a handwritten draft (HRC 36.3). In this sense, the sentence's form prefigures the geographical precarity experienced by Toni and her mother, who follow 'routes on maps that yield no sensible shape or figure when traced' (*Pale King* p. 56) – Wallace's sentence, similarly, evades the formation of a sensible shape as it is traced across the page.

This interrogation of the language of place is redoubled when the sentence goes on to describe the experience of 'seeing through the shifting parallax of saplings' branches sections then of trailers . . .' (*Pale King* p. 55). This clause draws attention to the act of seeing – and in one draft Wallace rendered this as 'espying then through parallax of thin limbs all sections then of trailers' (HRC 36.3), with 'espying' suggesting a furtiveness to the act and the doubling of 'then' giving a restless feel, suggesting that sight here is limited to a stolen glimpse. This attention to visuality is also underscored by the appearance of the word 'parallax'. In Chapter 3, I noted that the repeated appearances of this term in *Jest* provide a point of overlap between the paths and perspectives of different characters in the space of the metropolis, while also invoking a Joycean sense of coherence emerging from the shifts between differentiated points of view – and Wallace reminded himself of the definition of the term ('apparent change in the direction of an object caused by change in the observer's position & new line of sight') at the end of one of the 'electric girl' drafts (HRC 37.1). But here there is no multiplicity of perspectives for the reader to combine into a larger, collective perception of space; where the term had pointed towards the collective construction of the image of the city in *Jest*, here the emphasis is on a shifting and unstable relationship between sightlines and spaces, perspective and place – suggestive of a newly problematised relation between the text and the postindustrial geography it attempts to describe. This effect is redoubled by the opaque technicality of the word itself, which is also joined by the equally obscure 'stridulation' and 'anfractuous' as the sentence progresses. Recalling the dense language that frames A. Y. Rickey's architecture in *Jest*, these slippages into obscure registers underscore an important paradox at work in this descriptive passage: a surfeit of language, like the branches Wallace evokes, works to obscure rather than to elucidate the landscape.

As with the other signifiers of relationships to place in §8, though, this problematisation is not a one-directional process. The earliest handwritten 'Whispering Pines' draft mentions 'the stridulation of insects in the duff of the copse', a line revised slightly to give 'stridulation of *bugs*' in a subsequent handwritten version, as in the published text (HRC 36.3; *Pale King* p. 55, my emphasis). As well as countering the obscure 'stridulation' with the familiar vernacular note of 'bugs', this small revision shows Wallace embedding a fragment of strong internal rhythm that was less evident in the initial version – 'stridu*lat*ion of *bugs* in the *duff* of the *copse*' – within the larger diffuse sprawl of the sentence. This formal technique points to a tension between upheaval and settlement that is more obviously reflected in the subsequent description of the car in which unknown adults have sex, watched by assembled children: 'the shimmying motions resemble those of a car travelling at high speeds along a bad road, making the Buick's static aspect dreamy and freighted with something like romance or death' (*Pale King* p. 56). 'Freighted' here suggests weighing down in place, but also the movement of goods as 'freight', a fore-echo of the long-haul trucks that appear later in the section. Once again, both rootedness and mobility are in play as the section develops.

The composition of the 'Whispering Pines' passage, then, was marked by a complex tension between place-setting and displacement; a dense description whose language and syntax oscillate between evocation and obfuscation of space. Writing, here, seems to be a practice that disrupts and occludes place even as it seeks to invoke it; place and placelessness had become a duality embedded in the form of the developing text itself. This formal approach certainly seems appropriate to the semi-nomadic nature of the trailer park settings that dominate this section of the text: though the trailer park provides a home and locus for 'those who are poor in one place', this is a diffuse and centrifugal centre – as suggested by 'the trailers, [road] sign, and passing trucks', all associated with mobility, that form 'the furniture of their world' (*Pale King* p. 61). That Wallace associated this semi-itinerant setting with postindustrial conditions of work is indicated by a sketch in the 'Evidence' notebook, in which the social landscape of the trailer park is explicitly tied with a scene of labour poised between manufacturing remnants and service sectors:

> Jobs in Whispering Pines Mobile Home Park:
>
> Working state mental hospital, grain elevator, Solo Cup (cup design – P. Schaefer), drive wrecker for auto repair place, own video store, managing McDonald's (Pat J.), making tires (Steve K), domestic abuse cop (Doug P), Hector /AK apprentice (Bob A.), as Bond Enforcement Agent . . . medical transcriptionist (HRC 43.1)

The trailer park setting is doubly poised: between stasis and transience, and between manufacturing and service. In this respect, it is instructive to consider Wallace's writing of the tension between place and placelessness in relation to the social scene that framed this early phase of *Pale King*'s composition. Wallace, having moved to Bloomington in 1993 to complete *Jest* and teach at Illinois State University, found himself in a period of professional and geographical stability, as D. T. Max's biography relates; for the first time, he bought a house during this period – and wrote to Don DeLillo about his worry that he might become obsessed with his lawn.[44] As he remarked to Lipsky, Bloomington inspired in Wallace the 'weird warm full excitement of coming home'; a new-found rootedness and domesticity that must have been redoubled by the stability of his employment and the success of *Jest*.[45]

If this new sociospatial rootedness was part of the backdrop to this early phase of *Pale King*'s composition, then Wallace's working through of ambivalent relationships between character and place formed an experiment in writing against this settlement, undoing the grounding that he himself experienced. This experiment was perhaps linked to another aspect of the context of Wallace's writing at this point: his house was, according to Max, located near to 'trailer parks and a slaughterhouse', his new domesticity also placing him adjacent to the unfixed landscapes of work and life he described in the 'electric girl' drafts. Particular locations for this interaction between Wallace's professional rootedness and the conditions of postindustrial labour were, it seems, the chain restaurants on Bloomington's outskirts: the copyright page of *Brief Interviews* includes an acknowledgement of the 'generous and broad-minded support' of 'The Staff and Management of Denny's 24-Hour Family Restaurant, Bloomington, IL' (*Brief Interviews*, copyright page). The role of this interaction with postindustrial service labour in framing Wallace's early work on *Pale King* recalls the importance of the encounter with Boston's social alterity in *Jest*'s revived composition: a point of contact with a milieu outside his own sphere of privilege, through which the social effects of economic change entered into his compositional process. Wallace's own stability in work and place intersected with an awareness of different conditions of labour and life around him; an awareness that found expression in the process of constructing and deconstructing place in the 'electric girl' drafts. It is significant that Toni's name carries a clear echo of *Jest*'s Poor Tony – the figure of urban itinerance who had earlier provided a test case for the possibilities of empathetic social engagement in Wallace's fiction. In the nascent *Pale King*, too, the problem was one of aligning the possibilities of literary practice with the material consequences of economic change.

This problem finds its most explicit expression in §8 in a passage which lists Toni's mother's previous jobs, reminiscent of the list of trailer park jobs from the 'Evidence' notebook:

Mother's Stated Occupations, 1966–1972 (from IRS Form 669-D [Certificate of Subordination of Federal Tax Lien, District 063(a)], 1972): Cafeteria Dish and Food Area Cleaning Assistant, Rayburn-Thrapp Agronomics, Anthony IL; Skilled Operator of Silkscreen Press Until Injury to Wrist, All City Uniform Company, Alton IL; Cashier, Convenient Food Mart Corporation, Norman OK and Jacinto City TX . . . Hostess and Beverage Server, Double Deuce Live Stage Night Club, Lordsburg NM . . . Ticket Agent and Substitute Night Manager, Riske's Live XX Adult Entertainment, Las Cruces NM. (*Pale King* pp. 62–3)

Thematically, this segment reinforces the link between geographical precarity (indicated by the wide range of locations) and the transition from 'skilled' manufacturing labour, through the kind of service work Wallace witnessed in Bloomington's diners, to increasingly marginal forms of employment – and it is significant that the published version settles on a chronological placement in 1972, on the cusp of the post-Fordist transition. At the same time, the forms of employment registered here also point to a specifically female experience of service work and its precarity in postindustrial America; a reflection of the fact that 'women's labour and the conditions under which they enter the labour market as bearers of specifically "feminine" attributes is a central element of current restructuring', as Linda McDowell argued in 1991 – resulting in a 'new gender order of post-Fordism'[46] And, though it is important to avoid an automatic equation of sex work with victimhood, there is a clear intersection between precarious postindustrial labour and systematic sexualisation here; an association redoubled when, on the road, the mother's boyfriend uses 'an unsensual claw' to 'squeeze [Toni's] personal titty [. . .] with what seemed an absent dispassion' (*Pale King* p. 65). If the hubcap house conjoins industrial decline with an image of domestic neurosis, these moments suggest an engagement with the specifically gendered forms of precarity associated with the postindustrial economy.

In formal terms, though, the presentation of the mother's list of jobs presents a stark contrast with the ornate style that prevails in the 'electric girl' drafts, stripping its geographical references of all description or human detail and conveying nothing of the 'sense of place' that humanist geographers hoped to find in the novel. The experiential dimension of this personal geography has been effaced; this is geography drastically reduced to a function of the conditions of postindustrial work. It is noticeable that the form of the list – the initial heading followed by a colon and then an unembellished series of jobs – is very similar to the rough note in the 'Evidence' notebook: there seems to be relatively little compositional process involved in the move from sketch to drafted passage, the blunt facticity of this geography of work seeming to allow for minimal literary embellishment. This formal choice, then, seems to indicate an uncertainty about how the language and the process of the novel sit in relation to this material, class-inflected and gendered postindustrial geography.

Indeed, Wallace made this uncertainty explicit in a note he typed to himself, in block capitals, on one of the 'electric girl' drafts: 'THE TRICK WITH THIS THING WILL BE TO HAVE ENOUGH PLOT AND VIVID CONCRETENESS SO THE WHOLE THING DOESN'T JUST SEEM LIKE ALL LANGUAGE, SOME MCCARTHY EXERCISE' (HRC 36.3). That Wallace modelled the style that predominates in §8 partly on Cormac McCarthy's prose is clear from the 'Evidence' notebook, in which a number of descriptive sketches and fragments are labelled with that author's name (HRC 43.1); Chodat describes the section as an 'odd pastiche of Cormac McCarthy'.[47] But Wallace's note also signals an underlying concern with the efficacy of language in relation to the 'concreteness' of his historical and social subject matter, and with the work of writing itself – he wrote: 'THIS IS WHAT YOU DO, THIS IS YOUR JOB' (HRC 36.3). What work could the literary writing of place do among the postindustrial landscapes of the late twentieth century? Does any such project risk leaving the social world of postindustrial America behind, and sliding into 'all language'? The question also relates to the near-total silence of both Toni and her mother in §8; despite the verbosity of the section's prevailing style, only one line of direct speech is attributed to either character in the course of the section (*Pale King* p. 65). Though Toni acts as the focaliser for most of the section, the deployment of an elaborate, high-literary style seems calculated to sharply distinguish the narrative voice from hers even as she is positioned as the text's centre of consciousness. Wallace was deliberately opening up a gap between the literary language of the novel and the lived experience of these postindustrial working-class women; a gap that in turn raises the question of what kind of expression the novel form can give to the sociospatial landscape of postindustrial America.

In this earliest phase of Wallace's work on *Pale King*, then, a concern with the possibilities of place and its construction in the language of the novel was emerging as a central problem for the nascent project – a concern that was deeply connected with the relationship between literary composition and the postindustrial conditions of work and life that Wallace had seen in Bloomington. The development of the 'electric girl' drafts indicates that Wallace's sense of writing poised between 'vivid concreteness' and 'all language' can be read as generative as much as reflexive: his understanding of fiction as a practice of place now involved a difficult mediation between the material conditions of postindustrial life on the one hand, and the invocation of place through the descriptive capacities of the novel on the other. Postindustrial geographies of work were prompting not just a surface-level thematic concern but also a deep formal and compositional problem, implying searching new questions about the position of literary practice in relation to the landscapes of everyday life at the end of the twentieth century.

Lyric Opening: The Composition of §1

The problematic relationship between landscape description and postindustrial economy that shaped Wallace's work on the 'electric girl' drafts was also embedded in the short descriptive section that Pietsch selected as the opening to the published text, following Wallace's own draft annotation which suggests that this section was intended to form a 'lyric opening' (HRC 39.3). That this planned opening was related to the 'electric girl' drafts is indicated by its continuous placement with the 'Whispering Pines' description in one draft (HRC 40.3), and its publication alongside that section in *TriQuarterly* in 2002.[48] And, despite the changes in direction that the project would undertake, Wallace continued to entertain the idea of using these two sections for the introductory part of the novel: a note in one notebook suggests that there would be '3 intros': the 'read these intro' (§1) and the 'trailer park intro' ('Whispering Pines'), interspersed with a section labelled 'W105', which is an abandoned fragment narrated by a Regional Examination Center (REC) cart boy (HRC 41.4; see Pietsch's index, HRC 36.0). These ideas are contradicted by other structural notes elsewhere (e.g. HRC 39.5), reflecting the fluid nature of Wallace's composition; but these continued attempts to combine §1 with the 'Whispering Pines' passage clearly indicate their close affiliation, and their persistent role in Wallace's work on the project.

Section 1 is particularly notable for its flirtation with a mode markedly at odds with Wallace's more typical stylistic approach:

> Past the flannel plains and blacktop graphs and skylines of canted rust, and past the tobacco-brown river overhung with weeping trees and coins of sunlight through them on the water downriver, to the place beyond the windbreak, where untilled fields shimmer shrilly in the A.M. heat . . . Ale-colored sunshine and pale sky and whorls of cirrus so high they cast no shadow . . . Very old land. (*Pale King* p. 5)

The language here partly recalls that of the 'Whispering Pines' description, particularly in its combination of description and movement. But where 'Whispering Pines' also incorporates syntactic and lexical obscurity, here a much more distinct lyrical feel is imparted by the steady rhythm, the sentences that group lightly punctuated but manageable strings of clauses into mild crescendos, and the elements of rhyme and alliteration ('weeping trees', 'shimmer shrilly'). This 'very old land' seems, viewed this closely, to be a genuine grounding for affective engagement, and the two direct injunctions to the reader that appear in the section – 'look around you', 'read these' (pp. 5, 6) – seem to encourage such a reading; Brian McHale suggests that this section 'literally draws us into the landscape', while McGurl sees it as a 'strategic reembrace of rooted provinciality'.[49] Indeed, this section's unexpected lyricism and its contrast to the rest of the published material has drawn comment from a number of critics: Dorson points out that 'besides the first chapter, nature does not figure as a site of pastoral escape', while Levey notes that this 'invocation of a pastoral sublime' is absent from the rest of the novel, which 'seems more interested in the offices than the field'.[50] If *Broom* had critiqued Midwestern pastoralism as a commodified form of nostalgia offering a false promise of escape from the reality of globalised post-Fordist capitalism, this scene seems to promise a more genuine recuperation of a pastoral mode.

For a clearer view of what Wallace was doing in this section, and how it relates to the problematic intersection of language and place in §8, I want to examine its development across the composition process. In fact, this is a section that allows for a clearer view of Wallace's use of the 'Evidence' notebook in this early period of work on the novel, since a number of the individual details that make up the section were initially sketched there: 'the April night is a hand on your cheek', 'ale-colored' sunlight, the horizon 'trembling and shapeless', and the key image of 'crows turning up cowpatties to get the worms underneath' all appear both in §1 and as isolated fragments in the notebook (HRC 43.1). Max gives some indication of the role of notebooks in Wallace's practice: in his account, they allowed Wallace to 'write . . . anywhere – in the smoking room of the library, on a bench, in a cafe'.[51] The notebooks, then, are records of Wallace's composition in situ – traces of his writing as it literally took place, recording snatches of detail directly from the spatial environments around him. One earlier example connects this with a longer-running interest in places of work: According to Max, Wallace drafted the story 'Luckily the Accounts Representative Knew CPR' during a visit to Mark Costello's workplace, 'in an empty conference room . . . in a notebook', crafting his fiction directly within the spaces that inspired it.[52] Accordingly, we can see the 'Evidence' notebook as a record of Wallace's initial compositional encounters with the geographies he inhabited in the mid- and late 1990s – a literary spatial assemblage in process. The textual form of the notebook itself attests to this: a combination of notes written directly into the book and fragments on notepaper, evidently made separately and then taped onto its pages, the book appears to have functioned as a repository of impressions recorded in various locations, their collection and arrangement here forming a first stage in Wallace's compositional process. At the same time, as Daalder has established, these notebooks also record 'a collection of landscape descriptions that Wallace often lifted straight from the work of his Midwestern contemporaries, notably Michael Martone and William H. Gass' – adding an intertextual component to this assemblage of space.[53] That these were systematic elements of his composition, consciously tied with later drafting stages, is illustrated by the fact that one draft is appended with a specific reference to 'FBI-tape notebook [i.e. the 'Evidence' notebook] p. 101' (HRC 36.3).

It is §1, though, that provides the most extensive picture of this process: Wallace drawing together notes that had been sketched in isolation in the notebooks, fragments of the geography that framed his writing, and stitching them together to produce a developed passage of place description. This section, then, appears to have emerged particularly closely from Wallace's immediate experience of the Midwestern landscapes that formed the backdrop to his work on the novel, its pastoral lyricism an expression of his experiential engagement with place. Indeed, the notebook is replete with further examples of this kind of lyrical place-writing: 'loveliness of sunset on high ground. Shadows reach & reticulate & pool in valley below, while above everything is suffused with rose-colored light'; 'moon-blanched fields'; 'the beaten-gold light of late afternoon in mid summer', among numerous others (HRC 43.1). But at the same time, the notebook also contains a number of notes which indicate experiments in the merging of natural registers with distinctive aspects of late twentieth-century work and life, and their associated spatial experiences: 'bright moon – like a halogen light'; 'spring trees the color of a traffic light'; 'a severe-weather screensaver' (HRC 43.1). These notes were beginning to test the points of contact between the language of place and the experiences of postindustrial life – the same problematic intersection that had shaped the 'electric girl' drafts.

And, in what appears to be the earliest handwritten draft of §1, the process of working out this blending of pastoral and postindustrial is clearly in evidence. The more natural aspects of the scene form the basis of the draft, composed in pencil, with elements that signify contemporary forms of inhabitation of this geography worked through in superscript ink additions: 'blacktop graphs and skyline of rust', 'barbed wire and canted posts', 'the shush of the interstate off past the windbreak' (HRC 39.3, c.f. *Pale King* p. 5). Among these revisions, Wallace also added 'coins of sunlight' to go with 'weeping trees' as in the published version (HRC 39.3, *Pale King* p. 5), juxtaposing affective and economic registers. The process, then, was one of subtly corrupting the plainer natural lyricism with which Wallace began, using the signs of postindustrial life to break up an initially stronger sense of rooted pastoralism. At the same time, reprising the problematisation of sight in 'Whispering Pines', Wallace worked in moments of epistemological disconnection: 'insects at their business beneath the nodding heads of the green', with its strong visual emphasis, was revised to 'insects at their business unseen', while Wallace transposed 'the horizon trembling, shapeless' from the 'Evidence' notebook here (HRC 39.3). This form of revision was worked into the syntax of the passage itself as Wallace redrafted the section: the initial 'crows come over . . . corn-bound *past* the pasture's barbed wire' (HRC 39.3, my emphasis) becomes the published version's 'corn-bound *for* the pasture's wire' (*Pale King* p. 5, my emphasis): even as he invited his reader to 'read' his landscape, Wallace's revision of 'past' to 'for' introduced a confusion of the crows' direction – bound for the corn, or the wire? – that deliberately obscures the legibility of the scene. These moments of opacity, though, also serve to thread a sense of mysterious potentiality into the scene: the addition of the 'trembling' horizon is joined by a revision of 'the crows come over, silent' to 'the crows come over, their silence a coiled silence' (HRC

39.3), producing a tense potentiality like that of a 'coiled' spring. The composition of this first draft worked towards a carefully poised tension between signs of postindustrial life and the affective power of landscape.

This process continues in a second handwritten version of the section, in which Wallace added 'A.M.' to form 'in the A.M. heat' as in the published version (HRC 38.7, *Pale King* p. 5). This glimpse of distinctively human timekeeping, in an abbreviated form that jars slightly with the prevailing lyrical tone, suggests that the scene takes place at what would typically be the start of a working day; a signifier of contemporary experience which forms a counterpoint to the geological timeframe that Wallace simultaneously introduced in the form of a list of rock types comprising this 'very old land'. (HRC 38.7, *Pale King* p. 5). This balancing of geological and human is a reminder that, though Wallace worked from pastoral to postindustrial in the first draft, the process is not straightforwardly linear. Indeed, this second draft also adds the image of the 'arrow of starlings from the windbreak's thatch' – nature bursting out of a human component of the landscape, with 'arrow' ambiguously suggesting both a directional marker and a weapon (the latter emphasised more strongly in the addition of 'fired' to form 'fired from the windbreak's thatch' in the published version) (HRC 38.7, *Pale King* p. 5). Severs is right to note that nature holds its own in the passage, 'strongly asserting itself' to form a 'scene of competing economies'.[54] In fact, Wallace's handwritten amendments to a subsequent typed version show a slight reversal of the trajectory from natural to postindustrial: there, he revised out some of the more anthropocentric moments in the passage, amending 'breeze like a mother's hand on your cheek' to 'slight sideways breeze', and 'the interstate off past the windbreak' to 'the interstate off past the river' (HRC 40.4), suggesting a rebalancing of the scene towards a more assertively autonomous nature less heavily framed by the language of human experience and intervention. Though these revisions were not retained, they demonstrate that the process of place-setting in this passage was guided by a careful balancing of the landscape's natural facticity with experiential components of late twentieth-century human habitation.

This balancing indicates that the composition of §1 was framed by the same concern about the relationship between language and place in a postindustrial context that also shaped Wallace's work on the 'electric girl' drafts. Indeed, that the postindustrial scene Wallace developed in §8 was linked with the composition of §1 is indicated by a note on research materials on the inside back cover of the 'Evidence' notebook: 'stuff on mobile homes, history' appearing together with 'guide to Midwest flora esp. Central II.' (HRC 43.1). This latter aspect of his research presumably underpinned Wallace's composition of the long sentence that sits centrally in the first paragraph of the published version of §1, and lists plants visible in the field that the section describes: 'shattercane, lamb's-quarter, cutgrass, sawbrier . . .' (*Pale King* p. 5). This sentence has yielded revealingly opposed readings: for Severs, it carries 'Whitmanian associations, stylistic and thematic', contributing to a 'general Transcendentalist vibe'; for Wouters, its exhaustive cataloguing 'suggests that our technologically driven, human-organized present has somehow already superimposed itself on an eternal environment'.[55] It seems significant, and a testimony to the tension Wallace had worked into the passage as he developed it, that both interpretations hold: apparently connected with the project of writing trailer park precarity in §8, this sentence provides a moment in which a pastoral instinct unexpectedly overlaps with the informational labour of late twentieth-century capitalism.

That this was a central part of the process of §1 is further illustrated by the presence of a note at the bottom of the first handwritten draft, in the same pencil:

> Some sections w/ double colums [*sic*]. One column is just mind-bendingly dull catalogue of tax returns data to be input. Goes on in one column for ten pages – there is a backdrop of boredom that reader looks at just to be aware of but only very careful reader will actually "read." (HRC 39.3)

The note, which Wallace subsequently highlighted in the same pen he used to add the postindustrial registers to the passage itself, suggests a distinct ambivalence to the scene's invitation to 'read' the semi-pastoral landscape it describes: this act of reading, and the textual form of the novel itself, are at the same time beginning to blur with the deadening clerical labour of the postindustrial office. In Chapter 5, I will follow this 'double columns' idea, and the merging of literary and clerical labour that it suggests, into later stages of Wallace's work on the text. Where *Jest*'s reconstituted sociospatial image of the city had built on a constructive correlation between novelistic reading and urban walking, *Pale King* was tending towards a more searching interrogation of the nature of literary reading and its relationship to the labour of postindustrial bureaucracy. In its compositional development, then, §1 formed a pivot between Wallace's initial interest in the working-class precarity of the trailer park and his sharpening attention to the specifics of clerical and bureaucratic labour – and where the note to §8 had implied a hope of reconciling the 'vivid concreteness' of postindustrial America with the language of fiction, the double columns note on §1 indicates that the project was becoming increasingly concerned with ways of staging a collision between literary expression and the experience of postindustrial life.

Claude Sylvanshine's Fear of Falling

Wallace seems to have left off work on the Toni Ware section after composing the 'electric girl' drafts, only returning to Toni's story much later. Indeed, as Hering has established, Wallace appears to have considerably revised his vision of the project around 1999; and as he moved into this new compositional period, the focus on Toni's working-class experience of postindustrial precarity was supplanted by his writing of the IRS middle-manager Claude Sylvanshine's story – particularly in the segment that forms §2 of the published text, relating Sylvanshine's bumpy arrival at Peoria's regional airport.[56] Like Toni's story, though, this plotline also seems to have roots in the 'Evidence' notebook, where Wallace played with a narrative involving an 'accountant' and 'yuppie in Chi[cago]' who moves to Peoria, having failed a CPA (Certified Public Accountants) exam – the exam that Sylvanshine frets over in §2 (HRC 43.1, c.f. *Pale King* p. 11) as he arrives from New York via Chicago. Wallace went through at least two initial efforts at developing this idea, both much briefer than the version in the published text (HRC 40.7, 38.3), one of which is dated January–March 1999 (HRC 40.7). He then reworked the scene in two handwritten drafts, the more extensive of which is labelled 'rewrite 2' (HRC 39.1), followed by a typed version (HRC 39.7) which forms the basis of the section in the published text. One of the earlier handwritten versions (HRC 38.3) contains a mention of the 'IT'S SPRING, THINK FARM SAFETY' sign that also appears in the 'Whispering Pines' passage (*Pale King* p. 55), and a detail about a horse smelling another's behind which eventually settled in §1 (p. 5), suggesting that – despite Wallace's changes in compositional direction around this time – the writing of the earlier sections was connected with the new focus that Sylvanshine's story brought. Wallace's project may have been reconfigured in 1999, but these compositional continuities suggest that his work on §8 and §1 – with their ambivalence over the language of place – was still an integrated part of the project as he moved on to Sylvanshine's narrative.

Indeed, if the development of §1 had steered Wallace towards a focus on the relationship between place-writing and bureaucratic labour, then this milieu of late twentieth-century work comes into closer focus through §2. Found among the 'regional business travellers . . . on downstate sales calls or returning from the Chicago HQs of companies whose names end in "-co."' (*Pale King* p. 20), Sylvanshine is a member of the burgeoning clerical workforce of the late twentieth century. This section is concerned not with the precarity of the trailer park but the transience of the business commute – the futility of the plane's endless travel 'up and back again and again all day' (p. 22). At the same time, Sylvanshine's obsessive awareness of his own professional status is made plain in this section: acutely conscious of his position as a 'miserable and pathetic GS-9', he makes it his 'personal goal . . . to pass the CPA exam, thereby immediately advancing two paygrades' (p. 8). Notably, Sylvanshine's anxious interior monologue was added in the later rewrite of §2 together with a considerably more detailed account of the plane's progress towards Peoria than was included in the earlier versions, indicating a compositional connection between geographical experience and the psychology of postindustrial work.

Indeed, expanding on the futility of the commute, the section fuses class anxiety with physical space through Sylvanshine's own conflation of death and failure: 'which two things had collapsed in Sylvanshine's psyche to a single image of his silently, expressionlessly pushing a wide industrial mop down a corridor lined with frosted-glass doors bearing other men's names' (p. 13). As Issell pointed out in the 1980s, changes in the patterns and forms of work had 'sorted workers into categories more complex than traditional blue- and white-collar distinctions'; a process Levey traces into *Pale King*'s representation of 'the complexity of class in the postindustrial workplace, where white-collar workers try to distance themselves from blue-collar labor at the same time that automation and outsourcing threaten to hurl them towards it' – Sylvanshine's irony being that he initiates the process of automation that threatens his own status in the labour market (*Pale King* p. 15).[57] And in §2, Sylvanshine's anxiety over his precarious class identity is manifested in his vision of the workspace itself; a connection that is redoubled in the image of a janitor he sees 'at Midway, outside the men's room . . . the man fitted to his job like a man to the exact pocket of space he displaces' (*Pale King* p. 13). Work, class and space are deeply connected here.

The working of Sylvanshine's extensive interior monologue into this section presents a distinct contrast with the deliberate gap between Toni's voice and the language of the 'electric girl' drafts – and with the silence of Toni's mother, the figure for female and working-class precarity in the earlier composition. It is also notable that the field of real and imagined social interactions that feed Sylvanshine's class angst is decidedly masculine – the male janitor, the 'other men's names' that adorn his nightmare corridor – while at the same time, both visions of failure involve the performance of a type of service labour (cleaning) that is more traditionally associated with women. There are gendered contours to this postindustrial class anxiety; the 'new gender order' that McDowell identified in the post-Fordist restructuring of American capitalism is at work again here. At the same time, the conjoining of professional failure with death through Sylvanshine's image of the workspace links Wallace with a postwar tradition identified by Andrew Hoberek, in which the social and economic reconstitution of the American middle class is figured 'in terms that verge on the existential'– that Sylvanshine's fears take on this hue, where Toni's do not, suggests something of the class as well as gendered perspective implicit in *Pale King*.[58] The male, middle-class experience of postindustrial precarity is given an articulated psychological content and an existential tenor that are distinctly lacking from the stark materiality of female, working-class work and life, whose incorporation into the novel's language was problematised in the 'electric girl' drafts. As in *Jest*, Wallace's developing text had begun to overlap with gendered constructions that problematise the inclusion of the specific experiences of women in the form of the novel.

But if the tone and content of Sylvanshine's anxiety mark his experience as different from that of Toni and her mother, postindustrial geography and its experiences nonetheless form a line of continuity across the two sections. In particular, the corruption of domestic space and its relationship to wider geographical contexts that is figured in §8's hubcap house receives a clear echo in the 'Angler's Cove' apartment complex, in which REC employees are housed and about which Sylvanshine complains in §30. This complex appears only marginally in the published text, but a sketch in Wallace's 'Harvey Mudd' notebook – accompanied by a rough architectural diagram that shows Wallace visualising the space as he wrote it – underscores its association with a middle-class version of Toni's trailer park itinerance: 'Angler's Cove had clearly once been a motel, or designed by someone whose chief experience and expertise had been in the design of motels' (HRC 41.2). The motel, as Sarah Treadwell suggests, 'is a transit form that mediates between a fixed address and vagrancy'; in this sketch, the architectural form of the complex suspends its middle-class inhabitants between place and placelessness, much like the trailer parks in §8.[59] As Toffler suggested, both blue- and white-collar work are bound into the late twentieth-century decline of place. And where the hubcap house is severed from the landscape by its improvised postindustrial fortification, the fissure between Angler's Cove and its setting is embodied in the irony of its name: 'It makes a certain senseless sense – no lake in Lake James, and now where's the evidence of any water here around Angler's Cove' (HRC 41.2).

Severs suggests that the naming of Angler's Cove marks its inhabitants 'as fishermen, a profession leading to disciplehood' – but there is no fishing to be done here.[60] Instead, the Angler's Cove residents find themselves in a landscape consisting of 'the parking lot or the rear loading dock area of a KMart with Self-Storage Parkway in the distance . . . and another type of warehouse superstore, along the lines of Menard's or Target, that was under construction' (HRC 41.2). This dissonance between idealised name and material landscape implies a disconnection from place that is actualised in the climax of §2, where it is the 'cyclone of logistical problems' involved in setting up home in the Angler's Cove complex that tips Sylvanshine into panic, as he tries to 'merge his own awareness with the panoramic vista' (*Pale King* p. 26). Sylvanshine's spatial anxiety, compounded by the pseudo-domestic prospect of Angler's Cove, feeds a vision of the Midwestern landscape as 'the center of some huge and stagnant body of water, an oceanic impression so literally obliterating that Sylvanshine was cast or propelled back in on himself' (p. 26).

Geography, it seems, is the category through which the postindustrial angst of the late twentieth-century middle class is magnified into an existential condition. But does this discount the prospect of place entirely – or, indeed, the prospect of the novel as a practice of place-making? The question is confronted through the description of Sylvanshine's descent as his plane arrives in Peoria, the part of the section which most fully connects the contours of his class anxiety with the experience of space. His in-flight nerves have already been subtly registered in the free indirect speech that registers his obsessing over the meaning of 'yaw' and the 'word for pitching back and forth' (*Pale King* p. 11). That his anxieties over his professional and literal ascendance are entwined is suggested in the climactic 'yaw-wobbled horror' (p. 20) of the landing itself, rendered in a sentence that recalls the 'Whispering Pines' passage in its length and complexity:

> the interstate now rococo with exits and half-cloverleafs and the traffic denser and with something insistent about it . . . as there appeared a body of water below, a lake or delta, and Sylvanshine felt one of his feet was asleep as he tried to recall the particular crossed-arm configuration with which the figures on the card held their seat cushions to their chests in the unlikely event of a water landing, and now they did really and truly yaw and their speed became more evident in the rate of passage of things below in what had to be an older district of Peoria *qua* human city, close-packed blocks of sooty brick and angled roofs and a television antenna with a flag attached, and a flash of bourbon-colored river that was not the previous body of water but might have been connected to it . . . noting the steward-ess in her fold-down seat had her head down and arms about her own legs where at year's end the aggregate fair value of Brown's saleable securities exceeds the aggregate carrying amount at the beginning of the year as out of nowhere appeared an expanse of pale cement rising to meet them with no warning bell or announcement . . . (pp. 18–19)

The sentence's spiralling form deftly registers Sylvanshine's alarm at the suddenness of his descent, embedding his mounting panic into the breathless texture of the passage. And, veering abruptly and without punctuation or conjunction between the panic of the landing and the anxious rehearsal of a CPA exam question, the final part of the sentence – part of what Levey suggestively calls a 'postindustrial update of stream of consciousness' – engenders a climactic conflation of the two fears in Sylvanshine's mind.[61] His fear of flying enfolds the 'fear of falling' that Barbara Ehrenreich identified in the class consciousness of a professional workforce whose 'only "capital" is knowledge and skill' (here embodied in CPA accreditation) – a kind of capital 'far more effervescent than wealth', supporting an 'insecure and deeply anxious' elite.[62] Where Toni and her mother are subject to the horizontal precarity of senseless routes on maps, Sylvanshine's precarity is an appropriately vertical one.

But even as the sentence builds towards this conflation, its mounting speed is checked by the occasional invocation of the landscape of 'Peoria *qua* human city' glimpsed from the window. In the first draft of the revised scene, this is emphasised in a description of the city as 'like houses in a Victorian painting – very far away but very precisely lined' (HRC 39.1), terms which suggest a sense of static precision – in both perception and representation – that counters the plane's hastening descent and Sylvanshine's spiralling angst. In the published version, accordingly, his observations form a series of comparatively shorter and more carefully punctuated clauses that check the unfolding sense of panic dramatised in the overall syntax, so that it is the vision of the landscape that offsets this panic: the mention of Peoria's name is followed by a comma that breaks a particularly rapid string of unpunctuated clauses, with the subsequent descriptive clause ('close packed blocks . . .') offering a distraction from the fast-approaching landing. The details of place act as a formal calmative to the combined professional stress and vertical panic expressed in the form of the sentence. The humanist geographer Yi-Fu Tuan sees 'place' as arising from a 'pause' in the openness and fluidity of space, with 'each pause . . . mak[ing] it possible for location to be transformed into place' – pauses which the structure of Wallace's sentence seems to allow as Peoria's landscape comes into view.[63] If space is the dimension of postindustrial class anxiety, perhaps place is the ballast that can counter this anxiety – a possibility that is incorporated into Wallace's formal construction of this passage.

Place, then, seems to re-emerge as a corrective to the postindustrial anxieties that colour Sylvanshine's existentially charged spatiality. Is this what Peoria is for: an anchor that works against the geographical angst of postindustrial life? A problem is suggested earlier in the section, when Sylvanshine describes his 'effective concentration device': 'to summon into one's mind a soothing and low-pressure outdoor scene, either imagined or from memory' (*Pale King* p. 14). This 'device' reappears in §38, as Lane Dean, sat at his desk, 'flexed his buttocks and held to a count of ten and imagined a warm pretty beach with mellow surf as instructed in orientation the previous month' (p. 378). These are instances of the imagining of landscape reduced to a managerially sanctioned technique for maximising the productivity of clerical labour – Dorson suggests something of this when he remarks that in *Pale King* 'there is little friction between pastoral yearning and corporate ideology'.[64] Sylvanshine's anti-stress device is an indication that the traditional humanistic work of fostering a 'sense of place' is at risk of collapsing into the practices and conditions of postindustrial work.

Significantly, Wallace worked this detail into the section simultaneously with the extended description of the plane's landing. In the first version of the rewritten scene, Sylvanshine simply 'tried to imagine a soothing 60s scene' (HRC 39.1), without emphasis on this act as a 'concentration device' or on the scene as an 'outdoor' landscape. At the same time, in this version the landing itself is far more perfunctory: there is no long sentence or conflation with CPA exam worries, the passage instead simply reporting that 'The landing was not three-point' (HRC 39.1). Wallace's insertion of the more fully worked-out notion of landscape as a device for the management of postindustrial labour was simultaneous, then, with his formal use of place to offset the conjoined anxieties of descent and CPA examination later in the section. That the two are linked is further indicated by Sylvanshine's report that the 'concentration device' is 'even more effective if the scene comprised or included a pond lake brook or stream, as water had been proven to have a calming and centering effect' (*Pale King* p. 14); and sure enough, the most effectively calming aspect of the landscape Sylvanshine observes from the window is the 'body of water below', which ushers in a very short clause – 'a lake or delta' – that halts the sentence's spiral of panic precisely as it echoes the terms of the 'concentration device' (p. 19). The function of place as a psychic anchor for the postindustrial worker is pre-empted by its absorption into the conditions of labour that create the need for such an anchor in the first place.

This conflation of clerical work with the invocation of place finds another expression in a draft section that is not included in the published text, but which connects the composition of §2 with that of §1 and its tension between pastoral and postindustrial registers. The connection is indicated in a draft of §1, which is appended with the note: 'JUXTAPOSED W/ ACCOUNTANTS COMING TO WORK?' (HRC 38.7). The clearest candidate for this possible juxtaposition is an unpublished scene that opens with an injunction to 'look at the Internal Revenue Service agents coming to work at the Peoria/Lake James IL post', dated '10–1 to 3–99' (HRC 40.3). As Hering points out, this draft appears to comprise a new opening to the novel as Wallace was reconfiguring its direction in 1999.[65] The note about juxtaposition with §1, though, indicates that – rather than a completely new start for the project – this new composition was also shaped by attempts to combine the problem of place first developed in the earlier material with the new focus on Sylvanshine's clerical angst. The 'accountants' draft counters §1's gentle invitation to 'read' the landscape with an aggressively interrogative tone:

Examine a March sun that looks bright and clear but has no heart to it . . . What color is the lot? How well ploughed? What is its capacity? . . . Is the walkway continuous or composed of discreet rectangular slabs whose cracks cannot be ploughed free of rime? What is the yearly upkeep on the lot and walkways? How many windows face the promenade? Are there clouds, and if there are clouds do they look like anything and do they move or are they the creepy dull sort

of clouds that seem to hang motionless above the ground's wind? . . .
What's at the horizon? (HRC 40.3)

Though the clouds and horizon are traces of §1's lyricism (albeit
now more fully degraded to a 'creepy dull sort'), the mode here has
shifted towards something reminiscent of the CPA exam questions
over which Sylvanshine agonises; indeed, this draft is followed by
a note that reads 'INSERT OF FIDGETY STUFF, TRYING TO
STUDY FOR CPA EXAM', in turn followed in the same typescript
by a draft of §2 (HRC 40.3). At the same time as we are instructed
to 'imagine the stony mindlessness with which the Internal Revenue
Service employees negotiate the slick cement of the lot's system of
walkways . . . in a loose long herd to the institutional building's beige
facade', the use of an interrogative form of address to relay the scene
places us alongside these workers in their requirement to remain 'for
7.25 hours daily sensitive to pattern and discrepancy and the nuance
of attested fact' (HRC 40.3). This section forms a subtler instantiation of the idea behind the note about columns of data that Wallace
had appended to §1's landscape description; here, we can see place
taking up a central role in his experimental attempt to – as Levey
puts it – '[align] the work of the novelist and his readers with that
of the postindustrial professionals who are the focus of this text'.[66]
As in Sylvanshine's 'concentration device', this section indicates a
suffusion of the logic of accountancy and postindustrial bureaucracy
into the acts of perceiving and imagining places – and into literary
practice itself.

Wallace's reading of his Illinois State University colleague Curtis
White's critique of American culture at the turn of the twenty-
first century, *The Middle Mind: Why Americans Don't Think for
Themselves* (2003), appears to have been connected to his interest
here; Wallace read and annotated the book in manuscript form (his
copy is held in the Harry Ransom Center archive [HRC 32.5]), and
blurbed the eventual publication approvingly: 'Cogent, acute, beautiful, merciless, and true'.[67] In one passage, White writes:

> In contrast with the needs of capitalism, creativity (the work of the
> imagination) is a messy plurality of human possibilities not condu-
> cive to economic efficiency. And so capitalism has always to find
> ways to orient this messy plurality to the business at hand: work . . .
> In the twentieth and twenty-first centuries, this control has had less
> to do with the raw, repressive, physical obligation to work . . . and
> more to do with managing our creativity. We American workers are
> more beguiled than we are oppressed.[68]

Wallace underlined the last sentence of this passage in his manuscript copy, together with White's subsequent statement that 'what
capitalism can do is *manage* our creativity. Its primary strategy is to
provide the work of the imagination for us'; a sentiment connected
to Ash Amin's suggestion that the post-Fordist transition 'blur[red]
the traditional distinction between economics and cultural activity'.[69] Though the publication of *Middle Mind* postdates Wallace's
composition of §2 and the 'accountants' scene, White and Wallace
had been colleagues since the latter arrived in Bloomington in 1993,
and the two (in White's account) had 'a long and productive relationship' – so it is certainly possible that the ideas in *Middle Mind*
had been exchanged with Wallace earlier.[70] In any case, White's
critique resonates with Wallace's exploration of how the creative
and imaginative construction of place is co-opted into the practice
of labour management: place has become simply another means of
'beguiling' the American workforce. Clare Hayes-Brady connects
Pale King with a 'reflective romanticism Wallace adopted across the
board in his writing'.[71] But at the juncture of postindustrial work
and place, the traditional Romantic ideal of literary composition as
'one of the few enclaves in which the creative values expunged . . .
by industrial capitalism can be celebrated and affirmed' (as Terry
Eagleton puts it) is dissolved; no longer can literary practice play
its role as an 'image of non-alienated labour'.[72] In dialogue with the
kind of critique that White offers, Wallace was rethinking his own
work of writing place in line with an increasingly clear sense that
the novel, as a form and a practice, can claim no detached position
from which to approach the historical changes that had become his
explicit subject.

Conclusion

Wallace's work on these initial phases of *Pale King*'s composition
brought the theme of place and its loss in postindustrial America to
the foreground, developing this theme out of the interstitial economics and changing experiences of work with which he had begun in
the mid-1990s. The promise of a more human economy promoted
by the 'postindustrial' discourse of previous decades had been shown
to be a hollow one: precarity and anxiety were the actual results
of the late twentieth century's transition. But more than this, the
malaise that 'postindustrial' had come to signify was creeping into
Wallace's sense of literary practice itself: beginning with a disjunc-

ture between literary language and the precarious geographies of postindustrial work, and developing into the suspicion that creative practices of place-making were being subsumed into the regimes of clerical labour that now shaped the lives of the American middle class. *Jest*'s approach to the metropolis had been underpinned by a faith in the novel as cure as well as diagnosis; the language and form of fiction itself had seemed to present a means through which literary practice might intervene in the social atomisation of urban America. But the reconfigured geographies of work produced by the economic upheaval of the late twentieth century seemed to present a fundamental challenge to this earlier optimism: in *Pale King*, Wallace's practice of writing postindustrial landscapes had to find a way to negotiate its own imbrication within the sociospatial conditions it attempted to describe. It would not be until he reconfigured the project again in 2005 that he began to work in earnest towards a solution; and it is to this last period in the composition of *Pale King* that I will turn in the next chapter.

Notes

1. Hering, *Fiction and Form*, pp. 127–40.
2. Lipsky, *Although of Course*, p. 276.
3. Hering, *Fiction and Form*, p. 148.
4. Lipsky, *Although of Course*, p. 291, emphasis and last ellipsis original.
5. Issell, *Social Change*, pp. 57, 56.
6. For example: Marshall Boswell, 'Trickle-Down Citizenship: Taxes and Civic Responsibility in *The Pale King*', in Boswell (ed.), *Long Thing*, pp. 209–26; Adam Kelly, 'David Foster Wallace and the Novel of Ideas', in Boswell (ed.), *Long Thing*, pp. 3–22.
7. Issell, *Social Change*, p. 57.
8. Markusen and Carlson, 'Deindustrialization', p. 30.
9. Hering, *Fiction and Form*, p. 45; McGurl, 'Institution of Nothing', p. 28.
10. Daalder, 'Geographic Metafiction', p. 230.
11. Joseph F. Goeke, '"Everybody Knows It's About Something Else, Way Down": Boredom, Nihilism, and the Search for Meaning in David Foster Wallace's *The Pale King*', *Critique: Studies in Contemporary Fiction*, 58.3 (2017), 191–213 (p. 198).
12. Chodat, *High Words*, p. 298; James Dorson, 'The Neoliberal Machine in the Bureaucratic Garden: Pastoral States of Mind in David Foster Wallace's *The Pale King*', in Eric Erbacher, Nicole Maruo-Schröder and Florian Sedlmeier (eds.), *Rereading the Machine in the Garden: Nature and Technology in American Culture* (Frankfurt: Campus Verlag,

2014), pp. 211–30 (p. 212); Liam Connell, *Precarious Labour and the Contemporary Novel* (Palgrave MacMillan, 2017), p. 94.

13. Luc Herman and Toon Staes, 'Introduction: Can *The Pale King* (Please) be a Novel?', *English Studies*, 95.1 (2014), 1–6 (p. 3).

14. Alice Bennett, *Contemporary Fictions of Attention* (London: Bloomsbury, 2018), p. 36.

15. Richard Godden and Michael Szalay, 'The bodies in the bubble: David Foster Wallace's *The Pale King*', *Textual Practice*, 28.7 (2014), 1273–322 (p. 1273).

16. Hering, *Fiction and Form*, pp. 115–16.

17. Severs, *Balancing Books*, pp. 27, 89, 196.

18. Nick Levey, *Maximalism in Contemporary American Literature: The Uses of Detail* (New York: Routledge, 2017), p. 76.

19. Ehrman, *Eighties*, p. 103.

20. Yi-Fu Tuan, *Topophilia: A Study of Environmental Perception, Attitudes and Values* (Englewood Cliffs, New Jersey: Prentice-Hall, 1974).

21. Edward S. Casey, *The Fate of Place: A Philosophical History* (Berkeley: University of California Press, 1997); James Howard Kunstler, *Geography of Nowhere: The Rise and Decline of America's Man-Made Landscapes* (New York: Simon and Schuster, 1991).

22. Edward Relph, *Place and Placelessness* (London: Pion, 1976), p. 80.

23. Toffler, *Future Shock*, p. 69.

24. Ibid. pp. 74, 80.

25. David Harvey, 'From Space to Place and Back Again: Reflections on the Condition of Postmodernity', in Jon Bird, Barry Curtis, Tim Putnam, George Robertson and Lisa Tickner (eds.), *Mapping the Futures: Local Cultures, Global Change* (London: Routledge, 1993), pp. 2–29 (p. 24).

26. Toffler, *Future Shock*, p. 73.

27. Tom McCarthy, 'David Foster Wallace: The Last Audit', *New York Times* (11 April 2011), <https://www.nytimes.com/2011/04/17/books/review/book-review-the-pale-king-by-david-foster-wallace.html> [retrieved 28 February 2022]; Ralph Clare, 'The Politics of Boredom and the Boredom of Politics in *The Pale King*', in Boswell (ed.), *Long Thing*, pp. 187–208 (p. 188).

28. Levey, *Maximalism*, p. 76.

29. Severs, *Balancing Books*, p. 141; Jasper Bernes, 'Character, Genre, Labor: The Office Novel after Deindustrialization', *Post45*, 1.10 (January 2019), <http://post45.research.yale.edu/2019/01/character-genre-labor-the-office-novel-after-deindustrialization/> [retrieved 28 February 2022].

30. Daniel Bell, *The Coming of Post-Industrial Society: A Venture in Social Forecasting* (London: Heinemann, 1974), p. 37.

31. Boris Frankel, *The Post-Industrial Utopians* (Cambridge: Polity, 1987), p. 3.

32. Jarvis, *Postmodern Cartographies*, pp. 15, 21, 20.
33. Issell, *Social Change*, p. 59.
34. Robert J. Samuelson, 'America sings the postindustrial blues', *Washington Post* (18 June 2017), <https://www.washingtonpost.com/opinions/america-sings-the-postindustrial-blues/2017/06/18/d59a8a2c-52bb-11e7-91eb-9611861a988f_story.html> [retrieved 28 April 2022].
35. Gerald Howard, 'Infinite Jester: David Foster Wallace and his 1,079 mystical, brilliant pages', *Elle*, 11.6 (1996), p. 58.
36. David Foster Wallace, 'Exploring Inner Space', *Washington Post* (28 April 1991), <https://www.washingtonpost.com/archive/entertainment/books/1991/04/28/exploring-inner-space/39298a00–9030–4ae6-a3b9–03325e10b703/?utm_term=.db4d1fdc4713> [retrieved 28 February 2022].
37. See Hering, *Fiction and Form*, pp. 126 ff; Stephen J. Burn, '"A Paradigm for the Life of Consciousness": *The Pale King*', in Boswell (ed.), *Long Thing*, pp. 149–68 (p. 151); Tim Groenland, 'A King of Shreds and Patches: Assembling Wallace's Final Novel', in Coleman (ed.), *Critical Insights*, pp. 221–37 (p. 225).
38. Burn, *Reader's Guide*, p. 14; Hering, *Fiction and Form*, p. 67.
39. Severs, *Balancing Books*, p. 141.
40. Hering, *Fiction and Form*, p. 128.
41. David Foster Wallace, 'Peoria (9) "Whispering Pines"', *TriQuarterly*, 112 (Fall 2002), 132–3.
42. Haynes Johnson, *Sleepwalking Through History: America in the Reagan Years* (New York: Norton, 1991), p. 119.
43. Severs also notes this pun, also linking it to the commodification of the environment through the gypsum mining around the trailer park ('Ware' as a good for sale on the market). *Balancing Books*, p. 207.
44. Max, *Every Love Story*, pp. 177 ff, 200.
45. Lipsky, *Although of Course*, p. 300.
46. Linda McDowell, 'Life Without Father and Ford: The New Gender Order of Post-Fordism', *Transactions of the Institute of British Geographers*, 16.4 (1991), 400–19 (pp. 401, 417).
47. Chodat, *High Words*, p. 229.
48. David Foster Wallace, 'Peoria (4)', in *TriQuarterly*, 112 (Fall 2002), p. 131.
49. Brian McHale, '*The Pale King*, Or, The White Visitation', in Boswell and Burn (eds.), *Companion*, pp. 181–210 (p. 191); McGurl, 'Institution of Nothing', p. 28.
50. Dorson, 'Neoliberal Machine', p. 219; Levey, *Maximalism*, pp. 76, 77.
51. Max, *Every Love Story*, p. 55.
52. Ibid. p. 78.
53. Daalder, 'Geographic Metafiction', pp. 221–2.
54. Severs, *Balancing Books*, p. 228.

55. Ibid. p. 206; Courtney Wouters, '"What Am I, A Machine?": Humans and Information in *The Pale King*', in Boswell (ed.), *Long Thing*, p. 182.
56. Hering, *Fiction and Form*, pp. 130–1.
57. Issell, *Social Change*, p. 56; Levey, *Maximalism*, p. 79.
58. Andrew Hoberek, *Twilight of the Middle Class: Post-World War II Fiction and White-Collar Work* (Princeton: Princeton University Press, 2005), p. 11.
59. Sarah Treadwell, 'The Motel: An Image of Elsewhere', *Space and Culture*, 8.2 (May 2005), 214–24 (p. 215).
60. Severs, *Balancing Books*, p. 209.
61. Levey, *Maximalism*, pp. 82–3.
62. Barbara Ehrenreich, *Fear of Falling: The Inner Life of the Middle Class* (New York: Pantheon, 1989), p. 15.
63. Tuan, *Space and Place*, p. 6.
64. Dorson, 'Neoliberal Machine', p. 226.
65. Hering, *Fiction and Form*, p. 131.
66. Levey, *Maximalism*, p. 79.
67. Curtis White, *The Middle Mind: Why Americans Don't Think for Themselves* (New York: HarperCollins, 2003), frontmatter.
68. Ibid. p. 8.
69. Ibid. p. 9; Amin, 'Post-Fordism', p. 31.
70. Curtis White, 'Curtis White remembers David Foster Wallace', Melville House website (12 September 2016), <https://www.mhpbooks.com /curtis-white-remembers-david-foster-wallace/> [retrieved 28 February 2022].
71. Clare Hayes-Brady, '"Palely Loitering": On Not Finishing (in) *The Pale King*', in Clare (ed.), *Cambridge Companion*, pp. 142–58 (p. 143).
72. Terry Eagleton, *Literary Theory: An Introduction*, second edition (1996) (Oxford: Blackwell, 2001), p. 17.

Chapter 5

What is Peoria for? (II): Peoria, the Edge City and *The Pale King*

Introduction: Peoria and the 'Edge City'

Over the first decade of Wallace's work on *The Pale King*, the question 'what is Peoria for?' had opened the project onto searching questions about the efficacy of literary practice in the face of the geographical upheavals that characterised postindustrial life. Around 2005, though, the shape and status of the project itself began to come more fundamentally into question. In a note to himself dated 7 June 2005, Wallace reflected on the difficulty of incorporating his already drafted material into a coherent structure: he had been working to the assumption that 'the book were a puzzle and all these pieces fit into it', but '[t]his is not so' (HRC 39.1). And this pragmatic structural issue was also joined by more fundamental doubts about the purpose of the work Wallace had done and was doing on the project: 'The despair is that so much time and work has apparently gone into these nuggets, and so many of them just <u>stop</u>, as if the spirit just gave out' – 'I do not feel inspired' (HRC 39.1). Across the 'electric girl' drafts, §1 and the Claude Sylvanshine section, the question of place had provided a focal point for Wallace's renewed worry about the relationship between literary practice and the conditions of work and life in contemporary America. His 2005 note suggests that this conceptual concern had morphed into a compositional crisis.

David Hering places this note at the beginning of Wallace's third and last phase of work on the novel, running from 2005 to 2007. As Hering points out, the note 'clearly represents a crisis point in the life of *The Pale King*' – necessitating 'a new narrative strategy that [Wallace] clearly hoped would bring the disparate drafts together'.[1] In Hering's account, this strategy was the introduction of the character and narrative voice of 'David Wallace', who serves as the narrator of §9, §24 and §38 of the published text.[2] At the same time, though – and in §24 in particular – this character's appearance also coincides with a significantly more developed image of the Peoria Regional Examination Center and its surrounding landscape of 'Lake James', which began to form the geographical centre of the developing novel from this point. Did this clarifying geographical structure also play a role in the substantial reorganisation of the project? And how did Wallace's more focused vision of Peoria itself relate to the topographical arrangements produced by America's shifting postindustrial economy?

In the 'electric girl' drafts and Sylvanshine's arrival, Peoria had been a shared destination – the geographical centre of gravity towards which these fragments of narrative were tending. This location was already functioning as a means of connecting the different experiences of Toni (and her mother) and Sylvanshine, the figures for the overlapping precarity of the working class and of the rising clerical workforce that both characterised America's postindustrial economy. In both these sections, though, Peoria itself remains a distant and deferred presence rather than a realised location – appearing on Toni's road atlas and from the window of Sylvanshine's plane rather than as an immediate frame for the narrative. Wallace's progression towards a more concrete and sustained focus on the city itself is made visible in a diagrammatic map that he sketched on the cover of a cardboard folder (HRC 39.4), in which Peoria is shown as a circle, partly surrounded by a dotted line marked 'Self-Storage Parkway'. 'Lake James' is marked to the south, with rectangles to the south-east marked 'Anthony' (Toni's birthplace) and 'MWMW'– the latter indicating 'Mid West Mirror Works', the defunct manufacturing concern whose premises (as we hear in §24) are occupied by the REC in the novel's present (*Pale King* p. 267). In sketching out the geography of his re-imagined Peoria, Wallace was using the process of cartographic construction as a means of drawing together previously disparate ideas and strands of narrative. And as he began to lay out this topography, the diagram emphasises Wallace's attention to the peripheries of the city, with the key narrative locations placed on the outskirts and separated from the centre (simply represented by an empty circle) by the barrier of 'Self-Storage Parkway'. This marks a shift from notes in Wallace's 'Butterfly' notebook, which suggest a downtown location as the centre of the novel: 'Interstate came – killed Peoria downtown. REC in downtown factories by river?' (HRC 40.8); although this note also indicates Wallace's attention to how the construction of peripheral transport arteries was shifting economic activity towards the edges of former industrial cities. As he worked out his image of Peoria as the organising geographical centre for the novel, Wallace's attention was moving outwards, towards its outskirts and edgelands.

This attention to the topographical layout of the postindustrial city drew partly on work Wallace had done for 'The View from Mrs. Thompson's', the essay he wrote primarily in response to 9/11. This piece provided Wallace with an opportunity to work up the detailed attention to the economic geography and history of Midwestern cities that he had been recording in his notebooks, converting these fragments into a polished prose form as he depicted the city of Bloomington (where he continued to live until 2002). We hear that 'Three major interstates converge here, and several railway lines', and that 'its origins involve being an important train depot', before Wallace explains its turn-of-the-century 'recession-proof' prosperity with reference to the presence of 'the national HQ for State Farm Insurance, which is the great dark god of US consumer insurance and for all practical purposes owns the town' (*Consider* pp. 132–3). Following this, the essay sketches the current spatial form of the city, echoing Wallace's 'Butterfly' notebook entry as he reports that Bloomington's 'east side is now all smoked-glass complexes and Build to Suit developments and a six-lane beltway that's killing off the old downtown, plus an ever-wider split between the town's two basic classes and cultures'. (p. 133). These 'basic classes and cultures' recall Toni and Sylvanshine, figures of the semi-rural working class and the clerical professional milieu who form differentiated but linked social groups in *Pale King*'s vision of postindustrial life – and here this social landscape is re-focused around the altered form of the city itself, indicating the role that geography could play in organising Wallace's social vision. The essay's portrait of Bloomington represents an effort to condense and express the connections between the transition from manufacturing to service economies, the new physical shape of America's economic geography, and the social scene of Bloomington that had framed Wallace's work on the 'electric girl' drafts. It forms a first attempt to draw these aspects together into a cohesive form with a clear spatial focus.

It was not until the post-2005 period of work, though, that Peoria began to emerge as a realised locale in *Pale King* itself. Section 24 formed a primary focus for this, providing Wallace with an opportunity to deploy the lists of Peoria companies he had been collecting since 1996 in 'David's' inventory of 'notable businesses and industries based in metropolitan Peoria as of 1985' (*Pale King* p. 268). 'David' goes on to sketch out the economic geography that Wallace had been developing in note and diagram form: Peoria 'had come in the 1980s to assume the same basic donut shape as so many other formerly industrial cities'; 'a robust collection of malls, plazas, franchises, business and light-industrial parks . . . had pulled most of the city's life out into an exurban ring' (p. 274 n. 17). Building on the folder diagram and the portrait of Bloomington in 'View', this peripheral development places the explicitly postindustrial landscape of Lake James in an ambiguous hinterland: located in 'something between a suburb and an independent township of metropolitan Peoria', it is part of 'the city's inexorable expansion and encroachment into the rich agricultural land around it' (p. 258). It is unsurprising that one draft of this section is labelled 'WPF July 8 05' (HRC 38.6); nearly a decade on from the 'Evidence' notebook's first recording of the question of what Peoria is for, the city itself was at last coming fully into view.

Alongside the introduction of 'David Wallace', this focus on Peoria's geography as an organising centre for the novel appears to have been a crucial aspect of Wallace's effort to impart a renewed coherence to his project after 2005 – to rescue *Pale King* from the dead end that his earlier efforts seemed to have reached. The question of what Peoria is for had become a compositional as well as a thematic one; the role of this geographical location in structuring the novel's direction had come into the foreground of Wallace's work on the text. Indeed, although he had moved to California in 2002, Wallace kept a map of Peoria hung in his workspace, maintaining the geography of the city literally in sight as he continued to work on the text.[3] And at the same time, even if the geographical experiences of postindustrial America had prompted a deep concern over the efficacy of literary practice in relation to late twentieth-century capitalism in Wallace's earlier work on the novel, his 2005 note was adamant that only the labour of composition itself could resolve the problem: 'The truth is that the book must be written – started afresh, and continued with . . . The key here is time and effort. There is no substitute. . . . Do the footwork' (HRC 39.1). Despite the searching doubts the project had spawned, a fundamental faith in the practice of writing was still pushing the novel forward. How this faith in the labour of composition could be reconciled with a context in which the role and status of writing seemed to be coming into doubt, and how this reconciliation might relate to the newly centred geography of Peoria itself, are the questions I explore in this chapter.

At the same time, the new emphasis on Peoria's changing spatial structure serves to place this developing narrative geography in relation to the landscapes organised around the new industrial spaces of late twentieth-century America. These landscapes were characterised by a novel form of development situated, like *Pale King*'s Lake James, on the edges of old industrial cities: a 'decentralization of the most vital urban functions' that 'has profoundly transformed the basic urban ecology' of America, as Robert Fishman put it in 1987.[4] The result was what Joel Garreau dubbed the 'Edge City', a form distinguished from earlier suburbs by its peripheral concentration of economic activity rather than residential development: as Garreau observed, 'we have moved our means of creating wealth, the essence of our urbanism – our jobs – out to where most of us have lived . . . for two generations'.[5] As a result, as Peter O. Muller wrote in 1997, 'the American city has turned inside out since about 1970, thereby constituting the most profound social and economic transformation in its history'.[6] This conclusion was shared by other observers: Manuel Castells and Peter Hall noted that 'Scenes like these are now legion on the periphery of virtually every dynamic urban area' and remarked that 'What we are witnessing . . . is the emergence of a new industrial space'.[7] For Edward W. Soja, these new configurations were 'improbable cities where centrality is virtually ubiquitous and the solid familiarity of the urban melts into air' – 'a manufactured landscape of flexible economic specialization' that 'slips free of our old categories and stereotypes, resists conventional modes of explanation'.[8] The novelty of this form, and its challenge to established ways of imagining space, is reflected in the proliferation of neologisms that sprang up in the attempt to describe it: 'technoburbs' (Fishman), 'technopoles' (Castells and Hall), 'new technology city' (Muller), 'exopolis' (Soja). The established geographical lexicon seemed inadequate to grasp this radically new form of development; to begin to describe it would require a change in the language of built space itself.

This sense of radical novelty partly explains why the Edge City became a focal point for the loss of meaningful 'place' that humanist geographers bemoaned in the late twentieth century. For Fishman, it heralded 'a crucial loss of texture in modern society'.[9] For David R. Goldfield and Blaine A. Brownell, the new landscapes represented 'no towns'; for James Howard Kunstler, they formed a 'geography of nowhere, that has simply ceased to be a credible human habitat'.[10] Eugene Victor Walter complained in 1988 that 'for the first time in human history, people are systematically building meaningless places'.[11] In 1985 – the year in which *Pale King* is set – Leonard Lutwack lamented that 'the quality of traditionally honored places has deteriorated . . . and a whole set of questionable new places is being created by social and economic forces'.[12] This challenging new form of development also began to shape the literary imagination of urban space: discussing the literature of the 'peripheral city', Lieven Ameel, Jason Finch and Markku Salmela argue that 'the creation of post-industrial cities' has led the 'palimpsestic set of disorientating experiences erupting from the margins of the city' to become 'what defines, to a considerable extent, urban literature'.[13] And, like the hubcap house of Wallace's 'electric girl' drafts, this peripheral landscape seemed to embody a breakdown of the established relationships with place that had been enfolded within older industrial patterns of work and life.

This sense of loss was at work in Wallace's development of Lake James as a narrative locale: in one draft of §24, the district is named 'Big Hollow' (HRC 36.3), while in a separate sketch for a character's move to the IRS, Peoria is described as the 'country's midsection's hollow heart' (HRC 40.7). This is an existentially empty space as well as an ambiguously peripheral one. It is also a place of malaise: §24's mention of the other (fictional) Edge City of 'Sicklied Ore' (*Pale King* p. 258 n. 2) suggests industrial decay (the economic sickliness of mining and steel production) while echoing Shakespeare's *Hamlet*: 'sicklied o'er with the pale cast of thought' (3.1.86).[14] The name of 'Self-Storage Parkway', the road on which the REC is located, also expresses this sense of malaise: Jeffrey Severs suggests that the name indicates 'the logic . . . of the self . . . as a storage receptacle', but for me it carries a suggestion of place as a site for the 'storage' of the self – not an existential root or nurturing frame, but a temporary, sterile container.[15] In its connections with the material development of urban geography in postindustrial America, §24 marks a continuation of the interest in topographical and architectural forms that I have explored in both *Broom* and *Jest*; except that, where the legacy of I. M. Pei occasioned connections with longer histories of built space in those texts, Lake James represents a radically new kind of landscape, unmoored from the topographical heritages that help make sense of space.

'David Wallace' in the Edge City

If Peoria's geography was central to the revival of *Pale King*, the focus on this challenging Edge City landscape did not exactly promise a straightforward solution to the compositional difficulties that had come to a head in Wallace's 2005 note. Stephen J. Burn suggests that 'the geography of the suburb' forms part of the novel's 'underlying geometry', and Hering builds on this to argue that 'the spatial dialectic between Midwestern suburban and urban geography ... is representative of the centring/decentring tension that characterizes the narrative'[16] – but the topographical form of the Edge City in fact represents the undoing of this familiar urban/suburban geography, hardly suggesting a stable model around which to shape Wallace's unwieldy fragments of narrative. Indeed, in 'View' Wallace had begun to experiment with a deliberate awkwardness to the incorporation of the materiality of this space into the form of his prose:

> Bloomington is a city of 65,000 in the central part of a state that is extremely, emphatically flat ... The town's almost exactly halfway between Chicago and St. Louis, and its origins involve being an important train depot. .... It has a smaller twin city, Normal, that's built around a public university and is a whole different story. Both towns together are like 110,000 people. (*Consider* p. 132).

This passage is notable for its combination of hard geographical facts and figures with a chatty colloquial style, and a performance of vagueness and approximation ('its origins involve', 'a whole different story', 'like 110,000 people') that offsets the concrete detail it conveys, giving a sense of impatience with its own factual content. Here Wallace signals a distinct hesitancy about the inclusion of this raw spatial data in the conversational exchange that is suggested by the informal syntax and punctuation ('town's', 'that's'). As he honed in on the radically new space of the Edge City, Wallace had begun to suggest an ambiguous relationship between the materiality of this geography and the possibility of a human exchange enacted through the text. From *Broom*'s exploration of regional writing in a geographically decentred America to *Jest*'s problematised inheritance of the city novel tradition in post-Fordist Boston, geography had consistently provided a generative challenge rather than a straightforward basis for Wallace's writing. The Edge City, it seems, would be no different.

Indeed, this challenge is reflected in Wallace's approach to the description of Lake James in the post-2005 work on *Pale King*, and especially in those sections narrated by the new 'David Wallace' figure. It is evident, for example, in his introduction of footnotes as 'David' conveys the geographical data concentrated in §24. Printed at the bottom of the page (as they are in draft versions), these footnotes physically split the space of the text itself; and importantly, much of the detail on Lake James and Self-Storage Parkway relayed in this section is relegated to these footnotes, as 'David' worries over the reader's interest in 'the geographical minutiae of Peoria' – 'the possibility of which I have decided I can safely presume is remote' (*Pale King* p. 259 n. 3). The division of the text-space suggests a disjuncture between the material of place – pushed out to the textual periphery, much as the Edge City hovered at the margins of the old industrial city – and the narrative form of the novel. This strategy was part of Wallace's work on this section from an early stage: the placement of the footnote that describes Peoria as one of 'the two grimmest, most blighted and depressed old factory cities in Illinois' (p. 261) appears on a handwritten draft, where the marginal notes 'FN' (footnote) and 'FN cont[inued]', together with several arrows and lines, visualise a developing plan for the physical arrangement of the text. The result is that, as it reaches the material of the Edge City, the draft becomes distinctly messy and confusing – this landscape was producing complications in the compositional process that were embodied and extended in the formal strategy of the footnotes (HRC 38.8). Physically separating the details of place from the flow of 'David's' narrative, these footnotes are a textual instantiation of the late twentieth-century 'separation of man from landscape' of which the humanist geographer Edward Relph had complained.[17] They give formal expression to the sense that in the postindustrial Edge City, the 'geographical minutiae' of everyday American life had become disjoined from any established system of sociospatial meaning, and from any familiar sense of place.

This disjuncture reappears later in §24 as, alongside more details on Peoria's economic history, Wallace zooms in on the REC complex itself – although here the disconnection is less straightforward, as 'David' in fact provides a patiently and clearly expressed description:

> The IRS's Midwest Regional Examination Center is a roughly L shaped physical structure located off Self-Storage Parkway in the Lake James district of Peoria IL. What makes the facility's L shape only rough is that the REC's two perpendicular buildings are closely proximate but not continuous; they are, however, connected at the

second and third floors by elevated transoms that are enclosed in
olive-green fibreglass carbonate as a shield against inclement weather
. . . (*Pale King* p. 267)

Opening with a precise geographical placement, this passage presents
a distinct contrast to the alienating descriptions of A. Y. Rickey's
buildings in *Jest*, which I discussed in Chapter 2; here, a clarity of
syntax is matched by an obligingly explanatory tone ('what makes
the facility's L shape only rough is . . .'). A particular point of
divergence is the material of this space: where *Jest* emphasised the
obscure, alienating materiality of postmodern architecture, here we
have a much more quotidian and familiar 'olive-green fibreglass'.
This passage begins to render the space of the Edge City straightforwardly legible, incorporating this geography more seamlessly into
the language of the novel. And the passage also provides an apparent
connection, albeit somewhat banal, between postindustrial space and
American history: we hear that 'Neither heating nor air-conditioning
service was ever reliably achieved in these elevated tunnels, and in
summer months the Post's personnel refer to them as bataans, an
apparent reference to the Bataan Death March of World War II's
Pacific theatre' (p. 267). In turn, this larger frame of national history
is given a local grounding in a brief sketch of Peoria's own industrial origins: 'incorporated in 1845 and perhaps best known as the
birthplace of barbed wire in 1873' (p. 267). Here, despite the general
perception of the Edge City's radical historical novelty, 'David's'
narrative begins to suggest links between built form and historical
consciousness.

But both architecture and history are explicitly and jarringly
disconnected from 'David's' larger narrative when he introduces
this passage as 'a brief interpolation' containing 'some preliminary
general background that I have opted not to massage or smuggle in
through the sort of graceless dramatic contrivance so many stock
memoirs resort to', and ends it with 'end of interpolation; return
to mnemonic real time' (*Pale King* pp. 267, 268). As in its relega-
tion to footnotes elsewhere in the section, geographical detail is
disconnected from the procession of narrative events and the flow
'mnemonic real time'; presented as raw and unincorporated data
that stands apart from any 'dramatic contrivance' and that distracts
from, rather than anchors, the story that 'David' is telling. This is
a formal strategy appropriate to a landscape that was itself widely
seen as a kind of interpolation, an interruption to the historical flow
of geographical development, understanding and imagination – a

confirmation of Garreau's suggestion that 'Edge City's problem is history. It has none'.[18] Brian McHale has read §24 as 'an exercise in *cognitive mapping*' and 'a tour-de-force of *narrativized description*'; but Wallace's formal and textual approach in fact incorporates an opposite tendency, disjoining space from narrative.[19] Narratives of the Edge City are left to resemble Sylvanshine's CPA exam questions: 'little stories with all the human meat left out' (*Pale King* p. 12).

These formal strategies for disrupting the connections between geography, history and literary expression take up the problematisation of textual communication and its relationship with built space that began with the placement of the publishing industry in *Broom*'s Bombardini Building and continued through Rickey's buildings in *Jest*. In the early 1990s, the anthropologist Marc Augé, echoing the humanist discourse of place and placelessness, made a famous distinction between 'place' and 'non-place': 'If a place can be defined as relational, historical and concerned with identity, then a space which cannot be defined as . . . [such] will be a non-place'.[20] For Augé, 'non-places' are associated with the end of the twentieth century (a period he calls 'supermodernity'), and are characterised by a particular form of textuality:

> The link between individuals and their surroundings in the space of non-place is established through the mediation of words, or even texts . . . the real non-places of supermodernity – the ones we inhabit when we are driving down the motorway, wandering through the supermarket or sitting in an airport lounge . . . have the peculiarity that they are defined partly by the words and texts they offer us.[21]

Foregrounding the textuality of 'David's' geographical descriptions through the footnotes and the signposted 'interpolation' of the REC's form and history, §24 reproduces this textual overloading of space; text acts to divorce the postindustrial landscape from the ordinary practice and experiential texture of everyday life. If humanist geographers prized a generative interaction between geography and literary practice as a mechanism for producing a sense of place, the deeply problematised relationship between textuality and space that Augé associates with 'non-places' represents an opposite tendency: text does not create existential connections between people and place, but instead displaces these connections. Wallace's embedding of this denuded relationship between text and geography into the formal construction of §24 allowed him to fuse his new focus on the Edge City with an expansion of the concerns over literary composition and its relationship to space that had been developing in his earlier work on *Pale King*, extending these concerns into a more developed component of the novel's thematic structure as he reworked it after 2005.

As 'David' approaches the REC in §24, this alienating textuality becomes a feature of the space itself as well as the form of its description. Recalling Augé's analysis, this is a space characterised by an insistent textuality, from the parking lot's 'directional signs – ENTRANCE ONLY; EXIT ONLY' to the 'flags, coded signs, directional arrows' that adorn the main entrance (*Pale King* p. 278, 283). But, much as for Augé this textuality acts to disconnect people from their environments, these signs only serve to produce confusion: the entrance/exit signs are integral to the 'phenomenally bad planning' of the Center's parking system, described at comic length over five pages (pp. 278–83), while the flags and signs at the entrance only contribute to an overall 'complex and disorienting' effect (p. 283). This combination of hyper-abundant signification and overall incoherence continues in the interior of the building, 'a labyrinth of hallways, staircases, and fire doors with coded signs' (p. 291) – and again, 'David' attributes the confusion to the effect of the signs themselves: 'The array of directional signs at each hub was so detailed and complex that it seemed designed only to increase the confusion of anyone not already sure where they were going and why' (p. 297). And as these confusions proliferate, they mesh with 'David's' self-conscious comments on the limitations of his own efforts at textual expression: he admits that 'only a few' of these spatial details are 'relevant overall', resorts to a list of '[r]andom examples of recalled snippets', and then complains that 'the place was too overwhelming and complex and repetitive to describe one's first experience of in any detail' (pp. 290–1). The expression of spatial experience in narrative and descriptive forms self-consciously founders in the gap between excess textuality and genuine meaning.

As well as a new narrative centre for the novel, then, the Edge City came to form a new focus for the worries over the efficacy of literary form itself in relation to America's postindustrial geography that had been threaded through the earlier 'electric girl' and Sylvanshine drafts. Strikingly, alongside the introduction of the geographical footnotes, the handwritten draft of §24 also reprises the idea – earlier recorded on a draft of §1, as I have shown in Chapter 4 – of offsetting the text of the novel with a concurrent column of deadening clerical data. In the §24 draft, Wallace sketched this layout at the top of the page; and where the note on the §1 draft had suggested that the second column would include 'just [a] mind-bindingly dull catalogue of tax returns data' (HRC 39.3), in the §24 sketch the right-hand column reads: 'Here is the order of the largest cities of IL, excluding Chicago, in 1985:' (HRC 38.8) – detail that in the published text appears in a secondary footnote to a footnote, redoubling the awkward detachment of spatial detail from the procession of the text (*Pale King* p. 261 n. 5). Geography itself was now blending with the mass of clerical data against which the literary text was to be pitted.

This return to the status of the literary text in relation to the scene of clerical labour, linked as it is with the details of geographical space, suggests that the simultaneous introduction of Peoria's Edge City landscape and the 'David Wallace' character in 2005 was not coincidental. For Hering, the introduction of this character provided a conceit through which Wallace 'dramatized his attempted mastery of *The Pale King*'s prior baggy and disparate narrative', and 'the text . . . begins to formally model itself around the manner of its own composition'.[22] Indeed, §9 of the published text (also narrated by 'David') develops the anxiety over creative practice and its relationship to postindustrial work that had emerged around the question of place in the earlier drafts. This section traces a disarming subordination of the creative practice of literary composition to the demands of legal bureaucracy in particular, as 'David' insists that the text's claim to fictionality is in fact merely 'a legal device' whose 'whole and only purpose is to protect me, the book's publisher, and the publisher's assigned distributers from legal liability' (*Pale King* p. 70). Accordingly, 'features like shifting P.O.V.s, structural fragmentation, willed incongruities, &c' are to be understood as 'protective legal devices, not unlike the legal boilerplate that accompanies sweepstakes and civil contracts', and as such, they are 'not meant to be decoded or "read" so much as merely acquiesced to as part of the cost of our doing business together, so to speak, in today's commercial climate' (p. 75). As Henry Veggian puts it, this section 'depict[s] how the legal forces of postmodern literary markets have so thoroughly saturated the actual writing of books that even their aesthetic intentions are distorted by the legal arrangements that permit the production of their commodity form'.[23] The anxieties over literary practice and its relationship to conditions of labour in late twentieth-century America that had coloured the earlier work on the novel now extended into an explicitly self-reflexive commentary on the composition and form of *Pale King* itself, as they were shaped by the project's imbrication in this historical moment.

Perhaps the fullest expression of the connection between this anxiety and the form of postindustrial space is the REC's 'elaborate and obviously expensive facade' (*Pale King* p. 283), an absurd architectural invention that recalls A. Y. Rickey's strange facades in *Jest*. Appropriately, this facade is itself the result of a failure of textual communication: 'an uncaught typo in the enlarged construction and technology budget . . . mandating that Regional Service and Examination Centers' facades' "form specifications" rather than "form*al* specifications" be ". . . matched as closely as possible to the specific services the centers perform"' (pp. 282–3, original emphasis). The resulting edifice is composed of 'some kind of tile or mosaic representation of a blank IRS 1978 form 1040, both pages of it, complete in all detail' (p. 283); a piece of architectural humour that provides a neat focal point for the ambivalent relationship between text and postindustrial space that Wallace was working into the section. While the explicit pun is on architectural 'form' (in relation to 'function') and the tax 'form' as the archetypal bureaucratic text, hovering behind this surface is a suggestion of literary 'form' – the creative arrangement of language that is the stuff of fictional composition, but that seems to be subsumed into the sphere of legal bureaucracy as 'David' describes his own writing in §9. Extending the use of architecture as a vector for experimentation with the relationship between literary practice and material history that had appeared in both *Broom* and *Jest*, the REC's facade encapsulates the problematic combination of postindustrial bureaucracy, new economic geographies and literary creativity that had been developing over the course of the project.

The reconfiguration of *Pale King* in 2005, then, rested in part on the new spatial structure that Wallace constructed by developing Peoria from an unrealised destination into a more fully worked-out narrative location. But the introduction of the Edge City space of Lake James and the REC hardly provided a straightforward solution to the problems of language and place that had been shaping the project from the beginning; conversely, the simultaneous introduction of 'David Wallace' and Peoria itself into the novel allowed for a more complete expression and dramatisation of this problem, developing it into a major formal and compositional principle for the text. If the 2005 note expressed Wallace's need for a way out of the seemingly intractable compositional dilemmas that had brought the novel to a crisis point, the introduction of the spatial focus on the Edge City addressed this need not by resolving the searching questions that the earlier composition had raised, but by providing a framework through which these questions could be worked into the developing form of the text itself. Geography had never been a simple matter for Wallace, and if it was to be part of the solution for *Pale King*, it would not be one that could simply be imposed on the text from outside; instead, as the 2005 note had also suggested, it would have to become so through the work of composition and the construction of the text itself.

Postindustrial Hauntings: Space and the Return of History

Despite §9's explicit problematisation of literary practice, the suggestion that the labour of writing would ultimately allow for *Pale King*'s revival also appears to have been transposed from the 2005 note into this section of the text as 'David' himself refuses to disavow the traditional terms of literary creation. Instead, alongside his account of the bureaucratic pressures that apparently shape his text's composition, he points to 'the autobiographical fact that . . . I dreamt of becoming an "artist," i.e. somebody whose adult job was original and creative instead of tedious and dronelike' – and specifically, 'an immortally great fiction writer' (*Pale King* p. 75). To this he adds an insistence that his narrative 'has significant social and artistic value', and remarks that 'I wouldn't and couldn't have put three years' hard labor . . . into *The Pale King* if I were not convinced it was true' (p. 84). Though Adam Kelly is right to point out how *Pale King*'s 'thematization of its own status as a legal fiction and corporate commodity works against any simple embrace of . . . aesthetic autonomy', 'David's' defence of the artistic and social significance of his 'hard labor' suggests that the possibility of a literary practice valued in these terms is not to be entirely discounted.[24] Speaking with David Lipsky, Wallace had wondered 'what it means to be human and alive' in the 'fluorescent-lit rooms . . . [and] cubicles' of contemporary America – and declared that 'the trick for fiction . . . is gonna be to try to create a kind of texture and a language to show . . . that what's always been important is still important . . . in a world whose texture and sensuous feel is totally different'.[25] How, then, could the work of the text itself act to counter the profound disconnections between postindustrial geography, personal experience and historical consciousness that the Edge City had come to encapsulate?

Discernible signs of an effort to counter the disconnection between postindustrial space and historical meaning in fact stretch back

to Wallace's early work on the 'electric girl' drafts, where a brief
section (not included in the published text) describes Toni's friends
who 'coalesced along the park's recessed fence within sight of the
~~Caterpillar~~ Monsanto stacks off the envenomed river and the black
shell of the rug factory that abutted the IRS complex' (HRC 36.3).
The revision of 'Caterpillar' to 'Monsanto' is intriguing; Caterpillar
did have a major plant in Peoria, which went into decline and
halved its workforce between 1979 and 1986 – exactly the historical
moment with which the novel is concerned.[26] The reference suggests
that Wallace was already working with Peoria's real-world economic
history in mind, although its removal perhaps indicates a reluctance
to envelop the novel too tightly in the specifics of this historical geography. Nonetheless, the spatial adjacency of old and new industrial
space – the 'black shell' of the factory and the IRS complex – allows
for a tangible sense of historical continuity, drawing together these
different economic landscapes into a single vista. Describing the rise
of the Edge City as a new industrial space, Castells and Hall had contrasted the 'image of the nineteenth-century economy, familiar from
a hundred history textbooks: the coal mine and its neighbouring iron
foundry' with a corresponding spatial 'image for the new economy'
– one that was 'only just imprinting itself on our consciousness'.[27]
Even in the early stages of *Pale King*, though, Wallace was working
towards a way of stitching these images together into a single spatial
form through which the historical process that links them might
become legible. In the 'Evidence' notebook, indeed, Wallace played
with the idea that 'Reed Road' (an initial iteration of Self-Storage
Parkway) would be poised 'between airport and river – old & new'
(HRC 43.1). Elsewhere in the notebook, numerous notes record
snatches of an older industrial topography: 'plum-colored sunset
thru polluted city'; 'Edge of Peoria – huge German Expressionist
skyline of power plants, corn processing concerns, heavy equipment
manufacture' (HRC 43.1). While Brian Jarvis had reprimanded
Daniel Bell's forecast of the coming 'postindustrial society' for
eliding industrial capital's role in the creation of American landscapes, Wallace's early sketches of the REC's surroundings keep the
contours of this history visible; he kept in sight what Jarvis calls the
'evanescent factoryscapes of industrial capitalism'.[28]

This experimentation with the adjacency of old and new industrial spaces extended into Wallace's subsequent work on the novel
as he played with the idea of placing the REC within, rather than
simply next to, an older industrial space. In notes appended to
various drafts, Wallace worked through a range of possible former

uses for the building: an 'old department store' (HRC 40.7) or a
'defunct 50s shopping plaza' (HRC 40.3); an orphanage, school for
the blind, or soldiers' and sailors' home (HRC 36.2); a 'mansion
built by [a] millionaire' and perhaps the 'inventor of barbed wire',
linking with §24's report of Peoria's industrial history (HRC 38.8).
But he settled increasingly on the idea that the REC would be located
in a former manufacturing space (HRC 36.3, 40.3), and specifically
in a defunct mirror factory belonging to 'Mid West Mirror Works'
– the version of the building's history that appears in the published
text (*Pale King* p. 267). This idea was extended in Wallace's play
(in another note) with the idea of having the internal architecture of
the building marked by physical traces of its industrial past, an idea
he associated with Colin Harrison's thriller *Afterburn* (2000): 'REC
Center is former factory? . . . [Harrison's *Afterburn* – old factory
floor w/ signs of former machines.]' (HRC 36.3, square brackets
original). The development of the REC's history across these notes
shows Wallace attempting to connect this geographical centre with
the sociospatial legacy of the declining manufacturing economy,
simultaneously inscribing its architecture with old and new images
of industrial space. If the building's facade encapsulates a problematised textuality associated with the Edge City's disconnection from
established social and geographical meanings, these notes suggest the
possibility that a countervailing historical continuity could be built
into the physical fabric that underlies this surface.

This palimpsestic aspect of the REC space is linked to an intertextual connection developed in §24, when 'David' remarks that he had
imagined the complex 'ahead of time as a kind of ur-bureaucratic
version of Kafka's castle' (*Pale King* p. 263). Kafka's *The Castle*
(1926) takes place in a village setting that is poised between an agrar-
ian past and an advancing modernity – a historically interstitial space
whose central manifestation is the castle itself, which appears as a
kind of double-image of feudal empire and modern bureaucracy: 'It
was neither an old-style knight's castle, nor a modern palace, but an
extended complex consisting of a few two-storied but a great many
lower buildings set close together'.[29] This strange architectural form
is the spatial embodiment of Kafka's historically transitional narrative, caught up in the progression between the old Austro-Hungarian
empire and the new Republic of Czechoslovakia; a building that
simultaneously embodies the two poles of 'the experience of tradition' and 'the experience of the modern big city dweller' that Walter
Benjamin found counterposed in Kafka's work.[30] Severs has noted
that Wallace's 'creation of odd, often rhizomatic forms of architec-

ture' was 'inspired by his deep reading of Kafka'; and here this inspiration also allowed Wallace to borrow the notion of a transitional architectural form that was appropriate to the historical continuity he was trying to work into the texture of his novel's central space.[31] The space of the REC, then, is a focal point for the 'artistic project of updating Kafka's vision within late-capitalist America' that Lucas Thompson identifies in Wallace's work.[32]

The significance of this transitional architecture is also developed through the defunct company Wallace invented for his re-appropriated factory building. 'Mid West Mirror Works' connects the REC's space to the 'deeply ambivalent relationship . . . with the concept of visual reflection' that Hering explores across Wallace's work.[33] But notes in two different notebooks also suggest that Wallace intended this industrial past to be integrated into the space in a very literal way: 'mirrors on all the walls, but some covered over with cheesy 60s fake-wood panelling . . . some panelling falls off – so examiners now working in rooms with fragments of mirror on wall'; and elsewhere, 'inside filled with mirrored plate . . . but covered over with IRS fake-wood panelling. Some of the panelling falls off' (HRC 40.8, 41.6). The 'Butterfly' notebook also suggests a source for this idea, referring to 'User Illusion ch.12 – p. 320', with the note: 'mirrors start being produced in Renaissance, alongside idea of individual consciousness' (HRC 40.8). The reference is to Tor Nørretranders' *The User Illusion: Cutting Consciousness Down to Size* (1991, English translation 1998), two copies of which are included in Wallace's personal library at the Harry Ransom Center – Toon Staes has explored some aspects of Wallace's use of this source in the development of *Pale King*.[34] Specifically, though, page 320 of the book includes the passage:

> The use of mirrors became widespread during the Renaissance, the period imprinted with the rebirth of the individual – the beginning of the modern age. Looking at oneself in a mirror, seeing oneself from without, was a literal communication of self-awareness or *I*-awareness.[35]

Through the REC and its industrial history, Wallace adapted this historically specific account of the construction of consciousness, applying it to his own transitional time and space. Having the mirrors of Mid West Mirror Works exposed in this way would suggest the extent to which postindustrial life, and the workspaces that frame it, entail a historical reconfiguration of consciousness itself: the uncovering of the buried products of a manufacturing industry, which simultaneously unveils this history and makes the examiners visible to themselves, is the moment at which the selfhood of the postindustrial workers of the REC is reconstituted. Through revealed connections between old and new industry embedded in the architectural fabric of the REC itself, Wallace was playing with ways of reframing the relationships between consciousness, selfhood and postindustrial space that had been under question since the 'electric girl' drafts.

This historicisation of contemporary consciousness, and the uncovering of history literally beneath the surfaces of postindustrial space, indicate Wallace's project of reconstructing a lived sense of history in a landscape that appeared to be dislocated from historical narratives. Indeed, Wallace had been developing connections between the REC and a history of Peoria labour in notes that appear on drafts of various sections. One note reads: 'Fact: an IRS town is rather like a mining town or a town built around a fishery – the industry is extractive, blue-collar, heavily stratified, unpleasant' (HRC 39.6) Another, attached to a draft of §13 of the published text, suggests a more concrete plot-level connection: 'Mirrorworks and American Twine both shut down in early 80s; a fair number of examiners work at IRS because they're laid off from ATC or MMW and need the work' (HRC 36.3). And this idea of uncovering historically continuous legacies of labour in this space is also connected to the physical form of the REC building. Nick Levey notes the importance of the scene in §22 in which Chris Fogle recalls noticing the paintwork on the walls of his University of Illinois dorm in Chicago:

> their texture was mostly smooth, but if you really focused your attention there were also a lot of the little embodied strings and clots which painters tend to leave when they're paid by the job and not the hour . . . if you really look at something, you can almost always tell what type of wage structure the person who made it was on. (*Pale King* p. 184).

For Levey, this moment is crucial to the section's exploration of class and work in postindustrial America, effecting 'the unearthing of something like the repressed class content of the information age'.[36] And, in a similar reading of how Fogle's attention 'deliver[s] insight into his environment that links its physical materiality to the materialist structures of work', Liam Connell also directs attention to how this trace of constructive labour is built into the fabric of the architecture itself.[37] Indeed, this is not the only point at which spatial traces of blue-collar work appear in the novel. In §23, an unnamed narrator recalls their childhood school, in which 'each classroom . . . had flooring of white tile with insubstantial cloud-shapes of brown and gray that were discontinuous because whoever laid the tile didn't bother to match the patterns' (p. 257). Another example appears in §24: escorted through the REC's interior, 'David' notices that the floor 'reflected an endless series of shining parenthetical arcs where a custodian had swung his autowaxer from side to side in the empty hall at night' (p. 291), offering a trace of the lived experience of work that counters the general incoherence of the building (even if 'parenthetical' threatens to conflate this trace with the space's problematic textuality). At each of these points, lasting traces of blue-collar labour are momentarily glimpsed within the spatial environments of institutional settings. Building these details into different fragments of narrative space, Wallace's compositional process was engaged in a form of imaginative archaeology, uncovering the remains of older and enduring forms of work in the apparently ahistorical spaces of postindustrial life.

This endurance is most strikingly developed through the literal haunting of the REC building by the 'actual, non-hallucinatory' ghosts of Garrity and Blumquist (*Pale King* p. 317). For Connell, the presence of these ghosts reflects 'a trend in writing about office work in the US by entwining the idea of work with a prominent imagery of death'[38] – but it is also significant that these two ghosts represent two historically specific forms of work that relate to the novel's postindustrial setting. Blumquist, described by his supervisor as 'very focused and diligent . . . always absorbed in his work' (p. 30), is an earnest member of the postindustrial workforce; but his lonely and unnoticed death, 'sitting dead at his desk for four days before anyone asked if he was feeling all right' (p. 29), reflects the isolation and dissolution of social bonds associated with this sphere of labour, echoing Sylvanshine's existentially charged class consciousness. Garrity, on the other hand, 'is older . . . as in dating from an earlier historical period'. He is another trace, this time in human shape, of the building's industrial past: 'a line inspector for Mid West Mirror Works in the mid-twentieth century' (p. 317). His haunting is linked with the redundancy of skilled labour that accompanied the transition from manufacturing to service and information sectors, reprising the concern that had shaped Toni's backstory and manifested in her mother's employment history.

But the physical presence of Garrity's ghost suggests a tangible legacy that persists despite the fact of redundancy, and I read his spectral presence in line with the way in which literary hauntings offer a means to 'resist any finite end to the past, and instead encourage a new awareness of the role of the past in the present', as Katy Shaw suggests.[39] The function of Wallace's ghosts, similarly, is to make the historical consciousness to which the Edge City seems so inimical in §24 uncannily present in the text. Their collision with the novel's presiding quotidian focus – producing the paradoxical form of 'a realist novel teeming with ghosts' (as Clare Hayes-Brady puts it) – embodies the unexpected interruption of a visible socioeconomic history into this postindustrial space, as the traces of blue-collar labour are given a persistent human form.[40] More than the 'nostalgia' for 'the steady, routine-oriented worklife' of industrial capitalism that Jasper Bernes associates with *Pale King*, Wallace makes the industrial past unexpectedly present in the central space of his transitional Edge City, an attempt to bring about a re-orientation of the postindustrial landscape in relation to its history.[41] The effort to trace a continuity of human experience in the space of the REC, despite its apparent disconnection from historical and existential meaning, indicates Wallace's response to the need for a fictional form that could express a continued sense of human significance in the context of postindustrial America. Like the social relationships of the metropolis in *Jest*, this history was one that had to be forced into consciousness through the language of the novel – this time in supernatural form.

Relocating the Human in the Edge City

Could the reconnection of this space with the fabric of economic and social history, then, open onto a revival of the efficacy of the novel as an artistically and socially useful form – a return to the capacity for humanising intervention that Wallace's comments to Lipsky had suggested? Garrity himself seems an unpromising avenue; he is, in fact, a distinctly discomforting ghost. The story of his death is grotesque: tasked with examining mirrors for flaws, he 'sat on a stool next to a slow-moving belt and moved his upper body in a complex system of squares and butterfly shapes' until 'toward the end he evidently moved his body in the complex inspectorial system of squares and butterfly shapes even when he was off-duty' – and eventually 'hanged himself from a steam pipe in what is now the north hallway off the REC Annex's wriggle room' (*Pale King* pp. 317–18). There is a clear departure here from the industrial nostalgia that was associated with the Citgo sign in *Jest*.

Nonetheless, the emphasis on gesture in Garrity's haunting points to the notion that there is a set of spatial patterns and rhythms of work and life, healthy or not, that are associated with the declining manufacturing economy, and thus in the process of breaking down – but that are also given a form of persistence through Garrity's spectral presence. In his prophecy of postindustrial life, Daniel Bell pointed to the decline of the factory as an 'archetype' in the society and culture of the late twentieth century: in a manufacturing society 'the factory is archetypal because its rhythms, in subtle fashion, affect the general character of work', but in the emergent postindustrial society 'the distinctive archetype has gone . . . the rhythms are no longer that pervasive. The beat has been broken.'[42] And yet when Garrity reappears in §33, we recognise him (although he is not identified by the narrator) by the distinctive rhythm of his physical gestures: 'he kept moving his upper body around in a slight kind of shape or circle, and the movements left a little bit of a visual trail' (*Pale King* p. 384). His haunting makes present, in an unsettling form, the factory-based rhythms and patterns whose disappearance marked the postindustrial transition: a gestural trace of the redundant factory archetype.

For Henri Lefebvre, gestures like Garrity's play an important but ambiguous role in the production of space. According to Lefebvre, the 'gestures of labour – the gestures of peasants, craftsmen or industrial workers', whose 'chief *matériel* consists of *articulated* movements', are 'not simply performed in "physical" space' but 'themselves generate spaces' – so that 'social spaces are given rhythm by the gestures which are produced within them, and which produce them'.[43] In the mid-century Fordist organisation of industrial capitalism of which Lefebvre was writing, 'repetitious spaces are the outcome of repetitive gestures (those of the workers)' – the kind of dehumanising repetition unnervingly performed by Garrity's ghost.[44] And there is a crucial line of continuity between Garrity's gestures and the postindustrial labour of *Pale King* in §25 of the published text, in which multiple tax examiners repeatedly turn the pages of the returns in front of them: 'Chris Fogle turns a page. Howard Cardwell turns a page. Ken Wax turns a page . . .' (*Pale King* p. 312). This scene constructs a repetitive rhythm composed of short sentences that, for the most part, simply and repeatedly convey the bare fact of examiners' rote gestures; a formal patterning that mirrors Garrity's unnerving rhythmic motions, and serves to establish the room as a locus for Wallace's 'use [of] the novel's setting . . . to introduce a . . . kind of boredom produced by the rote, regimented, systematized postmodern world', as Ralph Clare puts it.[45] The mention of the room's 'Two clocks, two ghosts, one square acre of hidden mirror' (*Pale King* p. 314) is particularly significant: both the REC's buried industrial history and its haunting by Garrity's trace of manufacturing labour reach the explicit surface of the text precisely as its form begins to reproduce the deadening temporal rhythms of clerical work, of which the clocks are a reminder.

At the same time, the production of this repetitious space through the examiners' page-turning gestures – gestures shared by the reader of the literary text – seems to form yet another instance of the problematic relationship between textuality and postindustrial space. As Stephen Shapiro has noted, this section places the novel's reader uncomfortably close to the workers it describes: 'it is not simply the IRS agents steadily turning pages ... but we, the readers, as well, turning the pages of Wallace's non-narrative text in hopes of somehow finding perhaps interesting or narratively gripping details to read' – the act of reading itself is threatened with subsumption into the dehumanising gestural repetition of postindustrial work.[46] This is underscored in a draft of the section, in which Wallace inserted a more explicitly self-reflexive note among the repeated page-turning: 'The Pale King, by David Foster Wallace. "Irrelevant" Chris Fogle turns a page. All rights reserved. David Cusk turns a page'. (HRC 36.1). This naming of the novel itself amid the examiners' repetitive negotiations of bureaucratic texts indicates a clear link with the self-reflexive turn of the 'David Wallace' sections, connecting the production of a repetitious postindustrial space in this scene with the problematic compositional practice dramatised in §9.

It is notable, too, that this section represents Wallace's only eventual use of the idea of arranging the text in two columns, which began in the note to a draft of §1 and was reprised in relation to Peoria's geography in the handwritten draft of §24. Significantly, the double columns idea is also appended to a handwritten draft of another, unpublished examination room scene – possibly an earlier basis for §25 itself – where notes at the top of the draft's first page read: 'left column – narrative'; 'right column – numbing data they're reading' (HRC 40.7). Having begun as an idea associated with more general postindustrial landscapes in §1, and then with the specific geography of the Edge City in drafts of §24, the doubling of literary and bureaucratic texts was relocated to scenes focusing on REC workers in the act of reading within an interior room. In his draft copy of Curtis White's *Middle Mind* (whose connection with Wallace's project I have suggested in Chapter 4), Wallace underlined a passage in which White valorises 'the self-consciousness that reading provides', arguing that 'being able to read is a large part of what it means to be human as opposed to being a mere social function'.[47] Bringing reading into the sphere of repetitious work and its history, §25 seems to dramatise a crisis in this generative capacity of textual communication: here, in fact, it is reading itself that reduces the 'human' to a 'mere social function'. As Sylvanshine's landscape-envisioning technique overlaid place-writing with labour management, this section uses the physical gestures of reading to draw attention to literature as a practice that uncomfortably shares the same postindustrial space as these dehumanised clerks.

But gesture, as Lefebvre also insists, is an unpredictable space-making force: 'the linking of gestures corresponds to the articulation and linking of well-defined spatial segments, which repeat, but whose repetition also gives rise to novelty'.[48] Gesture can produce unexpected ruptures in industrial and postindustrial routines, disrupting the production of repetitive spaces. And in §25, the repetitive page-turning of the examiners is increasingly interspersed with more idiosyncratic and individuating gestures:

> Lane Dean Jr. rounds his lips and breathes deeply in and out like that and bends to a new file. Ken Wax turns a page. Anand Singh closes and opens his dominant hand several times while studying a muscle in his wrist. Sandra Pounder straightens slightly and swings her head in a neck-stretching arc . . . (*Pale King* p. 314).

These more personal gestures serve to reinscribe moments of individuality that emerge from the repetitive texture of the work itself; Andrew Bennett suggests that 'both comedy and suspense are in fact generated by the intricate attention to the dull, monotonous, repetitive act of turning pages and the possibility of its intricate variety'.[49] The gestures and rhythms of work, forming a line of continuity from the factory archetype to the postindustrial office, allow for glimpses of human presence even as they inscribe deadening and inhuman routines into the fabric of the text. And insofar as these gestures are also those of the physical act of reading, they suggest a symbiosis of textual practice and historical consciousness that starts to open onto the possibility of a space reinvested with human significance.

These glimpses are a stronger presence in earlier versions of the scene. In a longer typed draft, a deadening attention to the abstract geometric attributes of the room is followed directly by a note on the sense of embedded history that Wallace was working through the REC: 'The Pod's dimensions are 88 feet by 37 feet, a former dorm.

[History of IRS bldg.: former orphanage, then Joliet School for the Blind?? – ORPHANAGE, or SOLDIER'S AND SAILOR'S HOME.]' (HRC 36.2, square brackets original). It is interesting that Wallace wavered on the industrial lineage he was devising for the REC at this point, apparently favouring a previous use that would impart a more overtly humanistic purpose to the building's past – but still, the linking of the room's raw data with this historical note points once again to Wallace's effort to invest the material of postindustrial space with a felt sense of history. And in this draft, the trace of the building's history is also joined by glimpses of domestic and familial space that unfold between the repetitious page-turning gestures:

> Robbie van Note turns a page. Frank Brown turns a page. . . . Your own little world at 2am when everyone else is asleep. What you see behind closed eyes. Memories of your father's lap, his smell and shirt's textures. Your kitchen tile, the light in the alcove where they keep the home's phone. The feel of a rotary dial. (HRC 36.2).

Here, a focus on sensory experience and memory punctures the otherwise prevailing sense of bland facticity and deadening repetition, giving further weight to the hint of intimate lived experience that the detail provides. Wallace omitted this detail in a terser version of the scene that appears to form the basis of the published version, but the development of this section was clearly shaped by an effort to reinvest the interior of the REC with a tangible and meaningful human presence – one that emerges unexpectedly out of the repeated gestures that link these workers with a longer history of labour and its patterns and rhythms.

And, as Lefebvre suggests, the combination of a repetitious gestural regime with an element of lived experience can have profoundly transformative effects on space: 'when a gestural space comes into conjunction with a conception of the world possessed of its own symbolic system, a grand creation may result'; Lefebvre's example is that of the cloister, in which 'a gestural space has succeeded in mooring . . . a space of contemplation and theological abstraction . . . to the earth, thus allowing it to express itself symbolically and to become part of a practice'.[50] And indeed, in the longer draft of §25 Wallace included hints of the theological and metaphysical alongside the domestic and familial tenor of other details: 'Because they help break you and make you cry out to God in your brokenness and desolation' (HRC 36.2). Though minimised in the briefer published version, these glimpses persist: 'devils are actually angels . . . every love story is a ghost story' (*Pale King* p. 314). Even as the physical gestures of reading are made to seem uncomfortably like those of meaningless postindustrial labour, these moments point to a return – by way of the history of work that the scene invokes through its connection with Garrity's ghost – to the 'symbolic system' (to borrow Lefebvre's words) of the novel form, and its capacity to connect the quotidian with larger spheres of meaning. As they do so, they provide points at which the gestural production of postindustrial space pivots to become an engendering of lived, human place.

Illuminating the historical connectedness of the old factory archetype and the new postindustrial conditions of work, the co-existence of Garrity's ghost and the page-turning examiners of §25 within *Pale King*'s central space serves to draw Wallace's postindustrial landscape into a longer industrial history that is also a nexus of human stories. Uncovering spectres and traces of a longer history of work and life within the REC's space, *Pale King*'s post-2005 composition was driven by a project of reconnecting the postindustrial landscape of the Edge City with the economic and human histories from which it seemed to have come unmoored; a process that in turn opens this postindustrial landscape to a revived version of the humanising work of the novel. This again illustrates the importance of placing Wallace's project in relation to the development of the discourse of the 'postindustrial' around the turn of the century, which I suggested in Chapter 4: as the ahistorical utopianism of the early prophets of postindustrial society gave way to an increased awareness of the loss of the 'factory archetype', Wallace was using the construction of his novel to connect this historical understanding with the landscapes of postindustrial life. After the Midwestern myths satirised in *Broom*'s G.O.D. and the postmetropolitan nostalgia of *Jest*'s Citgo sign, *Pale King* represents a search for a new way of looking back. In his draft copy of White's *Middle Mind*, Wallace underlined the sentence: 'I am interested in the imagination as a social force that allows for critique and reinvention.'[51] Wallace's new-found historicism was the tactic that enabled him to reframe his own imaginative work as such a 'social force', linking the process of his novel with a rediscovery of the possibilities of place.

Limits: Gender and Race in *The Pale King*'s Spaces

How far could this strategy go? Where *Jest*'s reconstruction of shared metropolitan identity had found limits at the questions of race and gender, especially when combined in the figure of Ruth van

Cleve, could Wallace's strategy for a revived humanistic construction of place in *Pale King* allow for a wider reach? As I have shown in the previous chapter, Wallace's work on the 'electric girl' and Sylvanshine sections had already introduced a gendered differentiation to the novel's view of postindustrial work, with Sylvanshine's class anxieties afforded a direct expression and existential tenor less evident in the treatment of Toni and her mother. And, as the lineage of industrial and postindustrial forms of work became a focus for the novel's reconstitution of historical consciousness and human meaning, this gendered dynamic continued to run through Wallace's composition. For one thing, both of the ghosts who serve to establish a tangible presence of different forms of labour within the space of the REC are male, much as the field of reference that frames Sylvanshine's class angst is distinctly masculine. If historical legacies of work are so central to Wallace's reconfiguration of literary practice in relation to postindustrial geography, what are the implications of this gendering of labour for *Pale King*'s humanistic project?

The continuation of the gendered aspect of work into Wallace's post-2005 composition is particularly evident in the long section narrated by Chris Fogle (§22), which – as Hering has established – also belongs to this late period of work on the novel.[52] While not focused on the Edge City but rather on the older metropolitan geography of 'the Chicagoland area in the 1970s' (*Pale King* p. 158), this section plays a key role in developing the novel's engagement with American histories and ideas of work through its narrative of Fogle's transformation from 'the worst kind of nihilist' (p. 156) into a model IRS examiner. And this transformation is notably organised around Fogle's relationships with two older men: first his father, then the 'substitute Jesuit' teacher whose 'Advanced Tax' class Fogle accidentally attends (pp. 226–35). If Garrity's ghostly (male) presence in the REC is what makes visible the historic connections between forms of labour, this section of the novel frames the idea of meaningful work as an explicitly patrilinear inheritance.

At the same time, §22 also plays with the construction of narratively and existentially meaningful spaces in ways that complement the key scene in §25 – and that are tied in with the gendered lineage of labour and its ideals that §22 delineates. Fogle's relationship with his father culminates in the latter's death in a subway accident, described at length (*Pale King* pp. 199–205); a choice of setting that recalls the role of the subway space in *Jest*'s effort to instantiate a moment of empathy through the form of the text via Poor Tony's seizure. And here – as Severs describes it – 'to move Fogle toward the transformative ritualism of the REC, Wallace creates a mythical space in the Chicago subway system'; a space invested with strong narrative and symbolic meaning, forming a clear contrast to the excess of geographical data and the failed textual communication that characterise Lake James and the REC in §24.[53] At the same time, Fogle's relationship with his father, and its climax in this acutely significant space, are linked with a notion of character-forming labour: 'I feel quite sad at the thought that he's not around to see the career path I've chosen, and the changes in me as a person as a result' (p. 190). The production of symbolically meaningful space is tied to a father-son relationship that in turn plays a prominent role in the novel's expression of a mythology of work.

The encounter with the Jesuit teacher, meanwhile, is placed in a setting that explicitly echoes the descriptions of the REC that Wallace was composing in §24: 'DePaul's Lincoln Park campus had two newer buildings that . . . were literally almost mirror images of one another, by architectural design, and were connected . . . by an overhead transom not unlike our own at the Midwest REC' (*Pale King* p. 191). The notion of a 'mirrored' architectural form brings to mind Wallace's play with the REC and 'Mid West Mirror Works', and the idea he was developing for a relationship between this company's buried material legacy and the formation of the REC workers' reconfigured postindustrial consciousness. Here, significantly, it is the confusion arising from this mirrored form that leads to Fogle's accidental attendance at the tax class, where he recalls that 'nearly everyone in the room was male' (p. 219) – and it is within this heavily gendered space that he absorbs the Jesuit teacher's spiel about the heroism of work: 'True heroism is you, alone, in a designated work space . . . minutes, hours, weeks, year upon year of the precise, judicious experience of probity and care' (p. 232). The transformative effect of this speech is registered in Fogle's changed perception of the space itself: 'I was aware of how every detail in the classroom appeared very vivid and distinct, as though painstakingly drawn and shaded' (*Pale King* pp. 228, 232). The unexpected charging of quotidian space with a suggestion of intense significance – a clear echo of the REC examination room in §25 – is closely connected with the avowedly masculine valorisation of labour as a 'heroic' pursuit.

As if to underscore the connection with work as a patrilinear inheritance, a marginal note on a typed draft of the tax class scene suggests that Fogle 'gets over dad's death' at this point, the Jesuit teacher providing a substitute patriarch in a connection that also links this scene with the symbolically charged space of the subway

(HRC 38.6). Strikingly, moreover, the text of this draft itself is also interrupted in mid-flow by a bracketed note containing some of Wallace's ideas for the history of the REC building, with further marginal annotations setting out the 'Mid West Mirror Works' idea, including a visual sketch for the company's logo to appear 'on iron filigree over front gate' (HRC 38.6). The appearance of these notes here seems incongruous at first glance, but their placement suggests that the project of reconnecting the REC's space with a history of industrial work and life was also linked to the construction of this explicitly male-dominated setting for the articulation of an ideal of meaningful labour.

The gendering of the ideal of work in §22 is heightened further through the contrasting narrative of Fogle's mother, whose discovery of feminism leads her to divorce his father and begin a relationship with another woman. In contrast to the heroism that colours the masculine notion of work, Fogle's attitude to his mother's embrace of feminism and lesbianism is distinctly dismissive: 'she liked to believe that the feminist consciousness-raising and Joyce ... were the result of thinking, like a conscious change of life philosophy. But it was really emotional. She had a sort of nervous breakdown in 1971' (*Pale King* p. 194). A typically misogynistic pathologisation of feminism and female sexual autonomy, Fogle's judgement is carried through into the spatial dimensions of the section when he recounts the mother's move back to his father's house, where she becomes 'a virtual shut-in ... the first psychological symptom I can remember involving her growing preoccupation with the welfare of the birds in a nest ... over one of the joints on the large, open wooden porch' (p. 209). Fogle's voice is not to be simply conflated with Wallace's – but in contrast to the charged spaces associated with the heroic male discourse of labour, it is striking that Fogle's mother is confined to yet another gendered image of neurotic domestic enclosure that recalls Avril Incandenza and Joelle van Dyne in *Jest*, and Toni's grandmother and the 'hubcap house' in *Pale King*. The gendered distinction that had begun to emerge in the contrast between Sylvanshine's articulated class angst and Toni's mother's silence continued to crystallise in Wallace's post-2005 work: while male labour and its associated spaces are rich with significance, spaces associated with femininity are neurotic and dysfunctional.

This raises the question of how the specific geographical experiences of women in postindustrial America, to which the 'electric girl' drafts had attended sympathetically, might be incorporated into the revival of human meaning and significance that Wallace was developing within the spaces of the REC. In fact, Wallace returned to Toni's story in February 2007, drafting the section that describes the truck crash which kills Toni's mother (§45) – an attempt to construct a bridge between the earliest phase of composition and the Edge City-focused structure he had introduced in 2005. But the terms on which this connection was premised are revealing: a typed draft of this section is headed '**ELECTRIC GIRL REDUX** ROUGH STORY OF HOW TONI WARE (who's from the Peoria exurb of Anthony, hence Toni) came to be such a good immersive [tax examiner]' (HRC 37.1, original boldface). Toni's history and her complex relationship to place, which had posed such a rich formal problem for development of the earlier drafts, were apparently relevant to the novel's post-2005 organisation primarily insofar as they could explain her incorporation into the sphere of clerical work whose mythology – through §22 in particular – is heavily coded as masculine. In order to bring her into the transcendent fold of the REC's space and into the revived humanistic project of the novel, the specific spatial experience of being a working-class woman in postindustrial America needed to be subsumed into a narrative of labour and its history that is marked as distinctively, if not exclusively, male. Her mother's experience of gendered geographical precarity, it would seem, lay beyond the redemptive horizons of the project as Wallace had reconfigured after 2005.

If gender poses a problem for Wallace's humanistic revival of place in *Pale King*, race too raises some questions. Wallace's critics have noted what Jorge Araya calls 'the overwhelming whiteness of *The Pale King*', resulting from the lack of prominent characters of colour in the drafted material; Araya points out that 'this lack of racial diversity is especially striking in a novel that ... concerns itself with politics and citizenship in modern US society'.[54] In fact, Wallace's early work on the novel does seem to have included some tentative ideas for the inclusion of race as a factor in its narrative and geographical construction. One note in the 'Evidence' notebook, for example, refers to 'Black part of town – "Ruddytown"' (HRC 43.1), while notes that appear on the 'electric girl' drafts include 'Gorgeous black girl w/ big gap between her teeth' and 'Black Girls v. Scrunchy Girls' (HRC 36.3); a racial dimension to this working-class postindustrial landscape seems to have been an idea with which Wallace was toying at an early stage. Intriguingly, moreover, Jurrit Daalder has shown through archival research that drafts of Wallace's portrait of Bloomington in 'View' included descriptions of the city's predominantly African American district, and a discussion of the racial politics inscribed in its topography – but the exclusion of these sections from the final version of the essay amounts to 'a conscious decision to "read" any racial and socioeconomic differences out of his . . . account of Bloomington', as Daalder puts it.[55] Evidently, Wallace did have an interest in the racial construction of late twentieth-century geography; but the incorporation of this interest in the material that he actually produced was a hesitant and unfinished process, hovering at the margins of his writing without finding a firm foothold.

One small trace of a specifically racial aspect to the geography of Peoria that does appear in the published text comes in §6, in which Lane Dean and his girlfriend discuss the prospect of an abortion by the side of Lake James: here, Dean briefly notices the opposite side of the lake, 'where little forms on camp chairs sat there in a row in a way that meant they had lines in the water for crappie, which mostly only your blacks from the East Side ever did' (*Pale King* p. 43). Araya has noted the importance of spatial distance here, with the positioning of the figures on the lake's opposite side producing a sense that 'racial difference is associated with physical and psychological distance'[56] – and this coincides with a more implicit geographical distancing of the 'East Side', which (like the racialised Brighton Projects in *Jest*) is situated firmly on the outer edge of the novel's spatial range of view; the eastern part of Peoria, indeed, is a blank space in Wallace's folder diagram of his version of the city (HRC 39.4). This distancing of the African American district from the Edge City is not without historical grounding. As Robert D. Bullard has established, the emergence of a new economic geography had profound implications for the experience of African Americans, compounding the deep-rooted spatial segregation of the labour market on racial lines: 'As jobs have migrated out of the central city into suburban and edge-city locations, it has been increasingly difficult for African Americans to get to work', a factor contributing to a 'Metropolitan apartheid . . . exhibited in . . . the spatial location of jobs, and the extent to which jobs and economic activity centers are accessible to urban blacks'.[57] And when Lipsky remarked on the absence of African Americans in Bloomington in 1996, Wallace's response suggests an awareness of this new form of segregation: he noted that 'They all live on the west side of town, next to the Purina plant, in housing projects', and expanded by remarking that 'the racism here is very quiet, very systematic'.[58] Wallace was apparently aware of how America's postindustrial geography had heightened the racial divisions inscribed in American space.

There are, however, more troubling aspects to the way in which the mention of the 'East Side' in §6 is relayed. Where 'David's' descriptions of Lake James express a deep and formally generative anxiety about the incorporation of geographical fact into narrative form, this African American district registers as a distinctly unproblematic detail: the sentence in which it appears mixes a performance of authoritative knowledge ('in a way that meant') with vernacular construction ('mostly only') to suggest both certainty and familiarity. In contrast to the challenging novelty of the postindustrial Edge City, African American space is taken as read, registering as established and given fact. The racial reference first appears in a handwritten draft, where it forms a superscript addition: 'which only black people from the poor part of town ever did' (HRC 39.1). The changes between this and the published version are small but revealing. The move from 'black people' to 'your blacks', as it strengthens the scene's focalisation through Dean, couches the moment in racial language more reminiscent of the 1980s – seeming to draw the factor of race into the historicising project of the novel. At the same time, though, 'the poor part of town' becomes 'the East Side', effacing the contingent economic aspect of racially segregated geography and instead invoking the permanence and objectivity of the compass. If the haunting of the REC serves to reinvest postindustrial space with a felt sense of history, here the tendency is opposite: racial divisions resolve into a permanent and naturalised, rather than historically conditioned, aspect of American geography. The African American district thus registers as an ahistorical space in a very different sense to that of the radically novel Edge City: one invested with permanence and stability, readily knowable to Dean as he stands in the role of detached white observer. At the same time, the blandly empirical naming of the 'East Side' suggests none of the rich symbolic and associative toponymic possibilities with which Wallace played elsewhere in the development of the novel, from 'Whispering Pines' to 'Angler's Cove' to 'Sicklied Ore'. The space associated with African American communities seems unable to transcend its sheer facticity, situated beyond the reach of the symbolic action of language – and, by extension, of the place-making possibilities of novelistic form and practice that Wallace sought to revive through the composition of *Pale King*.

As the Brighton Projects had stood outside the emerging image of the city in *Jest*, racialised space in *Pale King* is positioned as a marginal presence that seems to exceed the novel's strategies for rehumanising the postindustrial landscape. Thus, rather than merely describing the racial segregation of postindustrial geography, the novel risks reproducing these divisions in the form of a limit to its own horizons of humanistic intervention. As the geographer Richard H. Schein has argued, even where we might 'honestly deny a racist intent in our daily activities . . . the very structures of the world that we live in can make us unconsciously complicit in perpetuating processes of racialization through our interaction with and through the landscape'.[59] Wallace's efforts to address both race and gender in *Pale King* may have been rooted in a sympathetic awareness of the positions of women and people of colour in the new postindustrial economy, but in organising his revived literary humanism around a connection of novelistic form and practice with a historical legacy of work that is explicitly coded as male, and placing this reconciliation in a space whose transcendent possibilities do not extend to geographies of African American workers and communities, his unfinished text was at risk of inheriting and reproducing the gendered and racialised fault lines of late twentieth-century American geography.

These questions of race and gender converge in the distinctly uncomfortable presentation of Chahla Neti-Neti, or 'The Iranian Crisis' – the 'visibly ethnic' Iranian refugee and IRS worker (*Pale King* p. 287) whose appearance in §24 has been identified as one of the most politically problematic moments in Wallace's body of work: Lucas Thompson calls it 'a deeply offensive portrayal . . . particularly misguided in a post-9/11 climate'.[60] That Neti-Neti functions as a figure for a combination of racial and sexual otherness is indicated in 'David's' ruminations on her supposed promiscuity: 'she seemed to emerge from a different wiggler's housing unit every morning during the month of August 1985', he relates (p. 296). Thompson notes that this presentation 'brazenly perpetuates various Orientalist tropes' that link race with a conception of female sexuality, and the connection between the racial and gendered aspects of the character is even more evident in a draft in which her name is given as 'Ms. Vajna' – a name whose echo of 'vagina' performs a distinctly crude conjunction of sexual othering and racial difference (HRC 36.3).[61] This is a figure that troublingly recalls Ruth van Cleve, whose presence as a sexually and racially othered figure at the margins of *Jest*'s community of urban walkers marked the limits to Wallace's strategy for reconstructing the sociospatial environment of the metropolis.

At the same time, in *Pale King* this combination of sexualisation and racialisation forms a point of contact with a larger geopolitical framing of the historical moment with which the novel is concerned, as 'David' reports that Neti-Neti's 'off-duty eccentricities' had 'origins in the Iranian upheavals of the late 1970s' (*Pale King* p. 296), and later clarifies that 'like many other nubile younger Iranian women' she 'had to basically "trade" or "barter" sexual activities with high-level functionaries in order to get herself . . . out of Iran during the tense period when the displacement of the Shah's regime was becoming . . . certain' (p. 310 n. 67). The Iranian Revolution of 1979 came at the end of a decade in which American influence in the Middle East – and access to its oil reserves – had been a major focus of US foreign policy, in part because of the influence of the Organization of Petroleum Exporting Countries (OPEC) on domestic energy supplies; the context that had been obliquely signalled in *Broom*'s Great Ohio Desert. The Revolution itself represented a significant loss of influence in the region – with the result that, at home, 'the inflationary spiral began to spin out of control', according to James Patterson.[62] In the figure of Neti-Neti, then, the combination of gendered and racial difference becomes a conduit through which the global context of America's economic upheavals enters the text – working, perhaps, against §24's disjuncture between the Edge City and historical consciousness, and aligning with the tangible presence of history that Garrity's gestures impart to the building's interior.

And yet Neti-Neti's presence in the REC itself hardly improves the legibility of the space. Instead, in §24 she plays the role of leading 'David' into the building's baffling interior, intensifying the disorientation that characterises this section (much as van Cleve's movement inaugurated the turn to spatial dissolution in *Jest*'s 'Inman' chapter); 'David' summarises his experience as 'my . . . dazed scurrying around with the Iranian Crisis' (*Pale King* p. 298), and we hear that at one point 'she herself apparently got confused or distracted', leading to a brief glimpse of an examinations room and its 'sensuous and incongruous silence' (pp. 291, 292). Just as her name suggests entanglement, Neti-Neti becomes closely associated with the labyrinthine confusion of the REC and, by implication, with the wider challenge to geographical understanding that the Edge City represents. As with van Cleve, the trope of the 'ungeographic' woman of colour – her presence and lived experience framed as incompatible with spatial knowledge – is again at work in this novel. Indeed, the echoes of van Cleve continue as we hear that Neti-Neti 'chattered along almost the whole length of the [REC's] facade' and then 'continued talking during much of the circuitous trip to Personnel' (pp. 290, 296) – but nothing of the content of her speech is reported, with 'David' instead admitting that 'most of what she said is no longer available to memory' (p. 296). Like that of van Cleve, Neti-Neti's speech itself apparently exceeds the range of the text – a factor that is linked with the self-conscious failure of textual communication dramatised in this section when 'David' laments that 'Some of what she was saying was probably helpful and apposite REC information' that 'would probably be useful and concise, memoir-wise' (p. 296).

Where van Cleve's movement through Boston's streets was associated with a collapse of topographical coherence and a limit to the shared image of the city, here another woman of colour is again framed as a presence that apparently unsettles the effort to give meaningful shape to postindustrial space. How, then, could this portrait of gendered and racialised difference fit with the recovery of a sense of place that *Pale King* was attempting? It is of course important to remember that the text is unfinished; but a rather disheartening suggestion of an answer arises when §24 ends with Neti-Neti fellating 'David' in a closet within the REC – what Araya calls 'one of the most uncomfortable moments in the novel'.[63] Here, we are presented with a debased version of the repetitive gestures that are so central to the engendering of surprisingly humanised space in §25 (which follows immediately from this moment in Pietsch's arrangement of the published text): 'the Iranian Crisis's forehead impacted my abdomen twelve times in rapid succession and then withdrew to a receptive distance that seemed, in that charged instant, much farther away than it really could have been' (*Pale King* p. 311). If this instant is 'charged', it is with something very different from the glimpses of transcendent significance that punctuate the page-turning of the examiners in §25. Rather than impart a humanistic sense of meaning to the REC's space, the repeated gestures associated with this figure of racial and gendered otherness only confirm her troublingly degraded and sexualised status. She thus comes to signify an apparent limit not only to spatial expression in the form of *Pale King*, but also to Wallace's approach to reinscribing human value and meaning into postindustrial space by means of this form. In both *Jest* and *Pale King*, Wallace's attempts to represent women of colour, inflected as they are with larger discourses of race, gender and space, threaten to collapse his strategies for realigning literary practice with the social landscape that emerged from America's post-Fordist transition.

Conclusion

What is Peoria for? The question remains open in the material
Wallace drafted, and may well have remained so had he finished the
novel; but it was *Pale King*'s uncovering of a history of work and
life connecting the experiences of the postindustrial present with
those of the industrial past that served to re-situate the novel itself as
a form through which the question might at least be posed. Across
this text's long and fraught compositional process, Wallace had laid
out core thematic problems of postindustrial place: transience and
precarity in Toni's backstory, class anxiety in Sylvanshine's arrival,
and disconnection from narrative and history in 'David's' depiction
of Lake James and the REC. These themes posed a challenge to the
interventionist philosophy of fiction that Boston's social encounters had engendered in *Jest*, questioning the constructive social
possibilities of the novel in a period when acts of the imagination
were increasingly subsumed by corporate ideology, and geographical experience seemed to have become disjoined from established
systems of meaning and value. But Wallace had not abandoned the
idea that his novels could play a useful role in the production of
human space: on the contrary, he made the REC itself central to his
project of rediscovering the contours of the human in the conditions
of postindustrial work and life. If Wallace's work on *Pale King* was
shaped by a concern with how the language and practice of the novel
are situated in relation to the altered geography of work at the turn
of the millennium, his effort to re-humanise the resulting landscapes
was inseparable from the effort to reconstitute 'postindustrial' as a
historical rather than a utopian marker. Finding a new role for the
novel in the inhabiting of American geographies, and in the production of a more human kind of space, required configuring it as a
means of imparting a tangible shape to a history of economic and
social change, and making felt the ways in which the postindustrial
present is haunted by the industrial past. Deploying 'postindustrial'
as a keyword for the reading of *Pale King* thus helps clarify the intimate connection between fiction as a form of history-telling and the
novel as a practice of place.

As tempting as it might be to see *Pale King* as a final culmination
of Wallace's deep interest in the interface between geography and
literary practice, the manner of his death and its abrupt curtailing
of his career ought to preclude such a conclusion. Nevertheless, this
project did extend and develop a central concern with geography,

and its connection to economic and social change, that had also shaped both his previous novels. From the 1980s to the 2000s, these texts gave particularly nuanced form to the structures of feeling that were associated with this material change: from the altered forms of regionalisation with which *Broom* was engaged, to the pressures on metropolitan space and identity that found expression in *Jest*'s Boston, to the problem of place in the postindustrial geography of *Pale King*, his texts provide particularly rich examples of the inter-connection of textual form, novelistic practice, and geographical space at the end of the twentieth century and the beginning of the twenty-first. The lens of historical geography brings into view how, in the wake of America's transition to a new economy of flexible accumulation that had begun in the 1970s, Wallace's writing formed an effort to reconnect literary practice both with concrete social reality and with the narratives and processes of history.

And geography also helps clarify the limitations inherent to this project, as it intersected with the discourses and ideologies of race, gender and space that were enmeshed with the changing structures of late twentieth-century capitalism. Both *Jest*'s attempts to reconstitute the metropolis as a lived social environment and *Pale King*'s effort to reconstruct a human sense of place in the Edge City encounter such troubling limitations – conspicuous difficulties in extending to the experiences of women and people of colour in America's post-Fordist landscapes – which, insofar as they are bound up with the ideologi-cal structures that shape the American geographical imagination, must be understood as part of the connection between Wallace's writing and the economic and social histories to which it attempts to give shape by way of space. To confront these difficulties is not merely to put Wallace himself in the dock, but neither does connect-ing them with their larger material and ideological contexts mean explaining away their problematic effects. Rather, these aspects of the novels demonstrate how, as Wallace's practice connected with the prevailing spatial structures of feeling that surrounded America's transitional geographies, they both inherited and reproduced exclu-sionary discourses in ways that trouble the formal and compositional strategies through which they respond to their historical moment. Like all cultural forms, Wallace's texts have their role in the produc-tion of space; a role inseparable from the wider social, political and economic forces that shape human geography.

All novelists are also geographers: their texts describe spaces and explore how these spaces are inhabited, and in doing so they produce geographies of their own. Wallace, though, was a novelist for whom geography formed an especially subtle and generative aspect of his fiction; both in terms of the complexities of narrative and descriptive form, and in terms of the role space played in shaping the compositional process of his texts. Through each of his novels, we can see a developing and dynamic intersection between historical geography, literary practice and textual expression. Embedded in geographies of economic and social transition and the shifting sociospatial forms they produced, his texts show us how the form and practice of the novel could be realigned with its social contexts, reforging an imaginative and affective connection with material conditions in a period of profound socioeconomic change – and they show us how this realignment could be tied up with entrenched ideological assumptions about the nature of geographical knowledge, the politics of urban space, and the mythology of work and its meanings. Both the possibilities and the limitations of Wallace's novels are revealed through his career-long attention to deep geographical questions – an attention that engendered a dynamic interface between spatial history and literary practice, and that opened his writing fully onto its historical moment.

Notes

1. Hering, *Fiction and Form*, p. 124.
2. Ibid. pp. 135–40.
3. The map is held in the Harry Ransom Center archive (HRC 41.8) but is too badly damaged to be consulted.
4. Robert Fishman, *Bourgeois Utopias: The Rise and Fall of Suburbia* (New York: Basic Books, 1987), p. 184.
5. Joel Garreau, *Edge City: Life on a New Frontier* (New York: Doubleday, 1991), p. 4.
6. Peter O. Muller, 'The Suburban Transformation of the Globalizing American City', *Annals of the American Academy of Political and Social Science*, 551 (May 1997), pp. 44–58 (p. 45).
7. Manuel Castells and Peter Hall, *Technopoles of the World: The Making of Twenty-First-Century Industrial Complexes* (London: Routledge, 1994), pp. 1, 6–7.
8. Edward W. Soja, 'Inside Exopolis: Scenes from Orange County', in Michael Sorkin (ed.), *Variations on a Theme Park: The New American City and the End of Public Space* (New York: Hill and Wang, 1992), pp. 94–122 (pp. 95, 97, 101).
9. Fishman, *Bourgeois Utopias*, p. 201.
10. David R. Goldfield and Blaine A. Brownell, *Urban America: From*

Downtown to No Town (Boston: Houghton Mifflin, 1979), p. 397; Kunstler, *Geography of Nowhere*, p. 15.

11. Eugene Victor Walter, *Placeways: A Theory of the Human Environment* (Chapel Hill: University of North Carolina Press, 1988), p. 2.

12. Leonard Lutwack, *The Role of Place in Literature* (Syracuse, New York: Syracuse University Press, 1984), p. 182.

13. Lieven Ameel, Jason Finch and Markku Salmela, 'Introduction: Peripherality and Literary Urban Studies', in Ameel et al. (eds.), *Literature and the Peripheral City* (New York: Palgrave MacMillan, 2015), pp. 1–17 (pp. 1, 6).

14. William Shakespeare, *Hamlet*, ed. G. R. Hibbard (Oxford: Oxford University Press, 1998), p. 241.

15. Severs, *Balancing Books*, p. 202.

16. Burn, '"Paradigm,"' p. 155; Hering, *Fiction and Form*, p. 152.

17. Relph, *Place and Placelessness*, p. 124.

18. Fishman, *Bourgeois Utopias*, p. 201; Garreau, *Edge City*, p. 9.

19. McHale, 'White Visitation', p. 197.

20. Marc Augé, *Non-Places: An Introduction to Supermodernity*, trans. John Howe (London: Verso, 2008), p. 63.

21. Ibid. p. 77.

22. Hering, *Fiction and Form*, pp. 136–7.

23. Henry Veggian, 'Anachronisms of Authority: Authorship, Exchange Value, and David Foster Wallace's *The Pale King*', *boundary2*, 39.3 (2012), pp. 97–124 (p. 111).

24. Adam Kelly, 'Formally Conventional Fiction', in Rachel Greenwald Smith (ed.), *American Literature in Transition, 2000–2010* (Cambridge: Cambridge University Press, 2018), pp. 46–60 (p. 55).

25. Lipsky, *Although of Course*, p. 291.

26. Teaford, *Cities of the Heartland*, p. 221.

27. Castells and Hall, *Technopoles of the World*, p. 1.

28. Jarvis, *Postmodern Cartographies*, p. 16.

29. Franz Kafka, *The Castle*, trans. J. A. Underwood (London: Penguin, 2000), pp. 8–9.

30. Walter Benjamin, 'Max Brod's Book on Kafka, and Some of My Own Reflections', in *Illuminations*, ed. Hannah Arendt and trans. Harry Zohn (1968) (London: Bodley Head, 2015), pp. 136–44 (p. 139).

31. Severs, 'Immanent Structures', p. 9.

32. Lucas Thompson, *Global Wallace: David Foster Wallace and World Literature* (New York: Bloomsbury, 2017), p. 134.

33. Hering, *Fiction and Form*, pp. 79 ff.

34. Staes, 'Work in Progress', pp. 72–3.

35. Tor Nørretranders, *The User Illusion: Cutting Consciousness Down to Size* (London: Allen Lane, 1998), p. 320.

36. Levey, *Maximalism*, p. 92.

37. Connell, *Precarious Labour*, p. 117.

38. Ibid. p. 94.
39. Katy Shaw, *Hauntology: The Presence of the Past in Twenty-First Century English Literature* (Palgrave MacMillan, 2018), p. 13.
40. Hayes-Brady, '"Palely Loitering,"' p. 143.
41. Bernes, 'Office Novel'.
42. Bell, *Post-industrial Society*, p. 162.
43. Lefebvre, *Production of Space*, pp. 212, 213, 216, original emphases.
44. Ibid. p. 75.
45. Clare, 'Politics of Boredom', p. 191.
46. Stephen Shapiro, 'From Capitalist to Communist Abstraction: *The Pale King*'s Cultural Fix', *Textual Practice*, 28.7 (2014), pp. 1249–71 (p. 1268).
47. White, *Middle Mind*, p. 44; see Wallace's copy in HRC 32.5.
48. Lefebvre, *Production of Space*, p. 216.
49. Andrew Bennett, *Suicide Century: Suicide and Literature from James Joyce to David Foster Wallace* (Cambridge: Cambridge University Press, 2017), p. 175.
50. Lefebvre, *Production of Space* pp. 216–7.
51. White, *Middle Mind*; see Wallace's copy in HRC 32.5.
52. Hering, *Fiction and Form*, p. 157.
53. Severs, *Balancing Books*, p. 212.
54. Araya, 'Why the Whiteness?', pp. 244, 239.
55. Daalder, 'Geographic Metafiction', pp. 227–8.
56. Araya, 'Why the Whiteness?', p. 239.
57. Robert D. Bullard, 'The Black Metropolis in the Era of Sprawl', in Bullard (ed.), *The Black Metropolis in the Twenty-First Century: Race, Power, and the Politics of Place* (Lanham, Maryland: Rowman & Littlefield, 2007), pp. 17–40 (pp. 26–7, 24).
58. Lipsky, *Although of Course*, p. 45.
59. Richard H. Schein, 'Race and Landscape in the United States', in Schein (ed.), *Landscape and Race in the United States* (New York: Routledge, 2006), pp. 1–21 (p. 9).
60. Thompson, 'Wallace and Race', p. 206.
61. Ibid. p. 205.
62. Patterson, *Restless Giant*, p. 127.
63. Araya, 'Why the Whiteness?', p. 243.

Bibliography

AL, 'The Write Stuff ALT-X Interview (1994)', in Michael Hemmingson (ed.), *William T. Vollmann: A Critical Study and Seven Interviews* (Jefferson, North Carolina: McFarland, 2009), pp. 114–23

Alexander, Neal, 'Senses of Place', in Robert T. Tally Jr. (ed.), *The Routledge Handbook of Space and Literature* (London: Routledge, 2017), EPUB edition accessed via British Library electronic legal deposit

Alonso, William, 'Deindustrialization and regional policy', in Lloyd Rodwin and Hideo Sazanami (eds.), *Deindustrialization and Regional Economic Transformation: The experience of the United States* (Boston: Unwin Hyman, 1989), pp. 221–40

Ameel, Lieven, Jason Finch and Markku Salmela, 'Introduction: Peripherality and Literary Urban Studies', in Ameel et al. (eds.), *Literature and the Peripheral City* (New York: Palgrave MacMillan, 2015), pp. 1–17

Amin, Ash, 'Post-Fordism: Models, Fantasies and Phantoms of Transition', in Amin (ed.), *Post-Fordism: A Reader* (Oxford: Blackwell, 1994), pp. 1–40

Araya, Jorge, 'Why the Whiteness? Race in *The Pale King*', in Phillip Coleman (ed.), *Critical Insights: David Foster Wallace* (Ipswich, Massachusetts: Salem Press, 2015), pp. 238–51

Arden, Patrick, 'David Foster Wallace Warms Up', in Stephen J. Burn (ed.), *Conversations with David Foster Wallace* (Jackson: University of Mississippi Press, 2012), pp. 94–100

Augé, Marc, *Non-Places: An Introduction to Supermodernity* (1992), trans. John Howe (1995) (London: Verso, 2008)

Austin, Mary, 'Regionalism in American Literature', *The English Journal*, 21.2 (February 1932), 97–107

Ayers, Edward L. and Peter S. Onuf, 'Introduction', in Edward L Ayers, Patricia Nelson Limerick, Stephen Nissenbaum and Peter S. Onuf (eds.), *All Over the Map: Rethinking American Regions* (Baltimore: Johns Hopkins University Press, 1996), pp. 1–10

Banner, Olivia, '"They're Literally Shit": Masculinity and the Work of Art in the Age of Waste Recycling', *Iowa Journal of Cultural Studies*, 10.1 (2009), 74–90

Baudelaire, Charles, 'The Painter of Modern Life' (1863), trans.

P. E. Charvet (1972), in *The Painter of Modern Life* (London: Penguin, 2010)

Bean, Tim, 'Infinite Jest Tour of Boston: A tour of the Boston loca-tions mentioned in Infinite Jest', Flikr.com account, <https://www.flickr.com/photos/25383051@N05/sets/72157612365092520/with/3182231319/> [retrieved 28 February 2022]

Beckson, Karl and Arthur Granz, *Literary Terms: A Dictionary*, third edition (London: Andre Deutsch, 1990)

Bell, Daniel, *The Coming of Post-Industrial Society: A Venture in Social Forecasting* (London: Heinemann, 1974)

Benjamin, Walter, 'Max Brod's Book on Kafka, and Some of My Own Reflections' (1938), in *Illuminations*, trans. Harry Zohn, ed. Hannah Arendt (1968) (London: Bodley Head, 2015)

—— 'On Some Motifs in Baudelaire' (1940), in *The Writer of Modern Life: Essays on Baudelaire*, ed. Michael W. Jennings, trans. Howard Eiland, Edmund Jephcott, Rodney Livingston and Harry Zohn (Cambridge, Massachusetts: Belknap Press, 2006)

—— 'Paris, Capital of the Nineteenth Century', in *The Writer of Modern Life: Essays on Baudelaire*, ed. Michael W. Jennings, trans. Howard Eiland, Edmund Jephcott, Rodney Livingston and Harry Zohn (Cambridge, Massachusetts: Belknap Press, 2006)

Bennett, Alice, *Contemporary Fictions of Attention* (London: Bloomsbury, 2018)

Bennett, Andrew, *Suicide Century: Suicide and Literature from James Joyce to David Foster Wallace* (Cambridge: Cambridge University Press, 2017)

Benzon, Kiki, 'David Foster Wallace and Millennial America', in Phillip Coleman (ed.), *Critical Insights: David Foster Wallace* (Ipswich, Massachusetts: Salem Press, 2015), pp. 29–45

—— '"Yet Another Example of the Porousness of Certain Borders": Chaos and Realism in *Infinite Jest*', in David Hering (ed.), *Consider David Foster Wallace: Critical Essays* (Los Angeles: Sideshow Media Group, 2010), pp. 101–12

Bernes, Jasper, 'Character, Genre, Labor: The Office Novel After Deindustrialization', in *Post-45*, 1, 10 January 2019, <http://post45.research.yale.edu/2019/01/character-genre-labor-the-office-novel-after-deindustrialization/> [retrieved 28 February 2022]

Berry, Wendell, 'Writer and Region', *The Hudson Review*, 40.1 (Spring 1987), 15–30

Beutler, William, 'Infinite Atlas', <http://www.infiniteatlas.com/> [retrieved 28 February 2022]

—— 'Infinite Boston' (July–September 2012), <http://www.infiniteboston.com/> [retrieved 28 February 2022]

Bidgood, Jess, 'Boston Takes Step to Elevate Citgo Sign From LED Beacon to Landmark', in *New York Times*, 13 July 2016, <https://www.nytimes

.com/2016/07/14/us/boston-citgo-sign-landmark.html> [retrieved 28 February 2022]

Boswell, Marshall, 'Preface', in Boswell (ed.), *David Foster Wallace and 'The Long Thing': New Essays on the Novels* (New York: Bloomsbury, 2014), pp. vi–xii

—— 'Trickle-Down Citizenship: Taxes and Civic Responsibility in *The Pale King*', in Boswell (ed.), *David Foster Wallace and 'The Long Thing': New Essays on the Novels* (New York: Bloomsbury, 2014), pp. 209–26

—— *Understanding David Foster Wallace* (Columbia, South Carolina: University of South Carolina Press, 2003)

—— *The Wallace Effect: David Foster Wallace and the Contemporary Literary Imagination* (New York: Bloomsbury, 2019), EPUB edition accessed via British Library electronic legal deposit

Brooks, H. Allen, *The Prairie School: Frank Lloyd Wright and his Midwest Contemporaries* (Toronto: University of Toronto Press, 1972)

Brosseau, Marc, 'Geography's Literature', *Progress in Human Geography*, 18.3 (1994), 333–353

Bullard, Robert D., 'The Black Metropolis in the Era of Sprawl', in Bullard (ed.), *The Black Metropolis in the Twenty-First Century: Race, Power, and the Politics of Place* (Lanham, Maryland: Rowman & Littlefield, 2007), pp. 17–40

Bulson, Eric, *Novels, Maps, Modernity: The Spatial Imagination, 1850–2000* (New York: Routledge, 2006)

Burn, Stephen J., *David Foster Wallace's Infinite Jest: A Reader's Guide*, second edition (London: Continuum, 2012)

—— '"A Paradigm for the Life of Consciousness": *The Pale King*', in Marshall Boswell (ed.), *David Foster Wallace and 'The Long Thing': New Essays on the Novels* (New York: Bloomsbury, 2014), pp. 149–68

Bushell, Sally, *Text as Process: Creative Composition in Wordsworth, Tennyson, and Dickenson* (Charlottesville: University of Virginia Press, 2009)

Butterfield, Fox, 'What You See is What You Get', in *New York Times*, 1 May 1988, <https://www.nytimes.com/1988/05/01/books/what-you-see-is-what-you-get.html> [retrieved 28 February 2022]

Cain, Caleb, 'Approaching Infinity', in Stephen J. Burn (ed.), *Conversations with David Foster Wallace* (Jackson: University of Mississippi Press, 2012), pp. 121–26

Campbell, Robert and Peter Vanderwarker, *Cityscapes of Boston: An American City Through Time* (Boston: Houghton Mifflin, 1992)

Campbell, Thomas F., 'Cleveland: The Struggle for Stability', in Richard M. Bernard (ed.), *Snowbelt Cities: Metropolitan Politics in the Northeast and Midwest since World War II* (Bloomington: Indiana University Press, 1990), pp. 109–36

Carlisle, Greg, 'Introduction: Consider David Foster Wallace Studies', in David Hering (ed.), *Consider David Foster Wallace: Critical Essays* (Los Angeles: Sideshow Media Group, 2010), pp. 12–23

Caro, Mark, 'The Next Big Thing: Can a Downstate Author Withstand the Sensation over His 1,079-Page Novel?', in Stephen J. Burn (ed.), *Conversations with David Foster Wallace* (Jackson: University of Mississippi Press, 2012), pp. 53–7

Casey, Edward S., *The Fate of Place: A Philosophical History* (Berkeley: University of California Press, 1997)

Castells, Manuel and Peter Hall, *Technopoles of the World: The Making of Twenty-First Century Industrial Complexes* (London: Routledge, 1994)

de Certeau, Michel, *The Practice of Everyday Life*, trans. Steven Rendall (1984) (Berkeley: University of California Press, 1988)

Chafe, William H., *The Unfinished Journey: America since World War II*, seventh edition (Oxford: Oxford University Press, 2011)

Chodat, Robert, *The Matter of High Words: Naturalism, Normativity, and the Postwar Sage* (Oxford: Oxford University Press, 2017)

Cioffi, Frank Louis, '"An Anguish Become Thing": Narrative as Performance in David Foster Wallace's "Infinite Jest"', *Narrative*, 8.2 (May 2000), 161–81

Clare, Ralph, 'Introduction: An Exquisite Corpus: Assembling a Wallace without Organs', in Ralph Clare (ed.), *The Cambridge Companion to David Foster Wallace* (Cambridge: Cambridge University Press, 2018), pp. 1–15

—— 'The Politics of Boredom and the Boredom of Politics in *The Pale King*', in Marshall Boswell (ed.), *David Foster Wallace and 'The Long Thing': New Essays on the Novels* (New York: Bloomsbury, 2014), pp. 187–208

Clayton, Andrew R. L. and Susan E. Gray, 'The Story of the Midwest: An Introduction', in Clayton and Gray (eds.), *The Identity of the American Midwest: Essays on Regional History* (Bloomington: Indiana University Press, 2001), pp. 1–26

Cohen, Samuel, 'The Whiteness of David Foster Wallace', in Len Platt and Sara Upstone (eds.), *Postmodern Literature and Race* (Cambridge: Cambridge University Press, 2015), pp. 228–44

Collins, Robert M., *Transforming America: Politics and Culture in the Reagan Years* (New York: Columbia University Press, 2007)

Connell, Liam, *Precarious Labour and the Contemporary Novel* (Palgrave MacMillan, 2017)

Conte, Joseph M., *Design and Debris: A Chaotics of Postmodern American Fiction* (Tuscaloosa: University of Alabama Press, 2002)

Cooper, David and Gary Priestnall, 'The Processural Intertextuality of Literary Cartographies: Critical and Digital Practices', *The Cartographic Journal*, 48.4 (2011), 250–62

Crain, Caleb, 'Approaching Infinity', in Stephen J. Burn (ed.), *Conversations with David Foster Wallace* (Jackson: University of Mississippi Press, 2012), pp. 121–6

Daalder, Jurrit, 'Wallace's Geographic Metafiction', in Ralph Clare (ed.), *The Cambridge Companion to David Foster Wallace* (Cambridge: Cambridge University Press, 2018), pp. 220–34

Danielson, Larry, 'Tornado Stories in the Breadbasket: Weather and Regional Identity', in Barbara Allen and Thomas J. Schlereth (eds.), *Sense of Place: American Regional Cultures* (Lexington: University of Kentucky Press, 1990), pp. 28–39

Davis, Lennard J., *Resisting Novels: Ideology and Fiction* (New York: Methuen, 1987)

De Lio, Jeffrey R., 'Sovereignty of the Dead: Authors, Editors, and the Aesthetic Text', *The Comparatist*, 36 (May 2012), 123–13

Dianotto, Roberto M., *Place in Literature: Regions, Cultures, Communities* (Ithaca: Cornell University Press, 2000)

Dorson, James, 'The Neoliberal Machine in the Bureaucratic Garden: Pastoral States of Mind in David Foster Wallace's *The Pale King*', in Eric Erbacher, Nicole Maruo-Schröder and Florian Sedlmeir (eds.), *Rereading the Machine in the Garden: Nature and Technology in American Culture* (Frankfurt: Campus Verlag, 2014), pp. 211–30

Drellinger, Danielle and Javier Zarracina, 'Boston's Infinite Jest: A David Foster Wallace Memorial Tour', in *Boston Globe*, undated, <http://www.boston.com/bostonglobe/ideas/graphics/092108_infinite_jest/> [retrieved 28 February 2022]

Dudar, Helen, 'A Whizz Kid and his Wacky First Novel' (1987), in Stephen J. Burn (ed.), *Conversations with David Foster Wallace* (Jackson: University of Mississippi Press, 2012), pp. 8–10

Eagleton, Terry, *Literary Theory: An Introduction*, second edition (1996) (Oxford: Blackwell, 2001)

Eco, Umberto, *Six Walks in the Fictional Woods* (Cambridge, Massachusetts: Harvard University Press, 1994)

Ehrenreich, Barbara, *Fear of Falling: The Inner Life of the Middle Class* (New York: Pantheon, 1989)

Ehrman, John, *The Eighties: America in the Age of Reagan* (New Haven: Yale University Press, 2005)

Elkin, Lauren, *Flâneuse: Women Walk the City in Paris, New York, Tokyo, Venice and London* (London: Chatto & Windus, 2016)

Fishman, Robert, *Bourgeois Utopias: The Rise and Fall of Suburbia* (New York: Basic Books, 1987)

Fetterley, Judith and Marjorie Pryse, *Writing Out of Place: Regionalism, Women, and American Literary Culture* (Urbana: University of Illinois Press, 2003)

Fordham, Finn, 'Katabasis in Danielewski's *House of Leaves* and Two Other Recent American Novels', in Joe Brady and Alison Gibbons (eds.),

Mark Z. Danielewski (Manchester: Manchester University Press, 2011), pp. 33–51

Foster, Graham, 'A Blasted Region: David Foster Wallace's Man-Made Landscapes', in David Hering (ed.), *Consider David Foster Wallace: Critical Essays* (Los Angeles: Sideshow Media Group, 2010), pp. 37–48

Frampton, Kenneth, 'Towards a Critical Regionalism: Six Points for an Architecture of Resistance', in Hal Foster (ed.), *Postmodern Culture* (London: Pluto Press, 1987), pp. 16–30

Frankel, Boris, *The Post-Industrial Utopians* (Cambridge: Polity, 1987)

Franzen, Jonathan, 'Why Bother?', in *How to Be Alone* (London: Fourth Estate, 2002)

French, Michael, *US Economic History since 1945* (Manchester: Manchester University Press, 1997)

Garreau, Joel, *Edge City: Life on a New Frontier* (New York: Doubleday, 1991)

Gelfant, Blanche Housman, *The American City Novel* (1954), second edition (Norman: University of Oklahoma Press, 1970)

Genette, Gérard, *Narrative Discourse Revisited* (1983), trans. Jane E. Lewin (Ithaca, New York: Cornell University Press, 1988)

Giles, Paul, 'All Swallowed Up: David Foster Wallace and American Literature', in Samuel Cohen and Lee Konstantinou (eds.), *The Legacy of David Foster Wallace* (Iowa City: University of Iowa Press, 2012), pp. 3–22

—— *The Global Remapping of American Literature* (Princeton: Princeton University Press, 2011)

Glaeser, Edward L., 'Reinventing Boston: 1630–2003', *Journal of Economic Geography*, 5.2 (2005), 119–53

Godden, Richard and Michael Szalay, 'The bodies in the bubble: David Foster Wallace's *The Pale King*', *Textual Practice*, 28.7 (2014), 1273–322

Goeke, Joseph F., '"Everybody Knows It's About Something Else, Way Down": Boredom, Nihilism, and the Search for Meaning in David Foster Wallace's *The Pale King*', *Critique: Studies in Contemporary Fiction*, 58.3 (2017), 191–213

Goldfarb, Michael, 'The Connection: David Foster Wallace', in Stephen J. Burn (ed.), *Conversations with David Foster Wallace* (Jackson: University of Mississippi Press, 2012), pp. 136–51

Goldfield, David R. and Blaine A. Brownell, *Urban America: From Downtown to No Town* (Boston: Houghton Mifflin, 1979)

Goodman, Robert, *The Last Entrepreneurs: America's Regional Wars for Jobs and Dollars* (1979) (Boston: South End Press, 1983)

Gordon, David M., 'Capitalist Development and the History of American Cities', in William K. Tabb and Larry Sawers (eds.), *Marxism and the Metropolis: New Perspectives in Urban Political Economy* (New York: Oxford University Press, 1984), pp. 21–53

Groenland, Tim, *The Art of Editing: David Foster Wallace and Raymond Carver* (New York: Bloomsbury, 2019)

—— 'A King of Shreds and Patches: Assembling Wallace's Final Novel', in Philip Coleman (ed.), *Critical Insights: David Foster Wallace* (Ipswich, Massachusetts: Salem Press, 2015), pp. 221–37

—— 'Recipe for a Brick: *The Pale King* in Progress', *Critique: Studies in Contemporary Fiction* 58.4 (2017), 365–367

Gullon, Ricardo, 'On Space in the Novel', *Critical Inquiry*, 2.1 (Autumn 1975), 11–28

Harvey, David, *The Condition of Postmodernity: An Enquiry into the Origins of Cultural Change* (Oxford: Basil Blackwell, 1989)

—— 'From Space to Place and Back Again: Reflections on the Condition of Postmodernity', in Jon Bird, Barry Curtis, Tim Putnam, George Robertson and Lisa Tickner (eds.), *Mapping the Futures: Local Cultures, Global Change* (London: Routledge, 1993), pp. 2–29

Hayden, Dolores, 'Capitalism, Socialism, and the Built Environment', in Stephen Rosskamm Shalom (ed.), *Socialist Visions* (Boston: South End Press, 1983), pp. 59–81

Hayes-Brady, Clare, '"Palely Loitering": On Not Finishing (in) *The Pale King*', in Ralph Clare (ed.), *The Cambridge Companion to David Foster Wallace* (Cambridge: Cambridge University Press, 2018), pp. 142–55

—— *The Unspeakable Failures of David Foster Wallace* (New York: Bloomsbury, 2016)

Heise, Thomas, *Urban Underworlds: A Geography of Twentieth-Century American Literature and Culture* (New Brunswick, New Jersey: Rutgers University Press, 2011)

Hering, David, *David Foster Wallace: Fiction and Form* (New York: Bloomsbury, 2016)

—— 'Form as Strategy in *Infinite Jest*', in Philip Coleman (ed.), *Critical Insights: David Foster Wallace* (Ipswich, Massachusetts: Salem Press, 2015), pp. 128–43

—— 'Infinite Jest: Triangles, Cycles, Choices & Chases', in Hering (ed.), *Consider David Foster Wallace: Critical Essays* (Los Angeles: Sideshow Media Group, 2010), pp. 89–100

—— 'Theorising David Foster Wallace's Toxic Postmodern Spaces', *US Studies Online*, 18 (Spring 2011), <http://www.baas.ac.uk/issue-18-spring-2011-article-2/> [retrieved 28 August 2022]

Herman, Luc and Toon Staes, 'Introduction: Can *The Pale King* (Please) be a Novel?', *English Studies* 95.1 (2014), 1–6

Hoberek, Andrew, *Twilight of the Middle Class: Post-World War II Fiction and White-Collar Work* (Princeton: Princeton University Press, 2005)

—— 'The Novel After David Foster Wallace', in Marshall Boswell and Stephen J. Burn (eds.), *A Companion to David Foster Wallace Studies* (New York: Palgrave MacMillan, 2013), pp. 211–28

—— 'Wallace and American Literature', in Ralph Clare (ed.), *The Cambridge*

Companion to David Foster Wallace (Cambridge: Cambridge University Press, 2018), pp. 33–48

Holland, Mary K., *Succeeding Postmodernism: Language and Humanism in Contemporary American Literature* (New York: Bloomsbury, 2013)

Holleran, Michael, *Boston's 'Changeful Times': Origins of Preservation & Planning in America* (Baltimore: John Hopkins University Press, 1998)

Hones, Sheila, *Literary Geographies: Narrative Space in* Let the Great World Spin (New York: Palgrave MacMillan, 2014)

Houser, Heather, '*Infinite Jest*'s Environmental Case for Disgust', in Samuel Cohen and Lee Konstantinou (eds.), *The Legacy of David Foster Wallace* (Iowa City: University of Iowa Press, 2012), pp. 118–42

—— 'Managing Information and Materiality in *Infinite Jest* and Running the Numbers', *American Literary History*, 26.4 (Winter 2014), 742–64

Howard, Gerald, 'Infinite Jester: David Foster Wallace and his 1,079 mystical, brilliant pages', *Elle*, 11.6 (1996), p. 58

Hsu, Hsuan L., *Geography and the Production of Space in Nineteenth-Century American Literature* (Cambridge: Cambridge University Press, 2010)

—— 'New Regionalisms: Literature and Uneven Development', in John T. Matthews (ed.), *A Companion to the Modern American Novel 1900–1950* (Malden, Massachusetts: Blackwell, 2009), pp. 218–39

Hungerford, Amy, *Making Literature Now* (Stanford: Stanford University Press, 2016)

Issell, William, *Social Change in the United States, 1945–1983* (Basingstoke, Hampshire: MacMillan, 1985)

Jackson, Edward, *David Foster Wallace's Toxic Sexuality: Hideousness, Neoliberalism, Spermatics* (New York: Bloomsbury, 2020), EPUB edition accessed via British Library electronic legal deposit

Jackson, Edward and Joel Nicholson-Roberts, 'White Guys: Questioning Infinite Jest's New Sincerity', *Orbit: A Journal of American Literature* 5.1 (2017), 1–28, <https://doi.org/10.16995/orbit.182> [retrieved 28 February 2022]

James, David, *Contemporary British Fiction and the Artistry of Space: Style, Landscape, Perception* (London: Continuum, 2008)

Jameson, Fredric, *Postmodernism: Or, The Cultural Logic of Late Capitalism* (London: Verso, 1991)

Jarvis, Brian, *Postmodern Cartographies: The Geographical Imagination in Contemporary American Culture* (London: Pluto, 1998)

Jasty, Kunal, 'A Lost 1996 Interview with David Foster Wallace' (21 December 2014), <https://medium.com/@kunaljasty/a-lost-1996-interview-with-david-foster-wallace-63987d93c2c> [retrieved 28 February 2022]

Jencks, Charles, *The Language of Postmodern Architecture*, sixth edition (London: Academy Editions, 1977)

Johnson, Haynes, *Sleepwalking Through History: America in the Reagan Years* (New York: Norton, 1991)

Kafka, Franz, *The Castle* (1926), trans. J. A. Underwood (1997) (London: Penguin, 2000)

Kelly, Adam, 'David Foster Wallace and the New Sincerity in American Fiction', in David Hering (ed.), *Consider David Foster Wallace: Critical Essays* (Los Angeles: Sideshow Media Group, 2010), pp. 131–46

—— 'David Foster Wallace and the Novel of Ideas', in Marshall Boswell (ed.), *David Foster Wallace and 'The Long Thing': New Essays on the Novels* (New York: Bloomsbury, 2014), pp. 3–22

—— 'David Foster Wallace: The Critical Reception', in Philip Coleman (ed.), *Critical Insights: David Foster Wallace* (Ipswich, Massachusetts: Salem Press, 2015), pp. 46–62

—— 'Dialectic of Sincerity: Lionel Trilling and David Foster Wallace', in *Post-45*, 17 October 2014, <http://post45.research.yale.edu/2014/10/dialectic-of-sincerity-lionel-trilling-and-david-foster-wallace/> [retrieved 28 February 2022]

—— 'Formally Conventional Fiction', in Rachel Greenwald Smith (ed.), *American Literature in Transition, 2000–2010* (Cambridge: Cambridge University Press, 2018), pp. 46–60

—— 'The Map and the Territory: Infinite Boston', *The Millions*, 13 August 2013, <https://themillions.com/2013/08/the-map-and-the-territory-infinite-boston.html> [retrieved 28 February 2022]

—— 'The New Sincerity', in Jason Gladstone, Andrew Hoberek and Daniel Worden (eds.), *Posmodern/Postwar – And After* (Iowa City: University of Iowa Press, 2016), pp. 197–208

Kennedy, Lawrence L., *Planning the City upon a Hill: Boston since 1630* (Amherst: University of Massachusetts Press, 1992)

Kern, Leslie, *Feminist City* (London: Verso, 2020)

Kestner, Joseph A., *The Spatiality of the Novel* (Detroit: Wayne State University Press, 1978)

Konstantinou, Lee, 'The World of David Foster Wallace', *boundary2*, 40.3 (2013), 59–86

Kowalewski, Michael, 'Writing in Place: The New American Regionalism', *American Literary History*, 6.1 (Spring 1994), 171–83

Kunstler, James Howard, *Geography of Nowhere: The Rise and Decline of America's Man-Made Landscapes* (New York: Simon and Schuster, 1991)

Lambert, Stephanie, '"The Real Dark Side, Baby": New Sincerity and Neoliberal Aesthetics in David Foster Wallace and Jennifer Egan', *Critique: Studies in Contemporary Fiction*, 61.4 (2020), 394–411

Lattanzi, Bill, 'Messing with Maps: Walking David Foster Wallace's Boston', in *Los Angeles Review of Books*, 6 February 2015, <https://lareviewofbooks.org/article/messing-maps-walking-david-foster-wallaces-boston/> [retrieved 28 February 2022]

Lefebvre, Henri, *The Production of Space* (1974), trans. Donald Nicholson-Smith (Oxford: Blackwell, 1991)

Lehan, Richard, *The City in Literature: An Intellectual and Cultural History* (Berkeley: University of California Press, 1998)

Levey, Diane Wolfe, 'City Signs: Toward a Definition of Urban Literature', *Modern Fiction Studies*, 24.1 (Spring 1978), 65–73

Levey, Nick, *Maximalism in Contemporary American Literature: The Uses of Detail* (New York: Routledge, 2017)

Lipsky, David, *Although of Course You End Up Becoming Yourself: A Road Trip with David Foster Wallace* (New York: Broadway Books, 2010)

Lloyd Wright, Frank, 'In the Cause of Architecture' (1908), in *In the Cause of Architecture*, ed. Hugh S. Donlan and Martin Filler (New York: Architectural Record Books, 1975)

Luter, Matthew, '*The Broom of the System* and *Girl with Curious Hair*', in Ralph Clare (ed.), *The Cambridge Companion to David Foster Wallace* (Cambridge: Cambridge University Press, 2018), pp. 67–81

Lutwack, Leonard, *The Role of Place in Literature* (Syracuse, New York: Syracuse University Press, 1984)

Lutz, Tom, *Cosmopolitan Vistas: American Regionalism and Literary Value* (Ithaca: Cornell University Press, 2004)

Lynch, Kevin, *The Image of the City* (Cambridge, Massachusetts: MIT Press, 1960)

MacLeod, Gordon and Martin Jones, 'Renewing the Geography of Regions', *Environment and Planning D: Society and Space*, 19 (2001), 669–95

Mallory, William E. and Paul Simpson-Housley (eds.), *Geography and Literature: A Meeting of the Disciplines* (Syracuse, New York: Syracuse University Press, 1987)

Markusen, Ann R., *Regions: The Economics and Politics of Territory* (Totowa, New Jersey: Rowman & Littlefield, 1987)

Markusen, Ann R. and Virginia Carlson, 'Deindustrialization in the American Midwest: Causes and Responses', in Lloyd Rodwin and Hidehiko Sazanami (eds.), *Deindustrialization and Regional Economic Transformation: The Experience of the United States* (Boston: Unwin Hyman, 1989), pp. 25–59

Massey, Doreen, *For Space* (London: SAGE, 2005)

Max, D. T., *Every Love Story Is a Ghost Story: A Life of David Foster Wallace* (London: Granta, 2012)

McCaffrey, Larry, 'An Expanded Interview with David Foster Wallace', in Stephen J. Burn (ed.), *Conversations with David Foster Wallace* (Jackson: University of Mississippi Press, 2012), pp. 21–52

—— 'Moth to the Flame', in Michael Hemmingson (ed.), *William T. Vollmann: A Critical Study and Seven Interviews* (Jefferson, North Carolina: McFarland, 2009), pp. 85–113

McCarthy, Tom, 'David Foster Wallace: The Last Audit', in *New York Times*, 11 April 2011, <https://www.nytimes.com/2011/04/17/books/review /book-review-the-pale-king-by-david-foster-wallace.html> [retrieved 28 February 2022]

McDowell, Linda, 'Life without Father and Ford: The New Gender Order of Post-Fordism', *Transactions of the Institute of British Geographers*, 16.4 (1991), 400–19

McGurl, Mark, 'The Institution of Nothing: David Foster Wallace in the Program', *boundary2*, 41.3 (Fall 2014), 27–54

McHale, Brian, '*The Pale King*, Or, The White Visitation', in Marshall Boswell and Stephen J. Burn (eds.), *A Companion to David Foster Wallace Studies* (New York: Palgrave MacMillan, 2013), pp. 181–210

McKittrick, Katherine, *Demonic Grounds: Black Women and the Cartographies of Struggle* (Minneapolis: University of Minnesota Press, 2006)

McLaughlin, Robert L., 'Post-Postmodern Discontent: Contemporary Fiction and the Social World', *Symploke*, 12.1–2 (2004), 53–68

'Metropolitan, n. and adj.', in *OED Online* (Oxford: Oxford University Press, December 2018), <http://www.oed.com.ezproxy01.rhul.ac.uk /view/Entry/117705?redirectedFrom=metropolitan#eid> [retrieved 28 February 2022]

Miller, Jim Wayne, 'Anytime the Ground is Uneven: The Outlook for Regional Studies and What to Look Out For', in William E. Mallory and Paul Simpson-Housley (eds.), *Geography and Literature: A Meeting of the Disciplines* (Syracuse, New York: Syracuse University Press, 1987), pp. 1–20

Miller, Naomi and Keith Morgan, *Boston Architecture 1975–1990* (Munich: Prestel-Verlag, 1990)

Miller, Laura, 'The Salon Interview' (1996), in Stephen J. Burn (ed.), *Conversations with David Foster Wallace* (Jackson: University of Mississippi Press, 2012), pp. 58–65

Moore, Steven, 'The First Draft Version of *Infinite Jest*', in *The Howling Fantods*, website, 2003, <http://www.thehowlingfantods.com/ij_first .htm> [retrieved 28 February 2022]

Morrissey, Tara and Lucas Thompson, '"The Rare White at the Window": A Reappraisal of Mark Costello and David Foster Wallace's *Signifying Rappers*', *Journal of American Studies*, 49.1 (2015), 77–97

Morton, Adam David, 'The Frontiers of Cormac McCarthy', in *Progress in Political Economy*, 15 December 2015, <http://ppesydney.net/the -frontiers-of-cormac-mccarthy/> [retrieved 28 February 2022]

Muller, Peter O., 'The Suburban Transformation of the Globalizing American City', *Annals of the American Academy of Political and Social Science*, 551 (May 1997), 44–58

Nadel, Ira B., 'Consider the Footnote', in Samuel Cohen and Lee

Konstantinou (eds.), *The Legacy of David Foster Wallace* (Iowa City: University of Iowa Press, 2012), pp. 218–40

Nørretranders, Tor, *The User Illusion: Cutting Consciousness Down to Size* (1991) (London: Allen Lane, 1998)

O'Connor, Flannery, 'The Regional Writer' (1963), in *Mystery and Manners: Occasional Prose*, ed. Sally and Robert Fitzgerald (1972) (London: Faber, 2014)

O'Gara, Aisling, 'An Understanding of One's Place in the System: An Introduction to The Broom of the System', in Philip Coleman (ed.), *Critical Insights: David Foster Wallace* (Salem Press: Ipswich, Massachusetts, 2015), pp. 97–111

Patterson, James T., *Restless Giant: The United States from Watergate to Bush v. Gore* (Oxford: Oxford University Press, 2005)

Paulson, Steve, 'David Foster Wallace in the #MeToo Era: A Conversation with Clare Hayes-Brady', *Los Angeles Review of Books* (10 September 2018), <https://www.lareviewofbooks.org/article/david-foster-wallace-in-the-metoo-era-a-conversation-with-clare-hayes-brady/> [retrieved 28 February 2022]

Perosa, Sergio, *American Theories of the Novel: 1793–1903* (New York: New York University Press, 1983)

Pike, Burton, *The Image of the City in Modern Literature* (Princeton: Princeton University Press, 1981)

Plank, Karl A., *The Fact of the Cage: Reading Infinite Jest* (New York, Routledge, 2021), EPUB edition accessed via British Library electronic legal deposit

Pocock, Douglas C. D., 'Geography and Literature', *Progress in Human Geography*, 12.1 (1988), 87–102

Porteous, Douglas, 'Literature and Humanist Geography', *Area*, 17.2 (June 1985), 117–22

Prieto, Eric, *Literature, Geography and the Postmodern Poetics of Space* (New York: Palgrave MacMillan, 2013)

Quinn, Paul, '"Location's Location": Placing David Foster Wallace', in Marshall Boswell and Stephen J. Burn (eds.), *A Companion to David Foster Wallace Studies* (New York: Palgrave MacMillan, 2013), pp. 87–106

Relph, Edward, *The Modern Urban Landscape* (London: Croom Helm, 1987)

—— *Place and Placelessness* (London: Pion, 1976)

Reynolds, Nedra, *Geographies of Writing: Inhabiting Places and Encountering Difference* (Carbondale: Southern Illinois University Press, 2004)

Roberts, Kevin, 'Prisoners of the City: Whatever Could a Postmodern City Be?' in Erica Carter, James Donald and Judith Squires (eds.), *Space and Place: Theories of Identity and Location* (London: Lawrence and Wishart, 1993), pp. 303–30

Roiland, Josh, 'Spiritually Midwestern: What Middle America Meant to David Foster Wallace' (7 August 2015), <https://medium.com/just-words/spiritually-midwestern-216d8041f50d> [retrieved 28 February 2022]

Rose, Gillian, *Feminism and Geography: The Limits of Geographical Knowledge* (Cambridge: Polity Press, 1993)

—— Review of Edward W. Soja, *Postmodern Geographies: The Reassertion of Space in Critical Social Theory* and David Harvey, *The Condition of Postmodernity: An Enquiry into the Origins of Cultural Change*, *Journal of Historical Geography*, 17.1 (1991), 118–21

Rossi, Aldo, *The Architecture of the City* (1966) (Cambridge, Massachusetts: MIT Press, 1982)

Rossinow, Doug, *The Reagan Era: A History of the 1980s* (New York: Columbia University Press, 2015)

Samuelson, Robert J., 'America sings the postindustrial blues', in *Washington Post*, 18 June 2017, <https://www.washingtonpost.com/opinions/america-sings-the-postindustrial-blues/2017/06/18/d59a8a2c-52bb-11e7-91eb-9611861a988f_story.html> [retrieved 28 April 2022]

Saunders, Angharad, 'The Spatial Event of Writing: John Galsworthy and the Creation of *Fraternity*', *Cultural Geographies*, 20.3 (July 2013), 285–98

—— *Place and the Scene of Literary Practice* (London: Routledge, 2018)

Saylor, Colson, 'Loosening the Jar: Contemplating Race in David Foster Wallace's Short Fiction', *The Journal of David Foster Wallace Studies* 1.1 (2018), pp. 119–49

Schein, Richard H., 'Race and Landscape in the United States', in Schein (ed.), *Landscape and Race in the United States* (New York: Routledge, 2006), pp. 1–21

Scott, A. J., *New Industrial Spaces: Flexible Production Organization and Regional Development in North America and Western Europe* (London: Pion, 1988)

Severs, Jeffrey, '"Blank as the Faces on Coins": Currency and Embodied Values(s) in David Foster Wallace's *The Pale King*', *Critique: Studies in Contemporary Fiction*, 57.1 (2016), 52–66

—— *David Foster Wallace's Balancing Books: Fictions of Value* (New York: Columbia University Press, 2017)

—— '"We've been inside what we wanted all along": David Foster Wallace's Immanent Structures', in Brynnar Swenson (ed.), *Literature and the Encounter with Immanence* (Leiden: Brill Rodopi, 2017), pp. 8–29

Shakespeare, William, *Hamlet*, ed. G. R. Hibbard (Oxford: Oxford University Press, 1998)

Shand-Tucci, Douglas, *Built in Boston: City and Suburb 1800–2000: Revised and Expanded Edition* (Amherst: University of Massachusetts Press, 1999)

Shapiro, Mary, *Wallace's Dialects* (New York: Bloomsbury, 2020)

Shapiro, Stephen, 'From Capitalist to Communist Abstraction: *The Pale King*'s Cultural Fix', *Textual Practice*, 28.7 (2014), 1249–71

Shaw, Katie, *Hauntology: The Presence of the Past in Twenty-First Century English Literature* (Palgrave MacMillan, 2018)

Shortridge, James R., *The Middle West: Its Meaning in American Culture* (Lawrence, Kansas: University Press of Kansas, 1989)

Soja, Edward W., 'Inside Exopolis: Scenes from Orange County', in Michael Sorkin (ed.), *Variations on a Theme Park: The New American City and the End of Public Space* (New York: Hill and Wang, 1992), pp. 94–122

—— *Postmetropolis: Critical Studies of Cities and Regions* (Oxford: Blackwell, 2000)

—— *Postmodern Geographies: The Reassertion of Space in Critical Social Theory* (London: Verso, 1989)

—— *Thirdspace: Journeys to Los Angeles and Other Real-and-Imagined Places* (Malden, Massachusetts: Blackwell, 1998)

Solnit, Rebecca, *Wanderlust: A History of Walking* (London: Verso, 2002)

Spenser, Douglas, *The Architecture of Neoliberalism: How Contemporary Architecture Became a Tool of Control and Compliance* (London: Bloomsbury, 2016)

Spurr, David Anton, *Architecture and Modern Literature* (Ann Arbor: University of Michigan Press, 2012)

Staes, Toon, 'Wallace and Empathy: A Narrative Approach', in Marshall Boswell (ed.), *David Foster Wallace and 'The Long Thing': New Essays on the Novels* (New York: Bloomsbury, 2014), pp. 23–42

Steinhilber, Dominic, 'Modernist Aims with Postmodern Means: Joycean Parallax and the Doppler Effect in Wallace's *Infinite Jest*', *The Journal of David Foster Wallace Studies*, 1.3 (2020), 41–78

Sugrue, Thomas J., *Origins of the Urban Crisis: Race and Inequality in Postwar Detroit* (Princeton, New Jersey: Princeton University Press, 1996)

Tally Jr., Robert T., *Spatiality* (London: Routledge, 2013)

Teaford, John C., *Cities of the Heartland: The Rise and Fall of the Industrial Midwest* (Bloomington: Indiana University Press, 1993)

Thacker, Andrew, 'The Idea of a Critical Literary Geography', *New Formations*, 57 (Winter 2005–2006), 56–73

—— *Moving Through Modernity: Geographies of Modernism* (2003) (Manchester: Manchester University Press, 2009)

Thompson, Lucas, '"Books Are Made out of Books:" David Foster Wallace and Cormac McCarthy', *The Cormac McCarthy Journal*, 13.1 (2015), 3–26

—— *Global Wallace: David Foster Wallace and World Literature* (New York: Bloomsbury, 2017)

—— 'Wallace and Race', in Ralph Clare (ed.), *The Cambridge Companion to David Foster Wallace* (Cambridge: Cambridge University Press, 2019), pp. 204–19

Toffler, Alvin, *Future Shock* (London: Bodley Head, 1970)

Treadwell, Sarah, 'The Motel: An Image of Elsewhere', *Space and Culture*, 8.2 (May 2005), 214–24

Tuan, Yi-Fu, *Space and Place: The Perspective of Experience* (1977) (London: Edward Arnold, 1979)

—— *Topophilia: A Study of Environmental Perception, Attitudes and Values* (Englewood Cliffs, New Jersey: Prentice-Hall, 1974)

Veggian, Henry, 'Anachronisms of Authority: Authorship, Exchange Value, and David Foster Wallace's *The Pale King*', *boundary2*, 39.3 (2012), 97–124

'Verstiegenheit', in M. Clark and O. Thyen (eds.), *Oxford German Dictionary*, third edition (Oxford: Oxford University Press, 2008)

Vollmann, William T., 'American Writing Today: A Diagnosis of the Disease', *Conjunctions*, 15 (1990), 355–58

—— *The Rainbow Stories* (1989) (New York: Penguin, 1992)

Wallace, David Foster, *A Supposedly Fun Thing I'll Never Do Again: Essays and Arguments* (1997) (London: Abacus, 2013)

—— *Brief Interviews with Hideous Men* (1999) (London: Abacus, 2013)

—— *The Broom of the System* (1987) (London: Abacus, 2011)

—— *Consider the Lobster and Other Essays* (2005) (London: Abacus, 2012)

—— 'Exploring Inner Space', *Washington Post*, 28 April 1991, <https://www.washingtonpost.com/archive/entertainment/books/1991/04/28/exploring-inner-space/39298a00-9030-4ae6-a3b9-03325e10b703/?utm_term=.db4d1fdc4713> [retrieved 28 February 2022]

—— Review of Michael Martone, *Fort Wayne Is Seventh on Hitler's List: Indiana Stories*, *Harvard Book Review* 15/16 (Winter/Spring 1990), pp. 12–13

—— *Infinite Jest: A Novel* (1996) (London: Abacus, 2016)

—— *The Pale King* (2011) (London: Penguin, 2012)

—— 'Peoria (4)' and 'Peoria (9) "Whispering Pines"', in *TriQuarterly*, 112 (Fall 2002), pp. 131–33

—— and Mark Costello, *Signifying Rappers* (1990) (New York: Back Bay Books, 2013)

Walter, Eugene Victor, *Placeways: A Theory of the Human Environment* (Chapel Hill: University of North Carolina Press, 1988)

Warren, Andrew, 'Modelling Community and Narrative in Infinite Jest and The Pale King', in Marshall Boswell (ed.), *David Foster Wallace and 'The Long Thing': New Essays on the Novels* (New York: Bloomsbury, 2014), pp. 61–84

Wegner, Phillip E., 'Spatial Criticism', in Julian Wolfreys (ed.), *Introducing Criticism in the 21st Century* (Edinburgh: Edinburgh University Press, 2015)

Westphal, Bertrand, *Geocriticism: Real and Fictional Spaces*, trans. Robert T. Tally Jr. (New York: Palgrave MacMillan, 2011)

White, Curtis, 'Curtis White remembers David Foster Wallace', Melville House website (12 September 2016), <https://www.mhpbooks.com /curtis-white-remembers-david-foster-wallace/> [retrieved 28 February 2022]

—— *The Middle Mind: Why Americans Don't Think for Themselves* (New York: HarperCollins, 2003)

Whitehall, Walter Muir and Lawrence W. Kennedy, *Boston: A Topographical History*, third edition (Cambridge, Massachusetts: Belknap Press/ Harvard University Press, 2000)

Williams, Raymond, *The Country and the City* (1973) (London: Hogarth Press, 1993)

—— *Keywords: A Vocabulary of Culture and Society* (1976) (London: Fontana, 1983)

—— *Marxism and Literature* (Oxford: Oxford University Press, 1977)

—— 'Metropolitan Perceptions and the Emergence of Modernism', in *The Politics of Modernism*, ed. Tony Pinkey (London: Verso, 1989)

—— 'Region and Class in the Novel', in Douglas Jefferson and Graham Martin (eds.), *The Uses of Fiction: Essays in Honour of Martin Kettle* (Milton Keynes: The Open University Press, 1982), pp. 59–68

Wirth-Nesher, Hannah, *City Codes: Reading the Modern Urban Novel* (Cambridge: Cambridge University Press, 1996)

Wolff, Janet, 'The Invisible Flâneuse: Women and the Literature of Modernity', *Theory, Culture & Society*, 2.3 (1985), 37–46

Wouters, Courtney, '"What Am I, A Machine?": Humans and Information in *The Pale King*', in Marshall Boswell (ed.), *David Foster Wallace and 'The Long Thing': New Essays on the Novels* (New York: Bloomsbury, 2014), pp. 169–86

Wylie, Herb, Christian Reigel, Karen Overbye and Don Perkins, 'Introduction: Regionalism Revisited', in Christian Riegel and Herb Wylie (eds.), *A Sense of Place: Re-Evaluating Regionalism in Canadian and American Writing* (Edmonton, Alberta: University of Alberta Press, 1998), pp. ix–xiv

Archival Source

Austin, Texas, University of Texas at Austin, Harry Ransom Center, 'David Foster Wallace Papers, 1971–2008', call number MS-5155

Index